MORALITY AND OUR COMPLICATED FORM OF LIFE

PEG O'CONNOR

MORALITY AND OUR COMPLICATED FORM OF LIFE:
FEMINIST WITTGENSTEINIAN METAETHICS

The Pennsylvania State University Press
University Park, Pennsylvania

Library of Congress Cataloging-in-Publication Data

O'Connor, Peg, 1965–
Morality and our complicated form of life : feminist Wittgensteinian metaethics
/ Peg O'Connor.
p.   cm.
Summary: "A reassessment of metaethics that attempts to undermine the
nature/normativity or world/language divide, and offer an alternative account of the
world-language relationship. Advocates the need to replace the metaphor of foundations
with a metaphor about stability. Incorporates Wittgenstein and contemporary feminist
ethicists"—Provided by publisher.
Includes bibliographical references and index.
ISBN 978-0-271-03379-2 (cloth : alk. paper)
1. Feminist ethics.
2. Ethics.
3. Wittgenstein, Ludwig, 1889–1951.
I. Title.

BJ1295.O26 2008
170′.42—dc22
2008000932

CONTENTS

IN HONOR OF MY PARENTS,
for all they continue to teach me.

IN THANKS TO LISA,
for all she is to me.

ACKNOWLEDGMENTS

I know that some believe that philosophy is a solitary activity, best done in a small room where one can have Big Thoughts. There's a paradox here; I just know it. Because of my inability to sit still inside for extended periods of time, this has never been my experience. I get too antsy. More important for me, philosophy is a collaborative activity. Hard work, yes, but also playful, fun, and best done in the company of others. I have benefited enormously from my intellectual companions, and to them I owe the greatest debt. They help me to be a better philosopher and a better person, a phenomenon that isn't surprising because, as Wittgenstein notes, philosophy really is about working on oneself.

I am fortunate to have many intellectual companions. First and foremost is Lisa Heldke, excellent philosopher and amazing partner all in one. She is the mainstay in all my pursuits.

I owe a special thanks to my architect friend Bruce Norelius. Bruce introduced me to the Maison à Bordeaux, patiently explaining with diagrams drawn on cocktail napkins how the house does not fall off the cliff. You will recognize this house as one of the central images.

My philosopher friends Corrinne Bedecarre, Melissa Burchard, Heidi Grasswick, and Abby Wilkerson have given me great comments and feedback over many years. They know that I have been wrangling with these questions since graduate school.

So many others have supported me in this project for the last several years in myriad ways. If the value of life is measured in the quality of friends, then I have the best life possible. From Minnesota, I thank Jim Bonilla and Carolyn O'Grady, Noreen Buhmann, Cynthia Hendricks, Julie Johnson, Brian Johnson, and Bob and Kay Moline. From Maine, I thank Landis Green, Roxanne Sly, Andy and Amy Vaughn, and Arthur and Nita Wood.

Barbara Heldke and Jay Benjamin belong in an outlaw category of their own.

Tennis-playing friends Patty, V. B. Chamberlain, and Janet DeMars deserve special thanks from this racquet-wielding philosopher.

Completion of this book was made possible by a yearlong sabbatical from Gustavus Adolphus College. I was also fortunate to receive a fellowship from the University of Connecticut Humanities Institute. My time at UConn was incredibly productive, and I am grateful for the opportunities to present parts of this work to the other fellows at the institute and to members of the department of philosophy and the women's studies program.

I am very grateful for the insightful and constructive comments from Wendy Lynne Lee and Alessandra Tanesini, who reviewed the manuscript for Penn State. I also thank Sandy Thatcher of Penn State for his expertise and enthusiasm for my work.

I owe thanks to the audience members of conferences sponsored by Feminist Ethics and Social Theory (FEAST), Feminist Methodologies, Metaphysics, and Science Studies (FEMMSS), Society for Analytic Feminism (SAF), and the Radical Philosophy Association (RPA).

I am also grateful to have been an invited fellow at the Philosophy, Politics, and Law Program at Binghamton University. The paper I presented helped me dissolve a problem about rules and responsibility that was driving me mad at the time. Thanks to Bat-Ami Bar On and Lisa Tessman for this wonderful opportunity.

Finally, I thank my family. My parents, Ann and Jack, have always made it clear that they are my biggest fans. My brother John and his partner, David Reichert, are my favorite traveling companions. I thank my sister, Anne, for showing me how important it is to get back on the bicycle.

As a kid at the movies, I always loved the previews of coming attractions. That may help to explain why I like a preface that gives a good snapshot of the upcoming main arguments. To that end, my purpose in this work is to effect a change of the dominant metaphor in metaethics. In metaethics, as well as in epistemology, foundation is the metaphor around which theory turns. There is massive disagreement about foundations: Is there one for moral judgment? If yes, then what's its nature? Is it universally or absolutely binding on all? How can we know it? And if the answer is negative, then how does morality function in the absence of it? Is it all a colossal error; is there really no foundation but we just act as if there is one? Within these trenchant disagreements, the commonality assumed is the coherence of a foundation.

I replace the image of a foundation with an architectural alternative that creates stability with various elements in relationship and tension with one another. My image is a villa in Bordeaux that is built into the side of a cliff. Not only does it not have a foundation in the typical sense, but also it appears to be launching itself off that cliff. I argue that we need stability of this sort rather than that which is purportedly provided by a foundation.

Foundations have a homogenous and monolithic character, whereas stability is heterogeneous. Stability comprises various elements; with respect to metaethics, I argue that it is what Wittgenstein describes as certainty. This certainty includes a variety of elements that in recent metaethics are shunted off to the side, ignored equally by both camps in the realist and antirealist debates. Wittgenstein warns us about the importance of starting points: start in the wrong place and you will quickly become mired in philosophical "problems" that are unsolvable. Some problems disappear or shift significantly when you begin an investigation in a different place. One example concerns the "problem of normativity." This problem gets off the ground so quickly and effectively because most assume that there is a dichotomy between natural features of the world (amenable to scientific inquiry) and normative features. We readily assume the realness or independence of the natural, and it is this assumption that makes the normative seem that much more strange and in need of explanation (if not apology). In light of this assumption, the relationship between normativity and the natural is as vexing and challenging as the other big relationship of radically different kinds in philosophy—the mind and body. Assumptions will always frame not only what counts as an intelligible description of a problem but also what *can* count as a solution. My approach rejects a sharp nature/normativity or world/language dualism, and borrowing from the world of knitting, I argue that the world has a felted character; nature and normativity are inextricably tangled. I call my position "felted contextualism."

This felted-contextualist view has a very different starting point, and so the normativity question takes on a very different cast. In short, I argue that there is really no fundamental difference in moral normativity from the normativity that governs our answering "four" to the question of "What is two plus two?" Moral necessity and normativity are no more mysterious (and in some ways duller) than normativity in other domains of life. We can generate an account of normativity that is nonsubjectivist but also nonobjectivist.

Rejecting a picture that simply assumes a sharp division between natural and normative, as well as a sharp distinction between humans and the objects of our knowledge, will effect a profound shift in our expectations for moral knowledge. If we take seriously the fact that the certainty that provides the stability comprises activities and practices, then we begin to see that moral knowledge is best understood as a kind of practical knowledge along the lines discussed by Plato and Aristotle. In resisting the pull to more theoretical and abstract ways of knowing, moral knowledge is fundamentally practical.

This position I develop relies heavily on Wittgenstein's concept of grammar, and the ways that it is both arbitrary and nonarbitrary. I also take very seriously the contingency of our world and our ways of being. Thus, my view is neither absolutist nor relativist, because these categories have their lives against a conception of the world that I reject explicitly. Instead, I call my position "stabilist" because it captures the complex interactions among the various elements in the world. Stabilism is equally as far removed from "anything-goes" relativism as it is to various forms of absolutism.

One criticism that I have heard from feminists is that metaethics seems to miss the important issues that define normative ethics. One response that greeted my work was "Why bother?" As I make clear, particularly in the context of discussions of Frederick Douglass's 1852 speech "What to the Slave Is the Fourth of July" and the demands for justice from Hurricane Katrina victims, we can only use our moral concepts in the ways we do in the stable felted world. And describing those elements and relations to one another is the subject of metaethics.

Metaethics, like other branches in philosophy, is rife with all sorts of "isms," and my aim is to untangle these various "isms" so that we can identify what we need and want in a metaphysics of morals. In the course of writing this book, I have found myself drawing various diagrams in the hope of charting the relationships connecting realism and antirealism; absolutism and relativism; and objectivism, subjectivism, and voluntarism. I had hoped a nice clear pattern might emerge—something in which the various strands stand clearly and independently—but I had no such luck. They weave together in all sorts of complicated, crisscrossing, and overlapping ways on multiple levels. There was no hope of separately pulling on one set of questions without the others coming right along. At the end of many a frustrating day, I came to see this as a virtue in a feminist metaethics. It is a mistake to treat something as separable when it is not. This is an often-neglected source of philosophical trouble.

I spend a fair amount of space diagnosing some fundamental problems in current metaethics, in order to help make my case for effecting a shift away from the foundation metaphor, and to dispel some of the captivating and bewitching pictures in metaethics. Clearly this is no small task, and I entertain no illusions that my position is itself immune to many of the same criticisms. I expect and welcome these, because this work, like everything else in our lives, is always an ongoing project. If I am wrong, I hope to be wrong in interesting and productive ways.

This book is philosophical therapy. And to be honest, it is psychological therapy too. How often does one get to revisit something she did years ago? We all fantasize about revisiting and repairing past mistakes in the hopes of scrubbing away the sticky residue of error and its accompanying embarrassment. This book does just that. I had a very unfortunate realization two weeks prior to the defense of my dissertation on moral realism: I was wrong. Dead wrong. What was I thinking (for roughly two hundred pages) trying to argue for a Wittgensteinian form of moral realism? I could hardly begin to count the ways I went wrong, though I had no doubt that members of my examination committee might be able to do so. While it is true that it could have been worse had I this realization ten minutes before my defense, two weeks to mount a repudiation of my own work and still maintain a positive argument was daunting, keeping me from nights of slumber, dogmatic or not.

At the opening of my defense, my committee chair invited me to make some preliminary comments. I launched a preemptive strike and said that I believed that a Wittgensteinian approach to moral realism was a mistaken strategy. I am not sure who was more stunned by this, members of my committee or me. Somehow, I managed to argue that my dissertation still could stand as a coherent whole even though my claims about realism were deeply misguided. My claims about objectivity still could stand and might in fact be stronger without the particular brand of realism I mistakenly advocated. The two hours passed in a blur, at the end of which my committee passed me unanimously.

After correcting some minor typos and producing a version that met the approval of the Graduate School Maven (after a fierce disagreement about the correct way to number front matter that I let her win only because she had more power and a big wooden ruler), I relegated it to my bookshelves. I snipped out a few pages, but otherwise I moved it only when I changed jobs or offices.

I left metaethics behind and turned to normative ethics. I wrote *Oppression and Responsibility*, focusing on the ways that systems of oppression maintain and reinforce themselves, and offering a model of responsibility that enables us to talk about the responsibilities that members of privileged groups have for the continued lives of those systems. That work, being a work in normative ethics, makes many recommendations and prescriptions. I had no reservations about claiming that one state of affairs is objectively better than another. And then it happened.

As much as I thought I had left metaethics behind, I realized that I was in the process of coming full circle. In *Oppression and Responsibility*, I presumed simply that the grounding of our moral lives are organized in a certain way. Like a mechanical monkey, I gave a few winks and nods in recognition of this, but it was time to undertake an investigation of that grounding, and offer a description of it. I am suspicious of grand system building, and so my aspirations are more humble. Like John Locke, I see myself as an underlaborer clearing the ground and removing some of the metaphysical detritus.

BB   Ludwig Wittgenstein, *Blue and Brown Books* (New York: Harper, 1965)

CV   Ludwig Wittgenstein, *Culture and Value,* ed. G. H. von Wright, trans. P. Winch (Chicago: University of Chicago Press, 1980)

LE   Ludwig Wittgenstein, "Lecture on Ethics," in *Philosophical Occasions, 1912–1951,* ed. James Klagge and Alfred Nordmann, 37–44 (Indianapolis, Ind.: Hackett, 1993)

LFM   Ludwig Wittgenstein, *Wittgenstein's Lectures on the Foundation of Mathematics, Cambridge, 1939,* from the notes of R. G. Bosanquet, N. Malcolm, R. Rhees, and Y. Smythies, ed. C. Diamond (Chicago: University of Chicago Press, 1975)

LW   Ludwig Wittgenstein, *Last Writings on the Philosophy of Psychology,* vol. 2, ed. G. H. von Wright and H. Nyman, trans. C. G. Luckhardt and M. A. E. Ane (Oxford: Blackwell, 1992)

OC   Ludwig Wittgenstein, *On Certainty,* ed. G. E. M. Anscombe and G. H. von Wright, trans. Denis Paul and G. E. M. Anscombe (New York: Harper and Row, 1969)

PG   Ludwig Wittgenstein, *Philosophical Grammar,* ed. R. Rhees, trans. A. J. P. Kenny (Oxford: Blackwell, 1974)

PI   Ludwig Wittgenstein, *Philosophical Investigations,* 3rd ed., trans. G. E. M. Anscombe (New York: Macmillan, 1968)

PR   Ludwig Wittgenstein, *Philosophical Remarks,* ed. R. Rhees, trans. R. Hargreaves and R. White (Oxford: Blackwell, 1975)

RC   Ludwig Wittgenstein, *Remarks on Colour,* ed. G. E. M. Anscombe, trans. L. L. McAlister and Margaret Schattle (Oxford: Blackwell, 1980)

RFM   Ludwig Wittgenstein, *Remarks on the Foundation of Mathematics,* rev. ed., ed. G. H. von Wright, R. Rhees, and G. E. M. Anscombe (Cambridge, Mass.: MIT Press, 1978)

RPP   Ludwig Wittgenstein, *Remarks on the Philosophy of Psychology,* vol.

2, ed. G. H. von Wright and H. Nyman, trans. C. G. Luckhardt and M. A. E. Ane (Oxford: Blackwell, 1980)

Z   Ludwig Wittgenstein, *Zettel*, ed. G. E. M. Anscombe and G. H. von Wright, trans. G. E. M. Anscombe (Berkeley and Los Angeles: University of California Press, 1970)

1 FEMINIST WITTGENSTEINIAN METAETHICS?
REVISING THE BIG BOOK

Disquiet in philosophy might be said to arise from looking at philosophy wrongly,
seeing it wrong, namely as if it were divided into (infinite) longitudinal strips instead of into
(finite) cross strips. This inversion in our conception produces the greatest difficulty.
So we try as it were to grasp the unlimited strips and complain that it cannot be done
piecemeal. To be sure it cannot, if by a piece one means an infinite longitudinal strip. But it
may well be done, if one means a cross-strip.—But in that case we never get to the end
of our work!—Of course not, for it has no end.
—WITTGENSTEIN, *ZETTEL*, § 447

I have arrived at the rock bottom of my convictions.
And one might almost say that these foundation-walls are carried by the whole house.
—WITTGENSTEIN, *ON CERTAINTY*, § 248

FEMINIST METAETHICS?

To many ethicists, "feminist metaethics" sounds odd. Yes, they may agree that feminists have made many significant contributions in normative and applied ethics. Feminist normative ethics has played a vital role in ethics; it has named, challenged, and corrected a long, pervasive history of male biases. These biases show up in a multitude of ways and have fortified certain canonical concepts such as impartiality and universality. Feminists have challenged the terms of traditional debates and categories by identifying and rejecting problematic assumptions. For example, feminist analyses have argued convincingly against an atomistic sense of self and the accompanying expectations for autonomy and dignity.

Feminist ethics has been both a critical enterprise and a creative one. Feminist ethics is perhaps at its best when creative and innovative, opening new avenues for exploration. The relatively short history of feminist ethics is quite illustrious. The importance of feminist work on the concept of care, the reclamation and recognition of certain virtues, and the advancement of feminist conceptions of moral inquiry, should neither be underestimated nor overlooked. Feminists have done an amazing job of arguing against the devaluation and neglect of those spheres of life that have been associated with women; at the same time, they have challenged the notions of "women's sphere" and "women's work."

But when it comes to metaethics and more recent debates about realism and antirealism, or questions about the possibility or conditions for objectivity in morals or moral knowledge, feminist voices have been relatively few compared to our presence in normative and applied ethics. Annette Baier, Virginia Held, Margaret Urban Walker, Alison Jaggar, Cora Diamond, and Sabina Lovibond stand out in their attempts to push metaethics in different directions. Virginia Held, for example, has been one of the most important critics of scientizing ethics, especially with respect to moral psychology and its subsumption to cognitive science.[1] Annette Baier and Margaret Urban Walker have argued for naturalistic approaches to ethics, ones that recognize that we begin and spend our entire lives in relationships of interdependency.[2] Alison Jaggar challenges us to find an immanent grounding that begins with our concrete experiences.[3] Sabina Lovibond and Cora Diamond have explored questions of ethical realism in relation to Wittgenstein.[4] Though this is an impressive list, it is short. Why might this be so?

One reason, I suspect, is that old-fashioned grounding questions, which now fall into the category of metaethics, have undergone a significant

---

1. Virginia Held, "Whose Agenda? Ethics Versus Cognitive Science," in *Mind and Morals: Essays on Ethics and Cognitive Science,* ed. Larry May, Marilyn Friedman, and Andy Clark (Cambridge, Mass.: The MIT Press, 1996), 69–87.

2. Annette C. Baier, "A Naturalist View of Persons," in *Moral Prejudices: Essays on Ethics* (Cambridge, Mass.: Harvard University Press, 1995), 313–26; Margaret Walker, "Naturalizing, Normativity, and Using What 'We' Know in Ethics," *Canadian Journal of Philosophy,* 26 suppl. (2000): 75–102. See also Walker's *Moral Understandings: A Feminist Study in Ethics* (New York: Routledge, 1998) and her *Moral Contexts* (Lanham, Md.: Rowman and Littlefield, 2003).

3. Alison Jaggar, "Feminist Ethics: Projects, Problems, Prospects," in *Feminist Ethics,* ed. Claudia Card (Lawrence: University Press of Kansas, 1991), 78–104. See also Jaggar's "Feminism in Ethics: Moral Justification," in *The Cambridge Companion to Feminism in Philosophy,* ed. Miranda Fricker and Jennifer Hornsby (Cambridge: Cambridge University Press, 2000), 225–44.

4. Sabina Lovibond, *Realism and Imagination in Ethics* (Minneapolis: University of Minnesota Press, 1983). See also Lovibond's *Ethical Formation* (Cambridge, Mass.: Harvard University Press, 2002). From Diamond, see "Wittgenstein, Mathematics, and Ethics: Resisting the Attraction of Realism," in *The Cambridge Companion to Wittgenstein,* ed. Hans Sluga and David Stern (Cambridge: Cambridge University Press, 1996), 226–60. See also Diamond's *The Realistic Spirit: Wittgenstein, Philosophy, and the Mind* (Cambridge, Mass.: The MIT Press, 1991).

transformation, at least since the analytic turn of the early twentieth century. Recent Anglo-American philosophy has narrowed the scope of examination, shifting from questions about human nature and human capacities to questions about the metaphysical and epistemological status of moral properties, considered independently of humans. This shift is significant, resulting in part from importing the expectations and methods of science into morals. Metaethicists ask a metaphysical question: "Can moral properties such as goodness or evil exist in the world independently of humans?" They also ask epistemological questions: "Can these properties be known, and if so, how?" The expectation is that moral properties, if they do exist, must act like natural properties and must play the same role in observation and explanation as do natural properties. Moral epistemology takes on an empiricist cast. Gilbert Harman and J. L. Mackie argue that such properties cannot exist and that therefore moral knowledge is impossible. This antirealist and noncognitivist view leads to relativism. David Brink and Nicholas Sturgeon, moral realists, argue that moral properties are real and can be known. This view rejects the relativistic conclusions of the antirealists but perhaps lends itself to absolutist expectations.

Metaethical investigations are now framed by the categories and debates about realism/antirealism, cognitivism/noncognitivism, and objectivism/relativism. Entering debates on these narrowly constructed terms can be profoundly alienating. My dissertation adventure, described in the "Prolegomenon" above, is a case in point. I really wanted to advance a metaethical approach of a different stripe. In the end, I capitulated to the existing categories. I pledged allegiance to a form of moral realism. I lacked the conceptual resources and the confidence to reject the terms of the debates. The best I could do was advance a position that was a little critical of and a little different from what I now regard as a fairly standard view. I understood exactly what Wittgenstein meant when he wrote, "It is very difficult to describe paths of thought where there are already many lines of thought laid down,—your own or other people's—and not get into the grooves. It is difficult to deviate from the old line of thought *just a little*" (Z § 349, emphasis in original). After my defense, I folded up my metaethical tent and went to normative ethics, a field that felt so much more real, exciting, and important. I also felt compelled by Wittgenstein's directing back to the rough ground. Metaethics seemed to me like a frictionless surface, high theory and abstraction in the world of ethics. With respect to normative ethics, metaethics seems like the ornamental knob that spins but that doesn't engage with anything. On this view, metaethics and normative ethics seem like separate enterprises. It becomes easy to imagine that, as J. L. Mackie asserts, one could be a skeptic about metaethical issues even as one remains committed to making normative claims and staking out moral positions. Feminist ethicists remain in the business of making important prescriptions, and so we remain in normative ethics.

Small wonder that I and other feminists, particularly of my generation, have been so disinclined to grapple with these issues.

The confining nature of the absolutist/relativist dichotomy also contributes to the lack of feminist participation. Within the confines of this opposition, we find ourselves caught between the extremes of two untenable positions. Feminists, as a consequence of our critiques of concepts such as impartiality and universalism, are often assumed to be relativists in the sense of holding that there are no moral demands incumbent on all people or that morality is simply a matter of choice or convention. The charge of relativism when lobbed at feminists is often an accusation that we must hold that "anything goes." Our purported relativism of this anything-goes variety then becomes a justification others deploy to justify rejecting our normative claims about inequality, discrimination, and oppression. Any claims that feminists make in normative ethics can be met with demands—often issued in a hostile manner—for justification about our grounds. But feminists must be able to discuss the nature of the grounding of our moral lives in all its complexity—the quintessential metaethical question—so that we can defend ourselves against charges of this sort of relativism in a systematic and not ad hoc manner. Our silence or invisibility threatens the progress we have made, not only in philosophy, especially in ethical theory and applied ethics, but also in the political sphere. Our normative claims intersect directly with politics and public policy.

In advancing a feminist approach to metaethics, I take seriously the warnings about moral theorizing that Virginia Held issues in her book *Feminist Morality*.[5] She counsels us feminists to avoid the problematic dichotomies and assumptions that have defined the shape of ethical theory. These are so familiar that I will only list them here: reason/emotion dichotomy, public/private split, and a conception of self as an autonomous, atomistic individual. Additionally, Held offers the following recommendations for what feminist inquiry should do:

1. Involve actual experience (as opposed to hypothetical thought experiments)

---

5. Virginia Held, *Feminist Morality: Transforming Culture, Society, and Politics* (Chicago: University of Chicago Press, 1993).

2. Have an ongoing dynamic character (as opposed to being finished when one fixes on a course of action and then acts; it is not a series of discrete actions)

3. Proceed not solely on a case-by-case basis (requires some level of generality)

4. Understand moral agents to be actual embodied persons standing in multiple relations (as opposed to the isolated inhabitant of the view from nowhere or the Archimedean point)

5. Include a dialogic conception of normative reasons (not the sole product of an exercise of an atomistic individual)

6. Conceptualize moral experience as being something other or more than empirical experience (without turning it into something occult or supernatural)

7. Recognize the pluralities within human moral life (to avoid the problems following from false universalizability and cultural imperialism)

In addition to these recommendations, I add the following, which I take to be consistent with and in the spirit of Held's. Feminist moral theory and inquiry should:

1. Create a moral epistemology that is consistent with much recent work in feminist epistemologies (resisting its reduction or assimilation to an overly scientistic model)

2. Have a robust conception of responsibility that includes evaluating our practices, including our practices of responsibility (because practices will provide the stability to our moral lives)

3. Bring us back to first-order moral questions (so that metaethics is not the spinning ornamental knob that engages with nothing)

4. Recognize the disputatious character of moral inquiry and not understand disagreement as a simply a temporary and undesirable state of affairs to be overcome (recognizes the diversity in human lives)

5. Not presume an unbridgeable divide between nature and normativity or world and language (all the while resisting the reduction of one to the other, which recently has been the reduction of normativity to nature)

This last recommendation is perhaps the most interesting and contentious. The tension will be to avoid the dualism without falling into a reductionist approach, whereby the moral is subsumed to the empirical. This reduction is Held's concern as well as my own. My hope is to show the ways in which nature and normativity are inseparable from one another, and how nature and normativity are, more strongly, mutually constitutive by their very nature. I aim to do this without assuming that this dualism will provide the normative authority our moral judgments require or make normativity into something metaphysically odd.

A WITTGENSTEINIAN METAETHICS?

My strategy in meeting Held's demands as well as the ones that I claim is to adopt a Wittgensteinian approach to metaethics. Metaethics—in its present state—would be greatly improved by Wittgensteinian therapies. But, if feminist metaethics sounds odd, Wittgensteinian metaethics is odder still. The final sentence of the *Tractatus* says it all: "What we cannot speak about we must pass over in silence" (7). A book on ethics claiming a Wittgensteinian influence should perhaps be full of blank pages. As I discuss below, however, there are good reasons to draw from the wealth of Wittgenstein's philosophy for the benefit of ethical investigation.

This work is Wittgensteinian in two related ways. First, I employ a Wittgensteinian methodology with respect to diagnosing "problems" and offering certain therapies. I make use of many of Wittgenstein's insights about certain tendencies in philosophy: to crave generality over particularity, to seek the ideal case rather than the ordinary one, to be bewitched by certain pictures, to assume that substantives must always have objects, to fail to recognize or reject limitations of language, and to create thorny problems by demanding that what holds in one context must also hold in another. Metaethics is much in need of Wittgensteinian therapies, and in this work, I aim to provide some.

This project is Wittgensteinian in a second and more contentious way. Reading the *Tractatus* and his 1929 "Lecture on Ethics," it is easy to see the philosophical inspiration for the analytic/logical positivist turn that metaethics took. In the very little he wrote about ethics, Wittgenstein seemingly supplied much of the fodder for the shape of the realist/antirealist debates. Wittgenstein's reason for writing remarkably little about ethics—especially intriguing given his own belief that ethics treats of the most serious matters—is that ethics concerns showing and not saying. Ethics is beyond the reach of our language and, "if it is anything, is supernatural and our words will only express facts; as a teacup will only hold a teacup full of water [even] if I were to pour out a gallon over it" (LE, 40). He asks his listeners at his "Lecture on Ethics" to imagine that an omniscient being could write down all the movements of objects and beings, all states of affairs and states of mind of all humans in the world. This big book would contain a whole description of the world, but "this book would contain nothing that we would call an ethical judgment or anything that would logically imply such a judgment" (LE, 39).[6] Descriptions about absolute good or absolute value are nonsensical, but not because we simply have not found the correct descriptions. Rather, the nonsensicality of such descriptions is their very essence. In attempting to offer descriptions of these absolutes, one tries to "go beyond the world and that is to say beyond significant language" (LE, 44).

There are two received ways of reading Wittgenstein on this subject. The first reading denies that moral judgments can be expressed in propositional form. Thus, moral judgments are nonsense; they lack meaning. The second reading shares much with the first. Yes, moral judgments are nonsense because they reach beyond what can be meaningfully said. But, due to the subject of ethics, it is nonsense of a very special and deep sort. This shows that Wittgenstein recognizes a "mystical, ineffable, realm of value, for which our words are, of necessity, inadequate."[7] Both of these views are lacking, but my intent is not to offer a refutation of them. Rather, I am interested in the picture of ethics that Wittgenstein discusses.

Wittgenstein contrasts ethical judgments with relative judgments about value. Relative judgments about value are those that can be made with reference to some certain predetermined standard, goal, or purpose. Being a good pianist, for example, means being able to perform pieces of a certain degree of difficulty with a degree of dexterity. The right road is the one that leads to the destination with ease and speed. Relative judgments are actually statements of facts that have the appearance of judgments of values (LE, 40). One can restate these judgments as descriptions of facts. Therefore, the inclusion of relative judgments of value in the big book is unproblematic.

Wittgenstein clearly identifies his expectations for what absolute moral properties would have to be. He says, "The absolute good, if it is a describable state of affairs, would be one which everybody, independent of his tastes and inclinations, would necessarily bring about or feel guilty for not

---

6. See also Wittgenstein, CV, 5, where he says, "You cannot lead people to the good; you can only lead them to some place or other; the good lies outside the space of facts." (Hereafter, all citations of CV in text.)

7. D. Z. Phillips, *Religion and Wittgenstein's Legacy* (Aldershot: Ashgate, 2005), 1. There is a good deal of secondary literature on these two different readings. For an overview and interesting discussion of them, see Phillips's "Introduction: On Reading Wittgenstein and Religion," 1–10.

bringing about. And I want to say that such a state of affairs is a chimera. No state of affairs has, in itself, what I would like to call the coercive power of an absolute judge" (LE, 40). A state of affairs cannot both be describable and possess the absolute noncontingent authority over individuals. No statement of facts can ever imply an absolute judgment (LE, 40). Therefore, there is a sharp distinction between facts and absolute values. Facts are expressible in propositions while absolute values are not. Absolute values, as mentioned above, are ineffable. We cannot speak of them. Absolute values are beyond the realm of language and therefore beyond the realm of inquiry. Anyone who tries to say something about the absolute good or the absolute meaning of life runs into the boundaries of language. It is a human tendency to want to make these sorts of claims, but for all of us—ethicist and nonethicist—"this running against the walls of our cage is perfectly, absolutely hopeless" (LE, 44).

This running into the bars of the cage is both a philosophical and practical problem. How are the two related? Wittgenstein wrote that "work on philosophy—like work in architecture in many respects—is really more work on oneself. On one's own conception. On how one sees things. (And what one expects of them.)" (CV, 24). For Wittgenstein, work on oneself is perhaps the highest calling, and this in the broadest sense for him is the substance of ethics.

This connection makes sense of Wittgenstein's own description of the *Tractatus* that its point is an ethical one. While many commentators have found this to be an odd comment and have glossed over it, Alessandra Tanesini takes Wittgenstein at face value and makes sense of it by making explicit the connections between the philosophical problems of the modern self and the alienation and isolation we experience in our lives.[8] Questions about the meaning of life are terribly important, and our philosophical concepts and orientations may deflect or misconstrue them, such that we end up frustrated, alienated, and isolated. The meaning of life is fundamentally connected to the "problem" of subjectivity that is characteristic of the modern period.

According to Tanesini, in the *Tractatus* and his "Lecture on Ethics" Wittgenstein offers a diagnosis of the illness of the modern autonomous self. Philosophical concepts and their problems often have very prosaic and unglamorous origins. Consider the problem of other minds, which arises

---

8. Alessandra Tanesini, *Wittgenstein: A Feminist Interpretation* (Cambridge: Polity Press, 2004), 69.

from some very ordinary experiences that, when in the hands of philosophers, become inexplicable and inexorable. Descartes' access to his own ideas led him to produce the philosophical picture of the modern self. This modern self has privileged access to his own ideas and recognizes that he has access that no one else can. Thus, it is but a short step to skepticism about other minds. Skepticism gains purchase when the subject is severed from the rest of the world, and that raises epistemological concerns about whether and how we can know others. Skepticism is born out of and then reinforces a lack of trust not only about other minds, but also about one's own abilities and capacities.

The continued separation of subjects continues with Kant, who trumpets the autonomy of this modern self. In Kant's hands, the modern autonomous self is a knowing subject who is capable of being self-legislating, because his reason is able to recognize what is required of him. The modern autonomous subject produced by Kant is alienated and isolated from itself, from others, and from the world around it.

What avenues are available for redressing this alienation and isolation? With both Descartes and Kant, there is a presumption that our reason has the potential to liberate us through transcendence from the contingent and from the ordinary. The hope is that we can achieve meaning and value by transcending our finitude and limitations. We cannot resist this impulse; we will try and try, but this is precisely when we keep hitting our heads against the cage. Hitting our heads repeatedly will only cause despair, and so what meaning can life have? The very attempt to escape the isolation and alienation through transcendence produces more alienation and isolation. The curative option offered within a solidly modern world only exacerbates the illness.

Tanesini elucidates well one of Wittgenstein's characteristic approaches to philosophical problems in her discussion of the alienation and isolation of the modern self. The cure for philosophical illnesses and problems is not solution but dissolution. Oftentimes this involves examining the philosophical pictures that have captivated or bewitched us. One dominant picture concerns limitations and finitude, namely, that they form a cage and that the ultimate meaning is what one finds outside it. Tanesini's reading of the *Tractatus* focuses on the limits of the expression of thought in language in order to show how it is that limits can be drawn. With respect to the limits of logic, we should not think of them as "a boundary separating what is possible from what is not."[9] Rather, we need to reconceive the

9. Ibid., 70.

limits of logic. Our logic gives rise to tautologies and contradictions, and these indicate that logical space has limits. Tanesini argues that because logic expresses the laws of human thought, human thought has limits too. It is tempting, however, to "misunderstand this phenomenon and to believe that these failures show that something lies beyond what we can grasp."[10] If we assume that there has to be something beyond these limits of language and thoughts, but that we just cannot get there because of our human finitude, we suffer the illness of the modern age.

Once liberated from the impulse to run into the bars of the cage in the hope of escaping, we can begin to recognize our limitations and finitude as something in which meaning and value are created. The meaning of life is not an objectified meaning. It certainly is not something found by the modern autonomous self, but rather something that is made by human beings.

Thus, this present work is Wittgensteinian in the sense of embracing limitations and finitude as features of our world and life. Embracing this as our condition results in a very different picture of the metaphysics of morals. On the rejected view, ethics understood as the absolute and the unsayable is unreachable by the pull of science and its modes of inquiry. One important feature of this alternative metaphysics I offer is that it locates ethics right at the heart of language; it is not outside it nor is it unreachable from language. On my Wittgensteinian view, the moral dimensions are so intertwined with other aspects of daily living that they are inseparable. No scientific autoclave will be able to spin out the moral dimensions from the nonmoral ones. The move to bring ethics home to language reveals the ways that moral life is inherently social, public, material, and ultimately practical. One could say that I am offering revisions to the big book, not from an outside vantage point (last I checked, I was not omniscient) but from the middle of our ordinary language use. Wittgenstein, more than any other philosopher with whom I am familiar, equips me with the tools for this undertaking. His treatments of ordinary language and concepts, forms of life, knowledge and certainty, and agreement and disagreement influence this work tremendously. I recognize that I am using Wittgenstein's work to make inquiries into areas that many Wittgenstein scholars would claim to be ineffable and incapable of description. My project, then, is both Wittgensteinian and perhaps very un-Wittgensteinian (though I do not think so), a paradox that provides a productive tension.

10. Ibid.

Tension is a recurring theme of this work. The tension in the use of Wittgenstein is matched by the tension in feminist ethics about the important and pressing issues in normative ethics. One of my goals is to show some of the indissoluble links between metaethics and normative ethics. These links will become most apparent in discussing the concepts of certainty and grammar from Wittgenstein. Tension is also central in the metaphor I develop below. Tension is often perceived to be a defect or burden, but I argue that tension—in architecture and moral inquiry—is an unavoidable and important productive force.

CHANGING THE DOMINANT METAPHOR: CREATING STABILITY VERSUS LOCATING FOUNDATIONS

Everyone has heard that you should not build a house on a foundation of sand. Sand shifts, and when that happens, down comes the entire structure. In ethics, we have preferred our foundations big and unmistakable, unshakeable and undeniable. We like bedrock and, though we have differed over what is the bedrock (reason that gives us the categorical imperative or the maximization of utility principle, rights, some sort of sentiment, or independently existing moral properties), we go for the unshifting every time. Something that was moveable certainly could not do the job. What else could provide stability to the structure of our moral lives? The important first move made in metaethics is to assume that foundations alone (or even primarily) provide stability. This is the move that escapes notice.

I spend summers with my architect friend Bruce Norelius. I told him that I was working on a project in metaethics and that I was looking for a different way to describe the stability in our moral lives. My goal, I proclaimed, was to reject foundationalism as it is typically understood. In support, I offered Wittgenstein's quotation that "I have arrived at the rock bottom of my convictions. And one might almost say that these foundation-walls are carried by the whole house" (OC § 248). Given Wittgenstein's interest in architecture and engineering, this insight—cryptic though it is—afforded a wonderful opportunity. I needed a great deal of help to *see* stability created in different ways in some contemporary cutting-edge architecture. Bruce became my guide and introduced me to some of the works of Rem Koolhaas and Cecil Balmond.

The influence of Descartes in architecture, especially through coordinate geometry, is immense. Descartes' influence is also apparent in his

demand and quest for absolute foundations, and the accompanying expectations for what can support a structure (be it physical or metaphysical).
This modernism in architecture has enjoyed a relatively unchallenged
status for quite some time. Recently, however, a movement in architecture
led by architect Rem Koolhaas and engineer Cecil Balmond has emerged
as a direct challenge. Rem Koolhaas was retained to design a house on a
cliff edge overlooking Bordeaux. The owner is a man who had recently had
a car accident that had confined him to a wheelchair. He tells Koolhaas,
"Contrary to what you might expect, I do not want a simple house. I want
a complex house because the house will define my world."[11] The house
design showed three houses or boxes on top of one another. The lowest is
described as being cave-like, with a series of caverns carved out from the
hill. The highest house was divided in half for the parents' bedrooms and
the children's bedrooms. The middle level is described by Koolhaas as
the most important. It is "almost invisible, sandwiched in-between a glass
room—half inside and half outside—for living."[12] An elevator moves
among the three levels, changing plan and performance depending on its
location. Each house is intersected by a single wall next to the elevator.
The single wall contains many of the things the owner wants ready at
hand, such as books and wine.

Enter engineer Cecil Balmond. Koolhaas wants the top house/box to
appear to be flying. Balmond says, "But gravity is a tyrant. Its pull cannot
be avoided, and the usual response for supporting a load in the air is to
configure legs to hold the weight up from below."[13] This is the paradigm
of "table," an idea that "brings with it implicit acceptance of static symme-
try."[14] Balmond calls this one of the elements of the formal, or the character
of the modern, that marches to strict rhythms. He asks, why is it necessary
to space out structure equally, "like soldiers marching on a parade
ground?" Why should the design of structural framing be limited to the
bar pattern of a cage? Is space so dull "that punctuating it means only the
regular monotonous beat of verticals and horizontals? Why not relax and
move towards a slip or jump in the arrangement of things?"[15]

Balmond recognizes that there are different ways to approach design,
and he contrasts two of them through metaphor. The first is tried-and-
true. He says, "At the bottom of the valley there is a point of tradition and

11. Rem Koolhaas, *OMA/Rem Koolhaas, 1987–1998* (Madrid: El Croquis, 1998), 134.
12. Ibid.
13. Cecil Balmond (with Jannuzzi Smith), *Informal* (Munich: Prestel Verlag, 2002), 23.
14. Ibid., 24.
15. Ibid., 62.

solid reference. No matter how far we experiment and get away from the location and move up the slope, we fall back and settle at the origin. Analysis always brings us back to the zero point. The solution cannot get away from its original reference."[16] The mistake is to assume that one must always begin at the same place. Consider what happens when we reject this assumption: "At the summit of a hill the point is one of departure, the outcome unpredictable. There is no way back to the origin. We roll into the unknown to chart a new course. In the cliff top scenario there is no safety of past reference, only the certainty of unfamiliar territory ahead."[17] The concern about changing the starting point in design resonates with Wittgenstein's concerns about where philosophical investigations begin. Wittgenstein says that "the axis of reference of our examination must be rotated, but about the fixed point of our real need" (*PI* § 108). When we neglect "our real need," our starting point will set a course riddled with just the sort of philosophical problems Wittgenstein was attempting to dissolve. For Balmond, the starting point in design is a consequence of the physical location, the design, and a whole host of other factors. For both Wittgenstein and Balmond, one should never assume that *this* must be the starting point.

So how did Balmond work with Koolhaas to make a house appear to fly? As stated above, the house design is three boxes on top of one another. One side of the lowest box opens into the landscape and the other side is buried against the natural cut of the landscape. Glass walls surround the second level. These glass walls can slide, making a moveable boundary between inside and outside. The third level is the one that appears to be lifting off. Running through all three levels are two columns, wrapped to appear as one. Had they positioned these columns so that they ran through the center of all three levels, they would have achieved stability (in the sense of table) but would have lost the launch Balmond and Koolhaas sought. Instead Balmond pushed these columns off to one side, a move that would cause that top box to tip unless it was counterbalanced. The counterbalance comes from several things. The first is a shelf beam that acts like a leg on which part of that top box sits. This leg does not go straight down but rather extends off to the side of the two lower levels. Running the width across the top box is a beam approximately 1.5 meters thick. The end of this beam extends off the side, and in the design a weight

16. Ibid., 28.
17. Ibid.

would hang. This beam and weight would provide the counterbalance to the off-centeredness of the columns. Due to costs during construction, the hanging weight became a tie-down, which functioned in the same way.[18]

The beam and the hanging weight/tie-down provide the stability due to their relationship to each other and to the other structural features. The beam running width-wise carries the weight of the two long walls (they hang from this beam). These long walls themselves function as beams, carrying the weight of floor and ceiling. The tie-down is essential, and its proper functioning depends on tension. The trick, as Balmond says, "is to keep the cable under tension at all times. A hot day, for example, will increase the length of the tie due to thermal expansion, slacken it, and tend to tip the box over to one side."[19] The solution is to make the cable over-tensioned in order to remain taut, thereby keeping the box horizontal. And if the cable is cut? Then "the box will tilt to one side; but the deflection is calculated and the material proportioned in such a way as to keep the structure stable in this extreme condition. Due to the elastic nature of materials (even concrete) once the cable force is reinstated the structure will ease back to the horizontal!"[20] As this Koolhaas and Balmond house shows, stability is not a matter of foundations alone. One would be hard-pressed to identify the foundations of the Bordeaux villa. Rather, this house shows that stability is a matter of balanced relationships among a whole host of factors, and that stability comes with a constant recognition of limitations and location. Concrete can only bend so much, steel can only hold so much weight, glass can only take so much pressure. Stability is not simply a matter of immobility but also flexibility; just consider the importance of movement in a tall building or bridge. Stability is not a given but rather an achievement of balance and tension.

In terms of examining the grounding of moral life, I am not looking for the table equivalent of absolute foundations. None exists, I believe.

---

18. The change to a buried tie-down from the hanging weight was a matter of financial necessity and safety concerns. The original hanging rock was initially replaced by a concrete deadweight that would be located in a pit and held down further by a buried foundation. But this changed too, and it was cheaper to have the cable tie disappear into the ground, attached to a lump of dead concrete. That meant that "only a plate on the surface would denote the passage through to the subterranean holding. It was expedient but not poetic, not our dare-devil vision of a hung weight in space denoting a danger moment" (Balmond, *Informal*, 43). Some might be tempted to say, "Ah ha! There is a foundation really; it is just buried!" I would ask them, "What is the foundation? The cable? The cement deadweight?" It is not just one thing, but rather structural elements in relation to one another, playing certain roles. This, I believe, is that to which Wittgenstein's quotation points.

19. Balmond, *Informal*, 30.

20. Ibid.

Rather, I am looking at some of the factors that can provide stability so long as they are in balance with one another. One factor is the equivalent of location; Koolhaas and Balmond accept the edge of the cliff. In terms of moral life, the location is human life in the natural world. Ironically or paradoxically, the importance of location seems to have been lost in recent metaethics. The work of Koolhaas and Balmond also shows the importance of tension. Tension produces stability and beauty in architecture; my hope is that it produces these in philosophy too.

There is also great tension in the abstract nature of metaethics and the pressing concerns of normative ethics. Much of this present work is abstract in ways that may initially appear somewhat alienating. Even the discussions of activities such as measuring, counting, identifying facial expressions, and acknowledging and recognizing others may not seem all that philosophically interesting and relevant. To many philosophers, these are the rags, so mundane and prosaic that our philosophical talk passes them right by as unimportant. But they are very important, especially acknowledgment and recognition. This will be apparent when I move to a discussion about the simultaneous acknowledgement and denial of the humanity of blacks by whites in the United States in the context of slavery. In the final chapter, I turn to the events of Hurricane Katrina, arguing for the obligations of justice that are created within what I will identify as the stable felted world of practices.

Chapters 2 and 3 offer a diagnosis and an analysis of metaethics through the lens of one set of dominant questions. Chapter 2, "Does the Fabric of the World Include Moral Properties? Realist/Antirealist Debates," is most in John Locke's spirit of being an underlaborer who clears the ground and removes confusions. This chapter examines the shape that antirealist/realist debates have taken in the exchanges between Gilbert Harman and Nicholas Sturgeon, a moral antirealist and moral realist respectively. These exchanges are, I submit, canonical in contemporary metaethics, and present the clearest framing of the main issues. These debates revolve around metaphysical and epistemological considerations of moral properties. The question is posed, do moral properties behave like scientific properties in our observations and explanations? If the answer is no, then moral relativism follows. A positive answer to this question is evidence for moral objectivism or absolutism. The asymmetrical framing of this question enshrines scientific expectations for moral phenomena. The ethical naturalist, no less so than the moral antirealist, has pledged allegiance to these expectations. With the focus on moral properties—how they exist and function and how they can be known—human nature and agency drop out of the picture. Whereas in the past metaethics has asked those sorts of questions, recent work in metaethics, operating under the influence of scientism, largely passes those questions by. The displacement of questions about human nature, agency, and location contributes to the problematic tendency to divorce metaethics from normative ethics.

This chapter also introduces the issues of normativity and normative authority, and the expectations that a naturalist has for objectivity. One prominent approach to normativity treats it as a matter of necessity. This approach rests on a naturalistic metaphysics, which is also a prominent theme in the next chapter.

The third chapter, "Neither a Realist nor an Antirealist Be," continues the critique begun in the previous chapter, challenging the coherence of the philosophical theses of realism and antirealism. Many of Wittgenstein's investigations aim to deflate metaphysical theses such as "realism," "naturalism," "idealism," and "conventionalism." As he notes, these are posited as explanations for the nature or essence of the world. He concludes that metaphysical theses or concepts oftentimes mask grammatical principles, and philosophers have failed to appreciate this. Thus, metaphysics produces some of the most vexing and long-lasting confusions in philosophy. The predicament in which philosophers (including me) find themselves is that we fail to recognize the fact that two sides of a dualism often rest on shared assumptions. Wittgenstein aims his investigations right at those shared assumptions. In this chapter, my aim is the assumption that world and language, or if you prefer, nature and normativity, are radically distinct. I use these expressions interchangeably.

It is precisely against the backdrop of this assumption of the world/language dichotomy that normativity becomes a problem, especially in regard to ethics. One can tack into the alleged problem from several fronts. How do norms produce or generate reasons that have objective authority that holds for all? Whence comes the power or authority of moral judgments? How does the ought exercise a pull on all of us? What are the sources of normativity? Another way to put the question is, In what ways is normativity authoritative for us (and in ways that we can come to know)? Morality is fundamentally concerned with prescriptions and recommendations, judgments and evaluations. Morality wears its normativity on its sleeve, and needs no apologies for doing so. It certainly does not need to obscure its constitutive role in moral practices. The overt normativity of morality gives rise to the charge that ethics bears a special burden, especially when someone wants to argue for objectivity in morals.

Wittgenstein reframes discussions of necessity, offering a deflationary account. Rather than apologizing for context dependence, and assuming that it negates its necessity, he posited that all forms of necessity are context dependent. The next question, of course, is, what is the context. It was tempting to think that logical and mathematical necessities are anchored in logical and mathematical facts. The same temptation holds for metaphysical necessity. These necessities, it is assumed, hold without exception and regardless of context. But Wittgenstein's critique against just this temptation is devastating. Wittgenstein shows that this demand for independence is exactly what makes them untenable.

Ultimately, neither realism nor antirealism provides a coherent account of normativity, one that is adequate to the task of providing any criterion for correctness. The failure of these metaphysical theses traces back to their shared assumption about the world/language relationship. Thus, we find ourselves needing to reconceive both the relationship between world and language and our expectations for normativity.

Reconceiving the relationship between world and language is one way to address the worry that John McDowell has about the ways that nature has been disenchanted. When we acquiesce in the disenchantment of nature and expel meaning from the "merely natural," we will be left with philosophical mysteries about how to bring meaning back into the world.[21]

The first step in resisting this acquiescence is to show the twin failings of realism and antirealism. Once the confusions have been cleared, it is important to note what *is* there; this is an important descriptive task. The fourth chapter, "Felted Contextualism: Heterogeneous Stability," develops the alternative to the dominant realist/antirealist dichotomy. The chapter begins with a new metaphor for understanding the nature of the world, one that does not presume the world/language gap discussed in the previous chapter. This chapter addresses explicitly the context in which any forms of necessity and normativity have their lives. Wittgenstein's discussions of forms of life and natural history serve as my starting points in generating the position I call "felted contextualism." Using language in certain ways is one of our characteristic human activities, and it enables us to engage in moral practices. I read Wittgenstein to be using the concept "form of life" in two different but related ways. The first way is to

21. John McDowell, *Mind and World* (Cambridge, Mass.: Harvard University Press, 1994), 72.

mark the differences between human and nonhuman animals. This usage is concerned with the similarities and commonalities in activities shared by humans and that distinguish us from other animals. In this context, "form of life" refers to what I call the human form of life. Wittgenstein is not so much concerned with biological inflexibilities as with what different animals can and cannot do.

The second way Wittgenstein uses the term is to mark differences among humans. Communities having widely different moral and non-moral practices would have different forms of life. These two interpretations of this concept (one human form of life among other natural kinds and multiple forms of life within humanity) are often set up in opposition to one another, with the assumption that only one can be right. I take the two usages to be consistent and compatible, however, and ultimately important to my argument that there is an immanent and real grounding of our moral practices and judgments, which also has a remarkable diversity.

In this Wittgensteinian view, there is no radical break between what we are and what we do. In order to understand the nature of morality, the importance of the embodiedness of humans cannot be underestimated. Morality, on this view, is created and maintained through the actions and interactions of humans with one another, other beings, and the physical and social environments.

On Certainty is a centrally important text for the arguments in this chapter. As opposed to Avrum Stroll, who argues that Wittgenstein advances a certain form of foundationalism, I argue that Wittgenstein shows that foundations—understood as separable and distinct from language—are impossible. Felted contextualism and what I will call "stabilism" emerge as an alternative to both absolutism and relativism.

Various elements make up the stability, and with respect to metaethics, I argue that it is what Wittgenstein describes as certainty. This certainty includes a diversity of elements that in recent metaethics are shunted off to the side, ignored equally by both camps in the realist and antirealist debates.

Chapter 5, "Normativity and Grammar," addresses explicitly what naturalists call "the problem of normativity." This "problem" gets off the ground so quickly and effectively due to the assumption there is a dichotomy between natural features of the world (amenable to scientific inquiry) and normative features. If the natural is real or independent, which we readily assume, the normative seems that much stranger and in need of explanation (if not apology). In light of this assumption, the relationship between normativity and the natural is as vexing and challenging as the other big relationship of radically different kinds in philosophy—the mind and body.

The discussions of necessity, certainty, and the stability of our felted world of practices as the context of our living are intended to provide a very different starting point for discussions of normativity. With the felted-contextualist view, the normativity question takes on a very different cast. My account of normativity will rely heavily on Wittgenstein's conception of grammar. I will argue that grammar is part of the certainty that provides the stability in our shared ways of living. Grammar is an ineliminable feature of any and all practices; it is that which provides the possibility of intelligibility and meaningfulness. Grammar, in Wittgenstein's hands, becomes a remarkably complex concept. Grammar cuts across and is infused in both dimensions of forms of life. Actions function grammatically, as can attitudes. Thus, grammar has a heterogeneous character, the existence of which can give rise to tensions. In our world, grammar is both arbitrary and nonarbitrary, and these dimensions are inseparable from each other. Some features of the world and life contribute to grammar's arbitrariness, while others contribute to its nonarbitrariness. One common mistake is to treat them as separable, or to isolate their dynamic elements and treat them either as absolute or as contingent. Contingency is centrally important here. Wittgenstein in *Philosophical Investigations* brings out the contingency (what can also be called the arbitrariness) of our actual ways of living. Wittgenstein insists that it is a contingent fact that the world exists and that it contains humans. He takes it that there are general facts about the world and human beings that are stable and sure but cautions against taking these as foundations or as absolutes that can justify first principles or prove the existence of the world. Wittgenstein understands it as a given that there have been long-term uses of ordinary languages, and that grammar presupposes these uses. But many of his examples in *On Certainty* and *Philosophical Investigations* show the contingency of our actual ways of living, thus warding off the claim that ours must be the *right* ones. This is why it is a mistake to read *On Certainty* in any foundationalist sense.

Grammar is both constitutive of practices along with their meanings and intelligibility and regulative within a practice. Grammar has a force and authority; it is that which provides a standard of correctness through use. Each individual, as she becomes a member of communities, begins to feel and operate under the pull of grammar. As we mature, each of us begins to exert its pull ourselves, an activity that is part of what it means to develop what John McDowell calls a second nature.[22] This grammatical account demystifies normativity, and shows its rather prosaic and plebian character. Normativity is not something metaphysically queer. I argue that there is really no difference in kind in moral normativity from the normativity that governs our answering "four" to the question of "What is two plus two?" Moral necessity is no more mysterious (and in some ways duller) than normativity in other domains of life.

Moral epistemology is in need of a curative in order to resist the pull to more theoretical and abstract ways of knowing. Rejecting a picture that simply assumes a sharp division between natural and normative, and a sharp distinction between humans and the objects of our knowledge, will effect a profound shift in our expectations for moral knowledge.

Chapter 6, "Philosophical Rags and Mice: Changing the Subject in Moral Epistemology," makes an argument for broadening what is included under the category of moral epistemology. Virginia Held argues that with respect to morality, we ought to retire the term "epistemology" because of its close associations with science and its empiricist roots. This limits moral knowledge to the propositional sort, with the accompanying expectations for inquiry and standards of justification and verification. Instead, the broader category of "moral understandings" is more appropriate to and reflective of what we do when engaged in myriad moral practices and activities. If we take seriously the fact that activities and practices composing the certainty are the felted context, then we see that moral knowledge is best understood as a kind of practical knowledge along the lines discussed by Plato. The "rags" are the basic preconditions, background conditions, and skills that a traditional propositional approach of "S knows that p" takes for granted. These rags, I argue, are philosophically significant.

Moral knowledge involves practical understandings that are necessarily public and shared. Only as embodied and engaged persons can people be participants in the practices of daily living who contribute to the makings of moral understandings and who show understandings in our actions. Moral problems are not theoretical problems requiring theoretical solutions. Rather, moral problems are practical problems that require practical wisdom and embodied solutions. This effects a significant change in our expectations for moral knowledge or understandings. Moral understanding neither requires some sort of special faculty for apprehending the

22. See ibid.

moral dimensions of a situation nor is it beholden to empiricism narrowly conceived.

Reasons and justifications, which play significant roles in our shared ways of living, are primary components of one important form of moral inquiry. Reasons, by their use and role in our lives, have normative authority. Reasons and justifications demonstrate our intelligibility and the meaningfulness of our actions. They involve myriad skills and, even more basically, the acknowledgment and recognition of others. And it is here that we see one way in which normative ethics and metaethics are deeply entwined.

Justifications assume that one has recognized another as being worthy of a justification. But what are the conditions under which individuals or groups are recognized as being worthy of justification? The final section of this chapter raises just this question, making use of Frederick Douglass's 1852 speech "What to the Slave Is the Fourth of July." This speech of Douglass is an instance of moral inquiry, pointing to very real, practical, and embodied problems that moral understandings need to address and transform. This speech brilliantly identifies the ways that acknowledgments and recognitions are shaped by structural injustices or systems of oppression.

In the final chapter, "Stability and Objectivity: The Felted World," I return most explicitly to a discussion of moral absolutes, on the one hand, and surface conventionalism/relativism on the other. Throughout this work, I will argue against the view that conventions are social and cultural creations in which individuals can choose to participate. Typically, these conventions are seen as arbitrary and, in some sense, free-floating. Unlike the laws, objects, or properties found in the natural world, conventions have a much less stable grounding; because they are in no way given or inevitable, they are likely to change. This surface conventionalism entails relativism of a certain sort, and this relativism has implications for how we understand the nature and importance as well as the resolution of moral disagreement. As much as I have disagreed (and will continue to disagree) with Gilbert Harman, he is right when he claims that relativism is really not about truth but about objectivity.

Harman's expectations for moral objectivity, however, are fundamentally misguided. Harman's characterizations of relativism and objectivity will serve as a foil against which I will generate an alternative account of objectivity that is consistent with felted contextualism. I call my alternative stabilism, and this account will provide feminists with much of what we want in order to make normative judgments.

To highlight what my stabilist account offers, I will examine some of the events and aftereffects of Hurricane Katrina. Hurricane Katrina is itself a set of felted phenomena. My intent is to show how our obligations of justice are generated and met in the stable felted world. That knowledge will enable us to make use of claims to objectivity. The possibility for and expectation of transformation of structural injustices and systems of oppression are centrally important to feminist ethics.

For feminist arguments about oppression to be philosophically (and politically) compelling, we need to have a well-developed metaethics. Feminists' silence on metaethical questions threatens the progress that we have made in normative ethics. Because we have chosen not to address the grounding question explicitly, we find ourselves charged with having embraced an anything-goes relativism and having rejected objectivity. We end up developing ad hoc metaethical positions in the process of defending ourselves against these charges. We need a stable grounding for our claims and judgments; this could be something more than feeling or surface convention but certainly not something like a metaphysical property, in part because this sort of realism is often accompanied by moral absolutism.

This work offers a diagnosis of the ways that metaethics has been practiced in the last twenty-five years, by asking what it is that we are hoping to find in our search for foundations. What purpose do we want our foundations to serve? Our shared need, I hope to show, is not a foundation comprising universal principles or metaphysical properties, but rather something different. Our real need is stability, and this work shows how our morality has its life in the stability that practices create.

2 DOES THE FABRIC OF THE WORLD INCLUDE MORAL PROPERTIES? REALIST/ANTIREALIST DEBATES

But the trouble with the realist is always that he does not solve but skip the difficulties which his adversaries see, though they too don't succeed in solving them.

—WITTGENSTEIN, *BLUE BOOK*, 48

In this chapter, I examine the state of affairs in the realist/antirealist debates about metaethical issues. I focus attention on J. L. Mackie's *Ethics* because it is a canonical text that clearly articulates many of the standing concerns of these debates. I also examine a set of exchanges between Gilbert Harman, who is a moral antirealist and relativist, and Nicholas Sturgeon, an ethical naturalist. While there have been many philosophers engaged with metaethical questions, my goal in this chapter is not to provide a comprehensive or exhaustive overview of these issues. My goals are more humble: to identify some of the important underlying assumptions, definitions, and expectations that frame these debates, and then to examine these in a critical manner. I argue that the very framing of these debates rests on a certain picture of the nature of the world and, by extension, the nature of morality. This picture is taken for granted by realists and antirealists alike. The current framing of these debates sharply constrains the options available in metaethics. By exposing the problematic nature of this picture, I will take the first steps in providing the background for the alternative approach I advocate in the following chapters.

J. L. MACKIE'S FURNITURE AND FABRIC

J. L. Mackie offers a bald and bold statement in the opening of "The Subjectivity of Values" when he says, "There are no objective values."[1] For Mackie, to be objective is to be part of the fabric of the world. Mackie includes in the category of moral values "not only moral goodness, which might be most naturally equated with moral value, but also other things

---

1. J. L. Mackie, *Ethics: Inventing Right and Wrong* (New York: Penguin, 1977), 15.

that could be more loosely called moral values or disvalues—rightness and wrongness, duty, obligation, an action's being rotten and contemptible, and so on."[2] These qualities—moral goodness, rightness, and so forth— are not objective in the sense of being prior to and logically independent of human activities. In other words, moral values are not part of the fabric of the world.

Mackie offers several approaches to show how moral values cannot be part of the fabric of the world. He asserts that the thesis "there are no objective values" can be understood as "value statements cannot be either true or false."[3] He offers a clarification; he is not denying that value statements can be true or false given determinate standards, but he is denying that they can be true or false with respect to standards that are absolute or independent. Mackie denies that these moral values can be action directing absolutely and not simply contingently, as Kant's categorical imperative demands. And finally, Mackie claims that the evaluative, prescriptive, and action-guiding character of these allegedly objective properties would be nonnatural.

Mackie recognizes that in the ordinary course of living, people act as if there are objective moral values underpinning their inquiries and disagreements. People using moral language want to say something that is not solely descriptive but "something that involves a call for action or from refraining from action, and one that is absolute, not contingent upon any desire or preference or policy or choice, his own or anyone else's."[4] The authority of morality depends to a large degree on people acting as if there are objective values that can either result in right action or determine whether a moral statement is true or false. All these expectations, and the ways that we act on them, are in error, according to Mackie.

Mackie recognizes that his error theory flies in the face of the moral experience of many people, so he offers two main arguments in support of this theory. The first argument is the argument from relativity. Its central premise is that there is a wide variation in moral codes from society to society. This variation supports indirectly the claim that there are no objective values. Mackie notes that "radical differences between first order moral judgments make it difficult to treat those judgments as apprehensions of objective truths."[5] The objectivist finds himself in the position of

2. Ibid.
3. Ibid., 25.
4. Ibid., 33.
5. Ibid., 36.

having to explain such variation. The burden is on him to explain what work these objective values are doing if people hold such conflicting and contradictory values.

The second and more important argument Mackie advances in support of his error theory is the argument from queerness. This argument has both metaphysical and epistemological considerations. If there were objective values, Mackie says, "they would be entities or qualities or relations of a very strange sort, utterly different from anything else in the universe."[6] Mackie offers Plato's Forms as an example of what objective values would have to be. He says,

> The Form of the Good is such that knowledge of it provides the knower both with a direction and an overriding motive; something's being good both tells the person who knows this to pursue it and makes him pursue it. An objective good would be sought by anyone who was acquainted with it, not because of any contingent fact that this person, or every person, is so constituted that he desires this end, but just because the end has to-be-pursuedness somehow built into it. Similarly, if there were objective principles of right and wrong, any wrong (possible) course of action would have not-to-be-doneness somehow built into it.[7]

This "built into" or inherent rightness or wrongness presents enormous puzzles. Unlike volume or extension, which are constitutive of physical objects, rightness and wrongness lack this materiality and are therefore odd. They are also odd because these properties of rightness, wrongness, or goodness are supposed to possess inherently motivational efficacy. The quality of the not-to-be-done or the to-be-pursued must be motivational for all people absolutely and not contingently. This is the only way these properties could be objective. Mackie's argument is that no such entity can exist in the world, and thus these properties would have to be radically different in kind (metaphysically queer) in order to exist and function in the way that an objectivist would claim.

This metaphysical queerness lends itself to another problem, namely, how is it that the nonnatural properties (the motivational and action-guiding ones) connect to the natural features? This connection must itself be

6. Ibid., 38.
7. Ibid., 40.

queer. To say that an act is wrong because it is an act of deliberate cruelty prompts Mackie to ask, "But just what *in the world* is signified by this 'because.'"[8] The causation would have to be of a very different sort from how physical objects have causal efficacy. For Mackie, the burden rests with the defender of objective values to specify this causal relationship. The relationship must be something more than intersubjective agreement, which by itself is not sufficient to show that there are objective values.

This problem of the relationship of the nonnatural properties to the natural ones raises important epistemological questions for Mackie. How is it that people are supposed to apprehend these objective moral values or to ascertain the moral features of a situation? In order to be aware of the values, one needs a special faculty of moral perception or intuition. Any moral objectivist must be committed to intuitionism, according to Mackie. Our normal ways of perceiving are not suitable to the task of apprehending the distinctive nonnatural aspects of objective values. Our common ways of knowing things—perceiving, confirming hypotheses, and so forth—cannot engage with the nonnatural properties. Taken together, the metaphysical and epistemological considerations demonstrate the implausibility of objective values for Mackie.[9]

HARMAN AND THE "PROBLEM WITH ETHICS"

Gilbert Harman charts a complementary course to Mackie's in his book *The Nature of Morality*.[10] Harman, like Mackie, is concerned with the nature of moral properties, observations, and the roles these play in moral judgments and explanations. More specifically, Harman investigates whether the relationship between moral principles and moral observations or judgments is the same as the relationship between scientific observations and scientific theories. Harman contends that scientific theories can be tested against the world by observation and experiments, and this prompts him to ask, "Can moral principles be tested in the same way, out

8. Ibid., 41, emphasis in the original.

9. Julia Annas is very critical of Mackie's treatment of the Forms. She says, "This hostile portrayal of the Forms of moral qualities as bizarre entities picked out by an equally peculiar faculty of intuition is clearly a coarse and imperceptive interpretation of Plato." See "Moral Knowledge as Practical Knowledge" in *Moral Knowledge*, ed. Ellen Frankel Paul, Fred D. Miller Jr., and Jeffrey Paul (Cambridge: Cambridge University Press, 2001), 238. I will address Annas's work in greater detail in Chapter 6.

10. Gilbert Harman, *The Nature of Morality* (New York: Oxford University Press, 1977). My focus is the first chapter, "Ethics and Observation."

in the world?"[11] The problem with ethics, according to Harman, is that moral principles cannot be so tested.

One of the key concepts Harman uses is "observation." By observation, Harman means an "immediate judgment made in response to the situation without any conscious reasoning having taken place."[12] An observation has occurred whenever an opinion is a direct result of perception and not the result of inference. In other words, what we perceive causes us to form a belief, and beliefs are the sort of things that are either true or false. Harman begins with what he takes to be an untroubling case in science; that case, however, will then serve as the paradigm against which a moral case will be judged. Harman asks us to consider the case of the physicist who sees a vapor trail in the cloud chamber and thinks, "There goes a proton." In this case, the physicist makes an observation (the vapor trail) and then, on the basis of this observation, he makes an inference (the proton). In Harman's view, what the physicist observes is a vapor trail that he interprets as having been left by the proton. The observation of the vapor trail serves as confirmation for his theory, which gives meaning to the term "proton." Such confirmation rests on inferring an explanation, according to Harman.

Justification in this scientific case involves an impressive gap-free circle, according to Harman: "You need to make assumptions about certain physical facts to explain the occurrence of the observation that supports the theory."[13] And the circle in scientific confirmation works as follows: the observation provides evidence for the theory that best explains the physical event that explains the observation. The observation counts as confirming evidence for the physicist's theory to the extent that it is reasonable to explain the observation by assuming, not only that he has a given psychological set and certain beliefs about the apparatus, but also that there really was a proton in the chamber causing the vapor trail.

A theory that does make an assumption about a physical fact is better than a theory that does not. And further, any explanation of the observation of the vapor trail that makes no assumption of physical facts but only appeals to the psychological set of the observer would count neither as evidence for the existence of the proton nor as confirmation for a theory. It is entirely reasonable to assume something about the world, in this case,

11. Ibid., 4.
12. Ibid., 6.
13. Ibid., 13.

that there really was a proton going through the cloud chamber, in order to have the best explanation.

The question Harman poses is whether it is reasonable to make such an assumption when it is a moral observation at issue. Harman places moral observation on par with scientific observation as being an immediate judgment as the result of perception without the benefit of any conscious reasoning. Harman offers two cases where someone would make judgments that the acts in question are wrong. First, an observer would judge that it is wrong for a doctor who has five dying patients in need of organ transplants to remove the necessary organs from the healthy patient in room 306. The second case involves a person who, rounding a street corner, sees a group of juvenile delinquents dousing a cat with gasoline and then igniting it. As Harman himself says, "You do not need to conclude that what they are doing is wrong, you do not need to figure anything else out; you can *see* that it is wrong."[14] What, Harman wants to know, is the nature of this "seeing"?

The question becomes whether or not your reaction that an act is wrong is the result of the actual wrongness out in the world imposing itself on you in some way or is a reflection or indication of your own moral sensibility in conjunction with some natural facts of the situation. Harman wants to know whether it is reasonable to make an assumption about the moral fact of wrongness in the same way that it is reasonable to make an assumption of the physical fact of the proton.

Harman's position is that in the case of moral observations, we do not need to assume anything about the world over and above the assumptions we make about the observer's psychology. As Harman strongly puts it, "An assumption about moral facts would seem to be totally irrelevant to the explanation of you making the judgment you make."[15] In Harman's view, moral observations do not indicate a moral reality but only the moral sensibility of the observer.

The case of moral observation and explanation, unlike the case of scientific observation and explanation, is not a gap-free circle. In the case of moral explanation, a moral observation can provide evidence for a moral theory, and while this might explain a "moral fact," this moral fact does not explain the observation. The "confirmed" moral theory does not explain the observation. Thus, the so-called fact really is not doing any work

14. Ibid., 4, emphasis in the original.
15. Ibid., 7.

in the confirmation. And in Harman's view, we can find an explanation for these moral observations, without positing the existence of moral facts, by embracing a moral antirealism. Those explanations that can explain moral observations without assuming moral facts are better than those that do assume them in terms of explanatory simplicity.

In a slightly later essay, "Moral Explanations of Natural Facts," Harman continues to compare moral cases against scientific ones. Once again, moral cases fail to make the grade.[16] Specifically, Harman focuses on the empirical testability of moral claims. In a field such as physics, it is possible to test a theory against the world by finding some results in the world that are most plausibly explained by the theory's being true. One particular observable effect that physical facts can have is on people who did not believe in them ahead of time. Observations in a physicist's lab of the vapor trail in the cloud chamber can cause someone who was previously skeptical of protons to change his or her mind.

Harman questions whether such tests can yield similar results in the case of moral observations. He explicitly asks, "Can the actual rightness or wrongness of a given action have observable effects that enable moral claims to be tested against the world in the same way as scientific claims can be tested?"[17] Harman does make the concession that in some cases moral facts do seem to be relevant to explanations, but the demand that he now makes is slightly different. Now the focus is on empirical testability and observable effects.

Harman uses the example of Albert, Jane, and Mary to demonstrate that moral facts do not have the same possible effect of causing one to change her mind that scientific facts can have. In Harman's example, Jane sees Albert hitting a cat with a stick. (One hopes in Harman's thought experiments that cats have nine lives.) The cat cries out piteously and Jane believes that Albert's act is wrong. A believer in moral facts would say that the actual wrongness of the act, the fact of the matter, is the cause of Jane's belief and is part of the best explanation of Jane's belief. Complicating the matter is a third person, Mary, who, unlike Jane, is not convinced that there is anything wrong with causing pain to animals. Mary can explain Jane's belief as being the consequence of Jane's moral sensibility in conjunction with Albert's action. Mary, however, finds nothing surprising in the situation. Because there is no surprise, lacking is the possibility that

16. Gilbert Harman, "Moral Explanations of Natural Facts," Spindel Conference 1986: Moral Realism, *The Southern Journal of Philosophy* 24, suppl. (1986): 56–68.

17. Ibid., 61.

Mary could undergo a change in her belief system as a consequence of observing the alleged wrongness of Albert's action. And if these moral "facts" do not have a similar sort of observable effect on people, they are not capable of being empirically tested. Harman concludes that something incapable of being empirically tested is not a fact.

STURGEON REPLIES TO HARMAN'S "PROBLEM"

In his essay "Moral Explanations," Nicholas Sturgeon addresses Harman's contentions that moral facts are completely irrelevant to moral explanations and that explanations that appeal to moral facts are not the best explanations available.[18] Sturgeon's goals in this essay are somewhat modest—namely, to show that explanations that appeal to moral facts are as gap free and as reasonable as scientific explanations and that Harman has not provided us with sufficient reason to think otherwise.

Sturgeon's strategy involves making a provisional assumption of moral facts and showing that moral facts do appear relevant in particular moral cases. He offers several cases where it seems plausible to cite moral facts in support or as an aspect of explanation of nonmoral facts. The cases cited, with the exception of Harman's unfortunate cat, tend to be historical examples as opposed to abstract thought experiments.

For Sturgeon, it is entirely plausible that the fact of Hitler's moral depravity forms part of our best explanation of our belief that Hitler was morally depraved. Depravity, in this case, consists in trying to eradicate entire populations of people. Here, Hitler's moral character is cited as part of an explanation for his deeds, and these deeds are part of the evidence leading to a correct assessment of Hitler's character. It is also plausible that it is the wrongness of the kids' action of igniting the cat that helps explain our judgment that the act was wrong. In this case, it is the moral feature of an act that plays an explanatory role. The difference between the cases is that in the Hitler example, we can judge that Hitler's actions were evil, and on the basis of the magnitude and atrocity of his actions, we make inferences about his character. In the case of the youths, we can see that the action was bad, but on the basis of this action alone, we might not make inferences to the depraved character of the children.

18. Nicholas Sturgeon, "Moral Explanations," in *Essays on Moral Realism*, ed. Geoffrey Sayre-McCord (Ithaca, N.Y.: Cornell University Press, 1988), 229–55.

To further demonstrate that moral facts are not completely irrelevant to moral explanation, Sturgeon employs counterfactual situations. The crucial question is whether we would have drawn the same moral conclusion had the moral facts been otherwise. Would we have believed Hitler to be morally depraved if he had not been? Sturgeon asks us to consider a situation where Hitler was not morally depraved, and to ask whether he would then have done what he did. The answer, for Sturgeon, is clearly no. This answer relies on an uncontroversial moral view that in any world that remotely resembles the actual world, only a morally depraved person could order the "final solution."[19]

Sturgeon takes himself to have shown that the relationship between moral observations and moral explanations is just as gap free as the relationship between scientific observations and explanations. Moral observations do confirm moral theories, and these then can explain moral facts that in turn explain our original observation. Not only is the moral case that appeals to moral facts gap free, but those explanations that do appeal to moral facts are also part of the best and reasonable explanations of our moral observations.

Sturgeon offers a direct reply to Harman's denial that moral claims are empirically testable in his essay "Harman on Moral Explanations of Natural Facts."[20] Sturgeon reads Harman to be asserting that because the potential to surprise or cause one to change one's mind is lacking in moral cases, this constitutes a special problem in ethics. Sturgeon argues that this lack of potential to surprise would be a special problem for ethics only if one of two things were true: either "(a) that no situation of this sort can arise *outside* ethics or (b) that—short of settling in advance on a naturalistic reduction for ethics—we can never do better than this *within* ethics."[21] Both of these claims are false according to Sturgeon. In this section I am more concerned with the first claim. The second claim concerning naturalistic reductions I will touch on briefly in a section below.

To show that the first claim is false one must show that in a variety of disciplines, situations arise where observational testing does not require that one changes her mind. Sturgeon uses Harman's own example from physics where Harry sees a vapor trail in the cloud chamber and thinks, "There goes a proton." Harry, however, is not the only person in the lab

19. Ibid., 249.

20. Nicholas Sturgeon, "Harman on Moral Explanations of Natural Facts," Spindel Conference 1986: Moral Realism, *The Southern Journal of Philosophy* 24, suppl. (1986): 69–78.

21. Ibid., 71.

on that day. Also present is Susan, "who has been listening to too many neopositivist arguments in a philosophy of science class. [She] is utterly agnostic about the existence of microphysical particles."[22] Susan observes Harry's observation in a similar manner as Mary had observed Jane's observation of Albert striking the cat. Harry's inference to the proton, according to Susan's explanation, is due to his "physical sensibility" in conjunction with his observation of the vapor trail in the cloud chamber. Explanations such as Susan's are, according to Sturgeon, instrumentalist explanations. Such instrumentalist explanations are found in many disciplines, including psychology and social theory. Freudians and Jungians draw different conclusions from the same evidence, but each can offer an instrumentalist explanation for the other's view. Marxists and liberals do the same in social theory.

It becomes clear, then, that this "problem" is not specific to ethics and that science itself is not immune. If what Harman points out as a problem is a problem for ethics, then physics is indicted as well.

OBJECTIVITY IN HARMAN'S AND STURGEON'S POSITIONS: CAUSALITY AND INDEPENDENCE

Both Harman and Sturgeon link causation to objectivity, which is linkage demanded by Mackie as well. Recall the picture Harman sketches for scientific observation and confirmation. The cycle is gap free: a physical fact, existing in the natural world, causes our observation; our observation in turn confirms a theory that best explains the observation. This model of causation requires that these objects or facts exist entirely independently of us the observers. Further, that these facts or objects have the causal power to result in observations is taken as evidence for the independence of these objects.

The example of Harry is meant to show that assuming the existence of the proton best explains Harry's observation of the vapor trail, and that observation is then taken as evidence for the existence of the proton. Harman demands that facts possess causal efficacy, and Sturgeon asserts that moral facts also exercise this same power with respect to our moral judgments and observations. The wrongness of the juveniles' act of igniting the cat causes our judgment that the act is wrong. Hitler's evilness causes

22. Ibid.

our judgment that he was evil. And if the vapor trail can exist independently of Harry's observation, Hitler's evilness or the wrongness of igniting the cat can exist independently as well. Thus for Sturgeon, the circle
for moral facts, observation, and confirmation is gap free, like the circle in
science. Moral facts and observations do meet the standard of causal efficacy that science demands, thus showing its objective character.

When it is accepted that objectivity is a matter of being causally explanatory, then one of two options must be true if moral facts are to be objective.
Either moral facts exist in nature—that is, they are somehow reducible to
natural facts—or moral facts have some sort of supernatural or metaphysically queer character. As an ethical naturalist, Sturgeon embraces the first
option; there is no hesitation on his part in saying that moral facts are
reducible to natural ones. An intuitionist such as Moore or Ross would
accept the second option. Whichever way a moral realist turns in these
debates, the moral antirealist is going to demand an account of the origin
of normativity and the ways in which norms exert a pull on us. In order to
satisfy the antirealist, the moral realist would need to make a convincing
case for objective normative reasons. In an unsurprising development,
nothing will satisfy a moral antirealist who is naturalist (for brevity's sake,
I shall abbreviate this as MAN).

THE DEMANDS FOR NORMATIVE AUTHORITY

In *The Authority of Reason,* Jean Hampton offers an insightful analysis of
the debates between objectivists about moral values or properties and
MANs who insist that no such values can exist.[23] This detailed analysis has
been remarkably useful for me, especially for the clarity and precision of
the characterizations of these opposing views. Hampton's analysis lays a
groundwork for my advancement of a genuine alternative to these two
stratified positions. Specifically, I want to play off her characterization of
what she claims are the commitments of an objectivist about moral norms.
I quote her at length:

> She must say, first of all, that there exist norms generating rea-
> sons to act that are directives applying to her no matter the contin-
> gencies of her situation. Second, she must say that these reasons,
> along with their authority, can be known by agents (for what

23. Jean E. Hampton, *The Authority of Reason* (Cambridge: Cambridge University Press,
1998).

would be the point of a theory that recognized these reasons, but despaired of our ability to know them)? Third, she must say that it is at least possible for us to sometimes act "on" or "for the sake of" these reasons, as when we say that "Elizabeth acted on her duty to visit Aunt Ethel in the hospital" or "Jane interfered with Albert's behavior because she thought it was her duty to stop cruelty to animals."[24]

In short, an objectivist account of moral reasons commits to the beliefs that (1) there is a course of action that must be, (2) humans can sense the rightness of this course, and (3) humans act for the sake of the rightness. The authority of the norms comes from a compellingness or mustness that is independent of us.

This position, Hampton argues, is distasteful to naturalists because it ultimately rests on an appeal to Aristotelian final causes, an idea that science has long found suspect. Three factors compose the suspicion: the assumption that there is an appropriate or fitting place for objects that has some compelling rightness; the assumption that the movement of the object is a response to this compelling rightness; and the assumption that object's movement is explained by some sort of sensitivity to this rightness.

Objections similar to those raised by Mackie about moral properties' resemblance to Platonic forms can be made against this Aristotelian final-cause explanation. Final causes, no less than forms, present epistemological and metaphysical problems. How do final causes compel us? What is the nature of this compulsion? How is it that we not only act in accordance with them, but more important, act for the sake of them?

Once again, the objectivist finds herself in an untenable position. For the objectivist about moral reasons, the authority of these reasons is somehow separate from us but yet is something to which we respond. Thus, the objectivist finds herself confronting more metaphysical and epistemological mysteries.

What are the commitments that a normative objectivist must hold? According to Hampton, in order not to be a subjectivist, one must hold that some norms are not culture dependent. The authority of these norms is

24. Ibid., 110. This second example is a reference to Harman's example in "Moral Explanations of Natural Facts."

independent of any social or psychological contingency. Reasons derived from such norms must hold regardless of any particular social or psychological conditions. The "must" means that these norms hold necessarily; their necessity comes from their cultural independence. Thus, necessity is not the invention of a particular human agent or the human community. This particular demand creates a gap among the necessity, compellingness, and authority of the norm, and human agents. It is this gap that an objectivist must bridge, and that the naturalist takes as proof that objectivism is wrong.

Hampton briefly discusses some necessity candidates to which an objectivist might appeal in her defense. One candidate is logical necessity. An objectivist may try to claim that there is a logical relation between a reason and an action being carried out in accordance with that reason. A naturalist, however, claims that such a relationship is shrouded in mystery. Because we cannot show or demonstrate such a logical connection, the naturalist says, the objectivist must still be covertly relying on some contingent psychological fact to explain the relation between reason and action. This reliance on a contingent fact means that it is not objective, thus failing to help the objectivist's case.

A second necessity candidate to which an objectivist might turn is metaphysical necessity of a Kripkean sort. An objectivist taking this tack might hold that to argue a reason is necessary is to say that it could not have been otherwise in certain respects. Necessity is about essences; it is necessary that H_2O is water. This kind of necessity, however, will not help the objectivist to explain normative authority to the naturalist. Metaphysical authority is about the relationship between two objects (water and molecules, for example). Metaphysical necessity about norms, in order to provide their authority, must be concerned with the relationship between human agents and various aspects of the world. Metaphysical necessity, as an explanation of objective normative authority, cannot make nor facilitate that connection. As such, it is incapable of proving the authority an objectivist requires.

Hampton offers a third option for necessity that an objectivist might consider. For lack of a better expression, I will call this inescapable necessity. Hampton describes the sense in which "moral norms generated by objectively authoritative moral norms are necessary in the sense that their governance over us is inescapable. And by 'inescapable' here I mean that

reasons 'apply' to us 'no matter what. . . .' And this governance is inescapable because there is no way we can throw it off, or change it by our actions, beliefs, or social systems."[25] There are two versions of this
inescapable necessity, each one of which locates the source of authority in
some sort of author/commander.

The first version posits God as the source or issuer of commands that
we cannot escape. Positing God as the source behind the authority invites
a host of problems: What if there is not a God? Whose God? And if one
posits a God who must be subject to these norms, then the original question on the origin of their authority still stands.

The second version of inescapable necessity has a more direct Kantian
influence, according to Hampton. An authority coming from reason that
"transcends particularities of our persons, and even is part of the world"
would provide the sort of authority an objectivist needs.[26] The naturalist,
however, will once again demand an account of this transcendent conception of reason, accusing the objectivist of shifting the mystery once again.

Due to the failures of an objectivist to provide an adequate account of
the source of norms and directives and to advance an account of why their
governance is inescapable, the naturalist claims victory. Naturalists argue
for a simpler account of normative authority that does not, in their estima-
tion, traffic in occult properties or entities. A naturalist offers instead that
authority is a psychosocial phenomenon. Human societies exert great
pressure on their members, compelling them to act in certain ways and to
believe in certain claims. For a naturalist, normative authority is a matter
of human psychology; we take on and internalize all sorts of requirements,
mandates, and norms. This being a matter of human psychology is what
makes it contingent and therefore not necessary. Thus, Hampton writes,
"The objectivist's inability to say anything that is as sensible and clear as
this account of authority may be the most damning indictment of the view
in the eyes of the naturalists, and a clear indication that authority is nothing more than a cause of the operations of the human mind."[27] And so the
naturalist sees herself as having vanquished any nonsubjectivist account
of normative authority.

As I stated above, I believe that Hampton intended to open a path
between the objectivists and the naturalists. This, too, is my plan. The
naturalist's claim to victory assumes that authority's being a human

25. Ibid., 105–6.
26. Ibid., 108.
27. Ibid., 109.

phenomenon entails that it cannot be necessary. This assumption seems to belong to the objectivist as well. Both the naturalist and the objectivist demand a norm purported to be objective must have a source that is in no way contingent. One drop of human contact seems to contaminate necessity and authority. An objectivist, having adopted a logical or metaphysical or inescapable necessity, attempts to preserve this purity. The naturalist claims that all such attempts to preserve purity fail; this failure is taken as strong support for their subjectivist position.

The account of necessity I advance in the following chapter neither introduces nor relies on any metaphysically suspect properties or entities. And in opposition to the naturalist's views, this necessity is not something that human psychology simply decides. The view I present rejects the assumption that human contact introduces contingency and precludes necessity. More strongly, I show that no domain of inquiry—logic, mathematics, science, and morals—can meet this sort of human-independence demand for necessity. Instead, we should reconceive our needs and demands for necessity and authority, and turn our focus to the elements in life that constitute the stable context of our living.

WHY SHOULD MORAL FACTS BEHAVE LIKE EMPIRICAL FACTS?

The MAN's demand for scientific models of observation and explanation, as well as the demand for no human element in an account of necessity, reveals the pervasiveness of the nature/normativity dualism. These demands are predicated on the belief that it is possible to sunder everything that is human—our meanings and conceptual schemes—from the anormative, independent world. The demand from the MAN is that normativity must itself have the same sort of independent existence as the world that science reveals. The expectations about the independent nature of the world and the ways in which our science interacts with the world and reveals it are clearly evident in the debates between Harman and Sturgeon. Harman sets the terms of the debate with Sturgeon by taking as a key issue the testability of moral principles, more specifically, the possibility of moral principles' being subject to empirical testing against the world. This focus on empirical testing by Harman makes sense given that Harman is a self-identified naturalist. And Sturgeon's acceptance of the terms and demands of testability make sense because he is an ethical naturalist. Harman and Sturgeon embrace naturalism, which at minimum makes the claim that the only facts or properties are those that are or can be, in principle, discovered by science. More strongly put, nothing exists beyond what science licenses us to suppose. Naturalists in this sense usually have a distaste for any properties that are nonnatural—Moore's properties of goodness or badness come quickly to mind. Mackie offered Plato's forms, even while admitting that they are "some of the wilder products of philosophical fancy."[28] This is just the sort of thing that gives philosophy a bad name.

BATTLING BEWITCHMENT AND THE CRAVING FOR GENERALITY

One obvious Wittgensteinian point to keep at the center of our examinations is that huge amounts of philosophical confusion follow from the application of one set of rules or expectations from one language-game to another. One reason that this occurs frequently is that the clothing of our language makes everything look the same (*PI*, 224).[29] In ordinary usage, we regularly and unproblematically refer to physical objects causing our observations. We also regularly speak of moral properties causing our observations. Mackie, for instance, recognizes this and says that it is all an error. But here, a Wittgensteinian would say, are two very different language-games standing in complicated relationships to each other. Briefly, the language-games have different points; science aims at explanation and description while morals aims at recommendations and prescriptions. But they are also connected; most would say that in order to make good recommendations, you need to have at least somewhat of a clear description or understanding of a situation. Language-games can be incredibly complicated, as can be the relationships among them. Two points need to be raised here. The first is that Mackie's error theory assumes that it is perfectly acceptable to apply the rules and expectations from one set of language-games (science) to another (morals), and then to conclude that

---

28. Mackie, *Ethics*, 40.

29. Consider the following example Wittgenstein offers in *Remarks on Colour*, ed. G. E. M. Anscombe, trans. L. L. McAlister and Margaret Schattle (Oxford: Blackwell, 1980), § 1:

> A language-game: Report whether a certain body is lighter or darker than another.—But now there's a related one: State the relationship between the lightness of certain shades of colour. (Compare with this: Determining the relationship between the lengths of two sticks—and the relationship between two numbers.)— The form of the propositions in both language-games is the same: "X is lighter than Y." But in the first it is an external relation and the proposition is temporal, in the second it is an internal relation and the proposition is timeless.

in the case of morals, we are committing an error. Perhaps on a scientific view we may be in error, but most people do not think of themselves as doing science when making moral judgments. The second point is that Wittgenstein recognizes an incredible diversity of language-games. The philosophical mistake is trying to reduce the very complicated relationships among language games into a single formula. The dominant "formula" in metaethical debates is one of subsuming ethics to science. This desire for *the* formula is a product of the craving for generality.

This craving for generality has a particular character and stems from our "preoccupations with the methods of science." Wittgenstein says that

> I mean the method of reducing the explanation of natural phenomena to the smallest possible number of primitive natural laws; and, in mathematics, of unifying the treatment of different topics by using a generalization. Philosophers constantly see the method of science before their eyes, and are irresistibly tempted to ask and answer questions in the way science does. This tendency is the real source of metaphysics, and leads the philosopher into complete darkness. (*BB*, 18)

This craving for generality has shaped the realist/antirealist debates in metaethics in some very particular ways, as I make evident below. And while I do not believe that the philosophers engaged in these debates in the ways I have described are in complete darkness, I do think that metaethics itself—how its questions are asked and answered—has suffered from the limitations imposed by the quest for the single formula of explanation.

Connected to this craving for generality is the temptation to believe that something must be the case. This temptation is quite evident in how we think about games, when we assume that all games must have something in common. There are various "must be's" that underpin the realist/antirealist debates, such as moral observations must be such that they play the same role in observation and confirmation as do observations of natural facts, and that moral properties must be perceived, apprehended, and known in the same ways as natural properties. One important consequence of these "must be's" is that moral experience is always in the position of being reduced to that which is amenable to science. This seriously challenges the autonomy of ethics.

Virginia Held in her essay "Whose Agenda? Ethics Versus Cognitive Science" argues that the normative is in danger of being swallowed by the empirical. Held begins her argument with the extremely important reminder that science and ethics have two very different points or purposes. Science is a descriptive set of enterprises, aiming at explanation, control, and prediction. Ethics is prescriptive, aiming at recommendations. Unchallenged is the assumption that science is the norm against which all other forms of inquiry will be judged. This assumption undergirds the importation of scientific concepts and methodologies to ethical practices.

The demand that moral observations or properties function in the same ways as their scientific counterparts sharply limits what can be included in the category of experience. Science limits experience to what can be empirically observed. Held claims that moral experience cannot be so limited. She includes in moral experience "deliberation and choice and responsibility for action; it includes the adoption of moral attitudes, the making of moral judgments about our own and others' actions and their consequences, and evaluation of the character and lives we and others have and aspire to. And it includes these as experienced as subjectively."[30] Held is concerned that subjectivity is disappearing from moral psychology, and that questions about how we come to hold beliefs now eclipse questions about the validity of these beliefs. The latter—the normative—is being erased. When the normative is erased or subsumed, then ethics has no autonomy.

WHERE TO GO FROM HERE

Limiting what can be included in the category of experience and stripping out the subjectivity and normativity of ethics are moves that anyone who wishes to preserve the autonomy of ethics ought to challenge. Similarly, Held notes that the introduction of the natural and non- or supernatural distinction is most troubling. This distinction is taken as an untroubling given. As a consequence of its status, this distinction does an enormous amount of work in the realist/antirealist debates. Where there are questions, most often they concern into which side of the divide a property might fit; they do not address the categories themselves. What would it mean not simply to redraw the lines between the two categories, but to challenge and undermine the very definitions of these categories? How might we adopt an alternative to this distinction? Held says that this is

30. Held, "Whose Agenda?" 32.

what we must do. We need to adopt and make use of other distinctions in ethics:

> the distinction between that which is specifically human and that which belongs to the natural world that would be as it is with no humans in it, or the distinction between the subjective point of view of the conscious self and the objective point of view of the observer studying nature and the human beings in it and seeking explanations of its events. These distinctions require us to recognize realms that are not supernatural but are not natural either in the sense just suggested.[31]

Held's worries resonate with those raised by McDowell. He warns that "if we acquiesce in the disenchantment of nature, if we let meaning be expelled from what I have called the 'merely natural,' we shall certainly need to work on bringing meaning back into the picture when we come to consider human interactions."[32] We create philosophical mysteries when we operate with a conception of nature as completely separate from human living. To further complicate matters, these mysteries only deepen when we attempt to solve them rather than to dissolve them. In the remainder of this work, and most explicitly in Chapter 4, I attempt to dissolve the mystery by offering a description of the world and human life that is neither natural (in the sense of "what there really is independent of humans") nor supernatural (in the sense of metaphysically suspect properties). My goals are both to put humanity and subjectivity back into metaethics by showing that the world has ineliminable normative elements, which in turn preserve the autonomy of ethics, and to argue for moral knowledge and moral objectivity. While these are lofty and ambitious goals, my hope is to stay grounded in our actual moral practices. I want to take seriously Wittgenstein's exhortation that "our motto might be: 'Let us not be bewitched'" (Z § 690).

---

31. Ibid., 85.
32. McDowell, *Mind and World*, 72.

From the very outset "Realism," "Idealism," etc. are names which belong to metaphysics.
That is, they indicate that their adherents believe they can say something specific
about the essence of the world.

—WITTGENSTEIN, *PHILOSOPHICAL REMARKS*, V § 55

It is as if this expressed the essence of form.—I say, however: if you talk about essence—,
you are merely noting a convention. But here one would like to retort: there is no
greater difference than that between a proposition about the depth of the essence and one
about—a mere convention. But what if I reply: to the depth that we see in the essence
there corresponds the *deep* need for the convention.

—WITTGENSTEIN, *REMARKS ON THE FOUNDATION OF MATHEMATICS*, I:74

In the previous chapter, I raised issue with the particular forms of moral antirealism advocated by Gilbert Harman and J. L. Mackie and the moral realism advanced by Nicholas Sturgeon. As different as these positions are, I showed that they share important assumptions about naturalism, causality, necessity, and the appropriateness of scientific expectations and methods for ethics. The short version of the naturalist's argument is:

1. The natural world is normatively inert.
2. Normativity must come from without.
3. We introduce normativity to the natural world.
4. If we introduce it, then it is contingent and could be otherwise.
5. If it is contingent and could be otherwise, then it is not necessary.
6. If it is not necessary, then it cannot have objective authority.
7. Therefore, it cannot have objective authority.

The crux of the matter is located in the first two premises, and these are precisely the ones on which we need to focus.

Underlying these shared assumptions is an even greater one, namely, that the world and language are radically separate. It is against this assumption that the categories "realist" and "antirealist" in the context of metaethics have their lives, their meanings.

It is also against this assumption that these categories have their failure. The categories of antirealist and realist are not adequate to the task they set for themselves. Neither the conventions postulated by the antirealist nor the properties of the moral realist can account for normativity. Their failure traces back to the world/language divide, though this is the move that escapes notice because it seems so innocent. Their acceptance of the world/language divide results in their locating causality, normativity, and priority in only one side. Each side fails to appreciate what the world is. The deflationary treatment I offer comes from Wittgenstein, and I intend for it to prompt us to rethink the ways in which world and language are not simply linked but mutually constitutive. Contemporary metaethics has failed, to a very significant degree, to offer an adequate description of our world and interactions. All our ways of living and acting are matters of our world, and our world is much a matter of our interactions. Challenging the world/language divide has a significant impact on our expectations for necessity. Whereas the naturalist of Chapter 2 demands context independence, a Wittgensteinian approach links necessity to human natural history. We have the necessity we do because of who and what we are and do. Reframing and describing anew this world/language relationship provides an alternative starting point for metaethics, one that is adequate to the task of accounting for normativity.

THE TWO-WORLD PICTURE

Realism (of which naturalism is a subset) and antirealism (of which conventionalism is a subset) are metaphysical theses that attempt to explain the nature of the world. Taken in opposition to each other, they represent views about the relationship between what is really real and human agency. A naturalist holds there is a world of fact that is real and does not depend on human agency for its existence. One can speak of metaphysical necessity concerning two independently existing objects. An ethical naturalist holds that moral properties do have a place in this world next to their cousins—the nonmoral natural properties. Necessity is understood in terms of independence from human agency. The ethical naturalist finds himself accepting the linkage of normativity and necessity, and may attempt to show that with respect to moral properties, they are objective (not dependent on humans) and therefore capable of necessity.

In contrast, the antirealist holds that human agency plays a far more constructive and constitutive role in creating reality. A conventionalist may well agree that there are physical objects, but these do not mean anything until we endow them with meaning. Objects in the world like this are in the raw, so to speak. It is language—our creation and invention—that is the dominant partner in the world/language transaction. In accepting the world/language divide, the antirealist ends up denying that there can be necessity because they deny the kind of independence from humans that a naturalist demands. Thus, the antirealist needs an account of normativity that has no appeal to necessity.

This world/language dichotomy leads to what the moral antirealist naturalist (the MAN from Chapter 2) identifies as the problem of normativity for the moral realist. Recall Gilbert Harman's position that a purported moral fact cannot function in the same way as an anormative fact. Harman's example is the physicist who sees a vapor trail in the cloud chamber and then asserts, "There goes a proton." The vapor-trail-producing proton *causes* our observation; the proton is a brute fact, an entity separate from the vapor trail and separate from the scientist. Harman wants to know if a purported real moral property can have both this causal power for observation and the additional power to motivate or to provide a reason for action. What would such a property look like? This is just the question that J. L. Mackie addresses.[1] For Mackie, if moral values are objective, then they must be like the Forms. Such entities are not part of the world accessible through our reason or experience. Thus, our epistemic access to the Forms must be different in kind from our other ways of knowing things. The only way we could know these otherworldly properties is via an intuition that requires some special sort of faculty. Furthermore, these otherworldly properties must provide "the knower with both a direction and an overriding motive; something's being good both tells the person who knows this to pursue it and makes him pursue it."[2] The concept of a moral property is from an objectively prescriptive category. Normativity is tied to the causal power of these queer properties or objective reasons. For Harman and Mackie both, the fundamental assumption is that properties have causal power for our observations, and so our moral observations would need to be the cause of our moral motivations. One might say that the normativity inheres in these properties and objects and then somehow the power of the "ought" latches on to us.

For Harman and Mackie, the puzzle of how to attach these two radically different substances is insurmountable and unsolvable. Thinking that

1. Mackie, *Ethics.*
2. Ibid., 40.

these demands for metaphysical necessity cannot be met, the MAN might well argue that normativity remains in need of a satisfactory explanation. For the MAN, a satisfactory explanation is that the authority of moral judgments and the source of their motivating force are matters of convention. Normativity, stripped away from the objects in the world and returned to the realm of human agency, is unproblematic. Thus, for the MAN, the social world of our judgments, meanings, standards, rules, conventions, and values is separate in kind from the world of brute fact.

Sturgeon, as a committed naturalist first and foremost, finds himself needing to explain how normativity can be a part of the natural world. His challenge is to show that moral properties, which are natural properties, can have the character or force that Harman denies any natural property can have. But here is the aporia in which Sturgeon finds himself: because of the world/language divide, the only available option is conventionalism, an approach that would locate normativity in just the ways that MAN describes. Normativity would be in us (either in our concepts, our rules, or our norms, which are all our creations). In order to avoid this conclusion, Sturgeon has to go through all sorts of metaphysical gymnastics to get normativity into the world and out of us. This is the only available option for preserving the objectivity of morals. So long as normativity is linked in terms of causal efficacy and necessity, any ethical naturalist will find himself confronting this "problem of normativity."

But, one can rightfully ask, If we accept Mackie's and Harman's framing of the normativity problem in ethics, do we also call into question normativity in nonmoral matters? In tying normativity and necessity in the ways they have, have they actually laid the foundation for a case against any kind of normativity? This is the direction in which Joseph Rouse moves, as I briefly discuss below. This is not my target, but we share common cause in rejecting the world/language distinction that frames the realist/antirealist debates.

Realist/naturalist and antirealist/conventionalist are both captivated by the same picture: the physical world acts as the foundation on or over which the social world sits. The social world in its guise as language attaches to and makes contact with the physical world, though how this happens is subject to debate. This two-world picture is Wittgenstein's target. His attack is directed against realism's and conventionalism's shared expectation that there is a perspective outside of language from which we can identify the features of reality that determine language and thus provide a standard of correctness, or that in the absence of such features that our linguistic conventions determine the standard of correctness.[3] This two-world picture gets it wrong about what the world is and how we humans are part of it, and this mistake entails that it also gets it wrong about what could provide a standard of correctness.

ILL EFFECTS OF THE LANGUAGE/WORLD DIVIDE

We might say that advocates on each side of the realism/antirealism dichotomy suffer the ill effects of too much of a one-sided diet. Consider the following passages:

> We have a color system as we have a number system.
> Do the systems reside in *our* nature or in the nature of things?
> How are we to put it?—*Not* in the nature of numbers or colors.
> Then is there something arbitrary about this system? Yes and no.
> It is akin both to what is arbitrary and to what is nonarbitrary.
> (Z §§ 357–58, emphasis in the original)

A realist response to this question is to claim that the systems reside in the nature of things while antirealists would say that they reside in our nature in the sense that they are something we create. What each side accepts is that the disjunction is exclusive; the systems can reside in one and only one side. The expectation is that only one side can be the dominant party in a world/language transaction.

Against the world/language divide, once you reject a metaphysical conception of objectivity and challenge the ways in which the world is "independent of humans," then the temptation is to assume that the only available option is to embrace an antirealist argument in the form of psychologism or conventionalism. This locates priority in language rather than in the world. Cause and effect, a conventionalist might be prepared to say, is really what we make it to be. It is not out there in the objects, but rather it is matter of custom and habit that we introduce as a pattern onto the world. Here the conventionalist might say that human agreement decides what is true and false. This color is called "red" because we agree that it is red. Thus, one might be tempted to conclude that the only way to account for normativity is in terms of agreement in opinions or conventions. The antirealist is ready to fill the void left by the rejection of realism

---

3. See Alice Crary, "Wittgenstein's Relation to Political Thought," in *The New Wittgenstein*, ed. Alice Crary and Rupert Read (London: Routledge, 2000), 137.

with a full-blown conventionalist theory of truth. We can say that what is true is what we decide or agree is true. We are saying "that human agreement decides that is true and what is false," to quote Wittgenstein's interlocutor (*PI* § 241). That should do the trick, the antirealist thinks.

There are at least two forms of antirealism. One is psychologism and the other conventionalism. Psychologism is individualistic; the locus of truth or correctness is within individuals. Frege flagged an important problem with psychologism in logic. This problem will appear—in whatever domain of inquiry—wherever one invokes a psychologistic account of normativity. He says,

> If every man designated something different by the name "moon," namely one of his own ideas, much as he expresses his own pain by the cry "ouch," then of course the psychological point of view would be justified; but an argument about the properties of the moon would be pointless. . . . If we could not grasp anything but what was in our own selves, then a conflict of opinion [based on] a mutual understanding would be impossible, because a common ground would be lacking, and no idea in the psychological sense can afford such a ground. There would be no logic to be appointed arbiter in the conflict of opinions.[4]

The point here is logical or grammatical, as Wittgenstein would say. There is only the possibility of disagreement against a context or background of agreement. One of the hopes in locating the standard of correctness in our psychology is that it would be able to adjudicate conflicts. But what Frege shows here is that there is neither accord nor conflict, and so a standard is impossible.

At this point, the antirealist may attempt to offer an alternative account of normativity by invoking shared conventions. Conventionalism is yet another philosophical term surrounded by a cloud of confusion. There is a fair amount of disagreement about what conventions are, how they function, where they come from, and how we participate in them. In some usages, a convention is a social or cultural creation or production in which people choose to participate. These are social productions that in many

---

4. Cited in Steve Gerrard, "A Philosophy of Mathematics Between Two Camps," in Sluga and Stern, *The Cambridge Companion to Wittgenstein*, 173. The original citation is Gottlob Frege, *The Basic Laws of Arithmetic*, trans. and ed. M. Wurth (Berkeley and Los Angeles: University of California Press, 1964), ix.

instances we intentionally create and in which we voluntarily participate. They are a matter of our agreement and assent and function as the loci of meaning and value. Conventions are contingent in the sense that they could be otherwise and that there is nothing natural or given about them. Unlike natural processes that are independent from us and hence not contingent on us, conventions are arbitrary and entirely dependent on us for their existence. This form of conventionalism is a first cousin to relativism: there are multiple schema or sets of values, which is a consequence of their being relative to a particular group's conventions. This sort of conventionalism I shall call surface conventionalism, because it supposes that conventions sit on the surface of and are separable from the real or natural world.

Conventionalism runs into the same problem as psychologism, only on a grander scale. In what sense are there agreements such that disagreements are possible? Can conventionalism provide the needed ground for agreement and disagreement, such that a standard to adjudicate would be both possible and useful? If nothing could play such a role, conventionalism fails to be able to provide a standard of correctness.

The realist, seeing the trouble in which the advocate of the psychologistic approach finds himself, may say, You were a bit too hasty in your repudiation of a realist metaphysics. In neglecting the role of real, independently existing objects, you gave away the very thing that can provide a standard. The way that the world is provides a criterion for correctness. The external world is shared; it is not idiosyncratic in the ways that each person's psychological states are. Nor is it simply agreement among some subset of humans. Thus, one can find a standard to adjudicate conflict in the objects themselves.

Interested in arguing for a realist view, one might respond that language is actually shaped by the underlying reality that is independent of human needs and practices. In such a view, our language mirrors reality or corresponds to it. In some sense, the independently existing reality has a kind of causal power; it shapes our language and constrains our concepts. Our words and concepts are read off these facts. Language's responsibility involves accurately reflecting or representing reality.

This "reading off of the facts" is what Harman demands of both natural properties and the alleged moral properties. To be real, the concepts "wrong" and "good" must attach to objects in the world in the way that "proton" attaches to the trail in the cloud chamber. More specifically, he might be happier with there being some sort of necessity between "wrong-ness" and a particular act. The object in some ways becomes the standard of correctness. We just compare our word to the object and see if the proper correspondence is present. If it is, then we have acted correctly. Thus, it seems that the naturalism of Harman, which is a kind of realism, requires that the standard of correctness be in the objects themselves, because introducing language, a human phenomenon, would introduce contingency in the role of necessity.

On this view, the world forces us to adopt certain concepts, frameworks, and norms of representation. And this is often the point that is made in favor of naturalism: mimicking Wittgenstein, the naturalist is tempted to say, Look at our agreement in color judgments. We agree because these are the colors of the spectrum. Our agreement does not make the color spectrum, but the color spectrum accounts for our having the color schemes that we do.

What is taken as unproblematic is the account of causality assumed by Harman. This concern was initially raised in Chapter 2. Here is the issue: can a realist account generate an account of causality that locates causal efficacy all and only in a brute world, without any influence of human agency? If no such account can be given, even or especially in the "unproblematic" cases of natural properties, then surely this counts against the extension of this demand to moral matters. This might point toward nature and normativity having a different sort of relationship than one of mutual exclusivity.

Joseph Rouse explores the possibility of a different relationship of nature and normativity from within philosophy of science, where his target is a now-familiar form of naturalism.[5] Rouse takes the less-trodden path that shows the ineliminable normativity of nature. The nature/normativity dualism, Rouse argues, is debilitating to naturalists, and he instead offers a more expansive naturalism that recognizes its normative dimensions. Rouse is not attempting to reduce nature to normativity, but rather is conceiving nature and normativity as matters of intra-active phenomena. That is to say, nature and normativity both are mutually implicated and constitutive of each other. Rouse changes the starting point. Instead of beginning with objects in the world, which we assume to already possess definite bounds, he starts with phenomena. Rouse's focus is scientific practices, which he claims disclose nature as irreducibly normative.

5. Joseph Rouse, *How Scientific Practices Matter: Reclaiming Philosophical Naturalism* (Chicago: University of Chicago Press, 2002).

Rouse argues that the naturalism of the sort I have been describing fails to deliver a workable account of causality. For Rouse, this naturalist account assumes that objects in the world already possess definite bounds. Most theories of causality take the boundaries of causally interacting systems (objects and events) to already be determinate. This lends support to the view that causality is independent of any intentional determination of our part. Rather than locating causes in already-determinate objects and effects in equally determinate events, Rouse argues that they are only cause and effect as a part of an intra-active phenomenon. The move that Rouse makes is twofold: causal significance is a matter of phenomena rather than objects and the boundaries of causally intra-active systems are determined by the overall configuration of phenomena and intra-actions. These intra-actions are not separable from language. The point raised here is similar to the one raised about mathematical and logical objects: if we grant the independence and definiteness of objects from our conceptual schemes, how can we even recognize them as anything? Such independent objects and events could not possibility do the work nor play the role that most naturalists assign to them.

With respect to a standard of correctness, the MAN has to claim that reality sets or determines language, and in the process provides a standard of reality that is independent of our conceptual schemes. From the MAN, it does seem fair that we demand an account of how these objects are supposed to generate and provide a standard of correctness. But Rouse's account challenges naturalism on just this point: can these objects—raw and by themselves—do the work that a naturalist claims they can? In an attempt to shift the terms some, the naturalist at this point might claim that the standard of correctness is a matter of its truth. He might claim that truth is independent of human conceptual schemes. But this answer too runs into the same problem of the world/language dualism. Our concept of truth cannot exist independently of our linguistic behavior. Truth is not itself an object in the world, though our ways of speaking may at times make it appear as if it is an object. We do speak of discovering the truth or that the truth is out there (to paraphrase from the X-Files). But objects are neither true nor false. Our propositions are, but propositions are formulated in language. But here the MAN may object that facts make propositions true, and these facts are independent of human agency. The mistake is to treat facts as objects in the world. Do facts somehow stand aside or above the objects about which they are facts? Fact objects would be as metaphysically queer as moral properties of the sort imagined by Mackie.

The "independent natural objects" endowed with their causal capacities now appear strange, equally so as moral objects. At minimum what we can say is that those objects alone cannot do the work that Harman's naturalism expects and demands of them. Thus we can rightly challenge the extension of this demand, now seen to be unmeetable—not just in a particular case, but also in principle—to the domain of moral properties.

A form of realism that presumes the world/language divide shows itself to be incoherent, issuing two demands that cannot be met. On the one hand, a naturalist such as Harman wants to preserve causality and necessity as separate from normativity. But it seemed as if he were stacking the deck against the moral realist in the ways that he tied normativity and causality. But it turns out that naturalism, even in those cases where it seems as if causality and necessity were obviously independent of any language use, cannot get off the ground. It turns out that what the naturalist easily accepted about the relationship between two objects—be it the relationship of cause and effect or the relationship of metaphysical necessity—requires normativity in order to be coherent. This normativity is a matter of language, not as something projected in from without, but rather constitutive of the very world of the intra-actions.

While conventionalism might seem the most plausible initially, especially when compared to the realist attempts at explaining normativity, Wittgenstein's arguments show the impossibility of conventions and regularities providing a sustainable account of normativity. No standard of correctness can come from such regularities and agreement. Conventionalism, like realism, is unable to account for the very thing it was supposed to guarantee, namely, a standard of correctness, even one that is local. To say that something is a part of a regularity or is the same as something else already requires normativity. Appealing to regularity to explain normativity is a tack that leads nowhere.

Neither a realist nor an antirealist approach is able to provide a standard of correctness. Their failure stems from a shared commitment to the nature/normativity dualism. Surface conventionalism's failure is the companion to realism's failure: it imputes too much to human agency as opposed to or at the expense of the world. Where realism misconstrues the roles of humans in causal relations, surface conventionalism has a tendency to underestimate and misunderstand the formative, defining, and shaping power of the world. The physical world is real, actual, and something in which we live as material objects ourselves.

The failure of these philosophical theses ought to prompt us to reject the dualistic starting point, which is what I do in the following chapter. Conventions, like the "real and independent" objects posited by the MAN, cannot operate autonomously; they need some sort of background against which their regularity, uniformity, or consistency can be judged. Conventions are not established by mere stipulation or verbal agreement, but rather by practices over time.[6] As was the case with realism, conventionalism as a philosophical thesis is unable to deliver a standard of correctness. The concerns raised by Wittgenstein once again point toward the relationship among objects, standards, and their use in the world. Of course, the very nature of the background or the world is precisely the matter at issue. But it is this background that both realism and conventionalism underestimate or misunderstand. What we need is a new description of this background.

ONE MORE ATTEMPT TO LOCATE NORMATIVITY

As devastating as Wittgenstein's critiques are against realism's and antirealism's attempts to generate accounts of normativity, one still might persist in attempting to place normativity and its origin. The temptation is too great; the hope is that if you can locate normativity in something or somewhere, you might be able to see how it operates. Locating normativity in rules is initially quite appealing. Rules and laws are important components of both realist and antirealist accounts.

Whether the rule is mathematical ($2 + 2 = 4$), logical (p and not-p is a contradiction), ethical (murder is wrong), or scientific ($E = mc^2$), it seems as if any kind of rule forces a usage on us and guides us in its correct use. Rules can be of a variety of sorts. They can appear to be universal or particular. They can be explicitly formulated in particular contexts or they can seem to transcend all contexts. In speaking about rules and their origins, we immediately confront yet another dualism: absolutism/relativism. But here again, this pair shares an important presupposition, which makes them vulnerable to the same critique.

---

6. For an excellent treatment of Wittgenstein's trajectory on the matter of conventions and the shift he makes in the *Blue Book*, see Jose Medina, *The Unity of Wittgenstein's Philosophy: Necessity, Intelligibility, and Normativity* (Albany: The State University of New York Press), 2002.

Both absolutism and relativism locate normativity in the rules or standards themselves. The difference is the kind of relationship that rules have to human communities. The absolutist will hold that a particular rule or standard with its normative force is binding on all of us equally. A relativist, while locating intrinsic normative force in a rule, differs about the scope of application or binding force of a rule. A rule's normativity is limited to those of us (individuals or communities) who have generated or signed on to that rule. But it is precisely this presumption—that normativity is intrinsic to rules—that we need to examine.

In a minimal sense, absolutism is the position that there is some ultimate ground or standard that is context independent. It functions as a super-idealized standard that is itself beyond justification but is that against which everything else is justified and measured. Relativism, in contrast, is the denial of any such standard. There is no ultimate ground or ideal standard that has this sort of independence and is capable of providing the justification for related claims. Because there is no absolute standard, there is nothing to which we can appeal to adjudicate between competing standards, especially those that cross contexts.

Relativism has several forms, though they share common features. One view is that standards are all a matter of an individual's choice, what Frege called psychologism. The other is a community view, in which particular standards arise because a particular community makes something be the case and function as a standard of correctness. With both of these versions, standards and norms, at rock bottom, seem a matter of caprice that we (individuals or communities) can take on and cast off at will. We can choose explicitly to adopt rules or not.

Relativism, according to its harshest critics, is akin to a kind of anarchy. When you deny the existence of an absolute standard, then you must accept that all standards are on par with one another. The best you can do is live with it or try to change others to adopt your standards in cases of disagreement. The nature, extent, and dynamics of moral disagreement is the subject of greater discussions in Chapter 7. My interest here is the location of normativity.

Rules seem already to contain the correct steps. Their applications are like a series of rails invisibly laid to infinity (*PI* §§ 218–19). What a rule requires, it requires necessarily. Consider, for example, the way in which the rule of noncontradiction seems to have intrinsic normative force. The law of noncontradiction is not simply a description or a generalization. It may well be the case that in our regular workings of the world that we don't encounter an assertion and its denial. But more strongly, we think the contradiction must necessarily be false because an assertion and its denial necessarily exclude each other. As Medina notes, we hold this as a conviction, as a "normative presupposition about how things ought to be done."[7] There is no choice of the matter here; we are prepared to say that "You must say the statement 'p and not-p' is false." There is a hardness to this logical must. Similarly in mathematics, you must answer "twelve" in response to "what is seven plus five?" Here it seems that when you are using the rules of addition, you are riding these rails to infinity, and it is the force of the rule that pulls you aboard.

Likewise, there seems to be some intrinsic force in the moral principle that you ought not to commit murder. In our regular dealings with the world, we do not encounter murder. Murders are outside the course of our regular workings with the world. When we do encounter murder, we react in horror and outrage, because it is such a violent upheaval of daily living. It has a certain status: its assertion (You should not commit murder) and its denial (It is not the case that you should not commit murder) form a contradiction, which is *necessarily* false.

As we have seen, there are those who deny that possibility of necessity in the moral case but are perfectly willing to accept the necessity and the hardness of the must in logic, mathematics, and science. But Wittgenstein offers a devastating critique of logical and mathematical necessity that, combined with his arguments against philosophical realism, deals a fatal blow to any account of necessity that presumes its context independence.

SO WHAT HAPPENS TO NECESSITY?

As I discussed in Chapter 2, normativity and necessity have been fused in a particular way in metaethics. It is assumed that normative authority is best understood in terms of realism and necessity, context independence and causal efficacy. My goal is to uncouple these concepts, and I will do so using Wittgenstein's arguments against any account of necessity that presupposes deep metaphysical truths. This deflationary treatment lays the groundwork for reconceiving context and its inescapability and ineliminability. This, in turn, will be important for an alternative conception of normativity and normative authority I offer in Chapter 5.

7. Ibid., 149.

Wittgenstein's treatment of logical necessity in his earlier writings is innovative on many levels. He is suspicious of the notion that logical necessities are not only simply true, but that their being false is inconceivable. This makes logical necessity into some sort of supertruth. Additionally, Wittgenstein is suspicious of the view that necessary propositions, of which logical propositions are a subset, are statements about objects or entities in the ways that empirical statements are. This would involve necessary objects or entities making necessary propositions true. Wittgenstein's treatment of necessity disabuses us of the notion that we need some sort of metaphysical justification for necessity. Wittgenstein's arguments against mathematical and logical realities might tempt one to conclude that there is an analog to Mackie's error theory in mathematics. All our mathematical propositions are false because nothing in the world makes them true. Mackie concludes that because they cannot be true, they must be false. What follows is not an error theory, however, because they are neither true nor false. Mackie misses Wittgenstein's point that there is a whole important class of propositions to which neither truth nor falsity attaches. I discuss below Wittgenstein's rejection of mathematical realism in order to lay the groundwork for the following chapter.

If anything strikes us as a candidate for independent existence, it would be numbers. The realist is going to say in an incredulous tone, "Oh, come on. Human agreement has nothing to do with the fact that two plus two equals four. That is true in any possible world, come what may! A mathematical proposition corresponds to mathematical reality." In a wonderful treatment of this question, Cora Diamond argues that there is an important slippage that happens in the course of understanding what mathematical propositions are about.[8] Drawing from Wittgenstein's 1939 lectures on mathematics, Diamond highlights the distinction that Wittgenstein drew concerning the relation between mathematical propositions to reality and experiential propositions to reality. Here is a case in which the initial appearance of a mathematical proposition such as "$30 \times 30 = 900$" is similar to "Prince has blue trousers." It is tempting to reach the conclusion that they must have the same relation to reality. Mathematical propositions make it appear that, in them, we are using the language of mathematics to describe mathematical reality. But, Wittgenstein shows, a mathematical proposition that "$30 \times 30 = 900$" is not about 30 in the way that the proposition "Prince has blue trousers" is about Prince's trousers. The

8. Diamond, "Wittgenstein, Mathematics, and Ethics."

aboutness is different in each case, and this means that we should be aware of different senses in which a proposition is responsible to reality. The target is the notion of correspondence to reality.[9]

With respect to the experiential proposition about Prince's trousers, we say a reality corresponds to it if it is true and we can assert it. Reality corresponds to a mathematical proposition in a way that is similar to reality corresponding to a word. With respect to words such as "perhaps," "and," as well as "plus," we could not say anything about what reality is supposed to correspond with them. Instead, Wittgenstein encourages us to see that the reality corresponding to these words is our having a use for them. This is similar to what he has said about the reality that corresponds to a rule. As Diamond says, "A rule is made important and justified by all sorts of facts, about the world and about us. . . . For there to be a reality corresponding to a word is then for there to be things (about us, about the world) which make it useful to have the word as part of our means of description."[10]

Wittgenstein effects a shift in how we see the function or use of a mathematical proposition. Mathematics is not different in kind from other activities in which there must be a means of description used in experiential propositions. Diamond offers the example of saying, "This is a chair," to someone unfamiliar with the meaning of "chair." This proposition functions as a "preparation" for descriptions like, "The chairs are all terribly uncomfortable."[11] Similarly, a proposition such as "$20 + 20 = 40$" is a preparation for description: "In mathematics, the signs do not yet have a

---

9. Wittgenstein, *LFM*, 247.
10. Diamond, "Wittgenstein, Mathematics, and Ethics," 233. Wittgenstein asserts,

> What I want to say is this. If one talks of the reality corresponding to a proposition of mathematics or of logic, it is like speaking of a reality corresponding to these *words*—"two" or "perhaps"—more than it is like talking of a reality corresponding to the *sentence* "It rains." Because the structure of a "true" mathematical proposition or a "true" logical proposition is entirely defined in language: it does not depend on any external fact at all. I don't say: "No reality corresponds." To say "A reality corresponds to '$2 + 2 = 4$'" is like saying a reality corresponds to "two." It is like saying a reality corresponds to a rule, which would come to saying: "It is a useful rule, *most* useful—we could not do without it for a thousand reasons, not just *one.*" (LFM, 249)

The practical consideration of rules is an important topic of examination in subsequent chapters. These reasons are not individual, but rather are shared, collective, and perhaps ultimately unjustified.

11. Diamond, "Wittgenstein, Mathematics, and Ethics," 233.

meaning; they are given a meaning. '300' is given meaning by the calculus—that meaning which it has in the sentence 'There are 300 men in this college'" (*LFM*, 249–50). Instead of some exotic or queer realm of numbers, Wittgenstein focuses our attention back on prosaic uses and applications. Laws of inference do not describe a reality. Rather, they lay down rules that are normative but not causal.

Wittgenstein's discussion about logical and mathematical necessity is deflationary and aims to remove philosophical confusion by pointing us back to the practices in which these play roles and have lives. Wittgenstein attempts to break the hold of a picture in which there is a realm of logical and mathematical objects. He also aims to undermine the assumption that logical and mathematical principles are independent of all contexts. Quite the contrary, both are context dependent. But here it is important to remember that the context is neither a realm of independently existing mathematical and logical objects nor a realm of surface conventions. Recall that the MAN argued that the fact that moral principles rely on or even come in contact with a human context was all it took to reject their necessity. Wittgenstein, on the other hand, conceives of necessity in terms of this context dependence. He is not offering any sort of apology for this dependence, but rather is saying that there can be no necessity *of any sort* in the absence of context. This is a radically innovative account of necessity.

CONCLUSION

The world/language dualism, as I have been arguing, plays an important role in the moral realist and antirealist debates. Against this dualism, language is conceived as a human invention that is projected into a world that is independent of us. The puzzle is how to attach two radically different substances: language and the world. On this view, normativity became mysterious, especially normativity in moral matters. When confronted with a philosophical mystery, the temptation is to introduce a metaphysical entity as the solution. To explain the necessity of mathematical and logical necessity, for example, some postulated a realm of logical and mathematical objects. Logical and mathematical propositions were taken to be anchored in these objects. With respect to moral properties, moral properties or moral facts were introduced so that they could function in the same ways as natural facts. In this regard, moral properties, like their natural cousins, are thought to possess a certain causal efficacy. But as we have seen, neither natural properties nor moral properties can provide any standard for correctness so long as the world/language dualism is maintained. Against that dualism, it turns out that natural properties are just as metaphysically suspicious as moral ones. Any form of realism predicated on the world/language dualism is unable to generate any standard of correctness. We also saw, however, that no form of surface conventionalism or regularism is able to provide a standard when the world/language dualism is maintained. This is the paradox of interpretation.

Nothing—no object, no rule, no regularity—is inherently normative. Something has normative authority and binding force in use. We need to shift the lens of our examination, using Rouse's expression, to the intraactions or to use the language that I have been developing, to the conditions providing stability and certainty. Rephrasing Wittgenstein's opening to the *Tractatus,* the world is all that is the case, and the world is the totality of intra-active phenomena. This presents a challenge to the naturalist whom we encountered in Chapter 2, especially concerning the description of objective normativity. And while it might be tempting for a naturalist of Harman's stripe to conclude that all my talk of practices and intra-active phenomena proves his case (because the human contact is inseparable from the normativity), then the same will hold true for any kind of normativity, including the sort we readily accept in logic, mathematics, and science.

If neither realism nor antirealism is tenable as a description of the world, and their weaknesses trace back to a shared presupposition, then there is good reason to reject that presupposition. This liberates us to ask more about the world: neither about nature apart from language nor about language separate from the world, but rather about their constant conjunction and imbrication. This in turn allows for a new conception of normativity and an alternative conception of context dependence that will not collapse into certain pernicious forms of relativism nor make pretences to absolutism.

Let me be very clear on one point: I do not deny the existence of an external world or all the sorts of natural givens or regularities I discuss in the next chapter. Rather, by using Wittgenstein, I am arguing that the philosophical theses of realism and conventionalism cannot deliver what they promise *because* of their reliance on a world/language separation. The fruitful and exciting challenge I find in Wittgenstein for metaethics is to reconfigure and redescribe the world in which we live. That world is neither the one posited by the realist nor the conventionalist.

Perhaps realtors have it right: location, location, location. My own one-line version of the argument of this book is: context, context, context. We are always within contexts, and these overlap, crisscross, and support one another. There are aspects that may come into conflict as well as aspects that may change over time. But the context as I describe it is one in which there is no radical break between world and language, nature and normativity. Ours is also a world of human animals, nonhuman animals, objects and processes, and language and values are in constant interaction. We live in a world of ongoing transactions between multiple participants, including much of what has been lumped into the category of "brute nature" or "raw materials." This is the context in which we always live and from which we can never escape or transcend. This context is one of deep contingency and deep conventions and agreement. As philosophical theses, both realism and surface conventionalism are woefully inadequate to the task of explaining the world and normativity. In the following chapter, I offer an alternative description of our world and practices, in order to provide an account of the ways that necessity, normativity, and normative authority are inseparably tied to our forms of life, shared ways of living, and practices. It is a world of interactions and relationships of myriad elements and objects.

4 FELTED CONTEXTUALISM: HETEROGENEOUS STABILITY

The difficult thing here is not, to dig down to the ground;
no, it is to recognize the ground that lies before us as the ground.
—WITTGENSTEIN, *REMARKS ON THE FOUNDATION OF MATHEMATICS*, VI:31

Like everything metaphysical the harmony between thought and reality is
to be found in the grammar of the language.
—WITTGENSTEIN, *ZETTEL*, § 55

Rejecting the nature/normativity dualism and the accompanying philosophical theses of realism and antirealism makes it incumbent on me to
offer something in their place. How can I describe the world in a way that
highlights the myriad ways in which all the elements of our world are
imbricated and mutually constitutive, dependent, and enmeshed? I
thought about some of Wittgenstein's ways of describing things as mish-
mash (mathematics), hurly-burly, weaves, or patterns, though none of
these satisfied me. Other language I considered and discarded included
entanglement, networks, and entwinement. These seemed too hard to de-
pict. And then I fixed on the image of a felted sweater. Felting is a process
that transforms wool fibers—often yarn—into a dense tangled mat, in
which the individual fibers can no longer be distinguished. Felting is utterly irreversible.[1]

A felted sweater is a wool sweater that has been immersed in very hot
water, usually with some sort of detergent. Felted sweaters, unlike regular
knitted wool sweaters, do not have neatly knit rows. Instead, there is a
network of overlapping and crisscrossing fibers that make the sweater incredibly dense. Any and all elasticity is lost in the felting process, and the
wool can become so dense that it becomes very water resistant.[2]

---

1. I owe a debt to Edi Thorstensson and Barbara Kaiser for their patient explanations
of the felting process in knitting.
2. Wool's properties, in combination with felting, were the inspiration for Velcro.

Felting is the interaction of wool, with its hooks-and-barbs construction, and agitation. Heat speeds up the process, as do certain chemical compounds, including soap.[3] The agitation and the rubbing cause the hooks and barbs on adjacent wool fiber shafts to tangle up, becoming tighter and tighter until they cannot be separated.[4]

The philosophical temptation, stoked especially by realism and antirealism, is to unravel the felted sweater, to perhaps pull away the overlapping and crisscrossing fibers in order to get to the neatly knit rows you assume *must* be there. Undergirding this temptation is the fact that felting can be a matter of degree—in some instances we do see what appear to be the underlying knit rows. But we can never get to these rows, and in fact they disappear in our attempts to do so. The sweater is ruined.[5]

Returning to the architecture and building materials discussed in Chapter 1, in order to provide protection against the elements, houses are often wrapped in high-density polyethylene, a substance that has a felted quality. This wrap is randomly distributed nondirectional fibers of polyethylene that are bonded together by heat and pressure. The relative speed of the process produces the different strength of the wrap.[6]

The felted world, as opposed to the worlds of the realists and antirealists, seems a far better way to understand our world. Of course, I duly recognize that metaphors have limitations. But the felting image works so well because it shows the intense imbrication of the various elements of a sweater and how their relationships constitute the sweater (or *are* the sweater).

Our world is one in which human agency, facts of nature, social practices, and so forth are felted together, where fibers have opened up and closed down over one another, creating a weave that cannot be untangled. Nature/normativity and world/language are just this way. This may seem deeply dissatisfying for some, those who want a more easily identifiable

---

3. Other chemical compounds that aid the felting process are urine and sweat. Socks that are old-fashioned, 100 percent wool felt with use.

4. So why doesn't the wool on sheep felt on hot rainy days? Why don't we see a bunch of felted-up sheep? The lanolin on the wool has not been stripped away, which keeps the hooks and barbs down. Once stripped, however, the barbs of the fibers are ready for tangling and tightening.

5. The knit rows themselves are a mix of material and human agency. Anything that is knit is an intra-active phenomenon. See Rouse, *How Scientific Practices Matter*.

6. Tyvek, produced by DuPont, is the best-known brand in the United States. It is interesting to note that fiberglass is also felted. Glass fibers are cut in half-inch or one-inch pieces and then felted in much the same way that paper is made. Thanks to my chemist friend Mary Henderson for the building-material primer.

starting point or those who want a more glamorous or sophisticated solution to the nature/normativity dualism. But here we do well to heed Wittgenstein's warnings against philosophers' tendencies to want to get before the beginning in our philosophical quests (*PR* VII:58). Our problems, however, are not confined to starting points. Solutions and starting points are connected; a "solution" obtained from a tainted starting point is suspicious. About solutions, Wittgenstein says, "Here we come up against a remarkable and characteristic phenomenon in philosophical investigation: the difficulty—I might say—is not that of finding the solution but rather that of recognizing as the solution something that looks as if it were only a preliminary to it. 'We have already said everything.—Not anything that follows from this, no, this itself is the solution! . . . The difficulty here is: to stop'" (*Z* § 314). This captures much of what I have found distressful about treatments of the question of normativity. So much energy has been directed at "solving" the nature/normativity dualism, treating elements as discreet and showing how they could possibly (or not) interact.

My position is that the felted world is the only context in which there are norms and normative authority. In the absence of this context, there can never be any rules and standards of correctness in any domain of inquiry, including logic, mathematics, science, and morals.

In this chapter, I explore various heterogeneous elements of the felted world, primarily through Wittgenstein's concept of "form of life." Wittgenstein is expressly concerned with what human beings can do with and through language use in our shared world. Discussions of human activities and practices have front-and-center questions about (dare I say it) human nature. Wittgenstein does not discuss human nature per se, but his discussions of natural history and forms of life can be taken as descriptions of the kinds of activities in which humans engage. Most explicitly, he focuses on our uses of language. Using language in certain ways is one of our characteristic activities and, as I hope to show, enables us to engage in moral practices.

I read Wittgenstein to be using the concept "form of life" in two different but related ways. The first way is to mark the differences between humans and nonhuman animals. The second way Wittgenstein uses the term is to mark differences among humans. Communities having widely different moral and nonmoral practices would have different forms of life. These two interpretations of this concept (one human form of life among other natural kinds and multiple forms of life within humanity) are often set up in opposition to each other, with the assumption that only one can be right. I take the two usages, however, to be consistent, compatible, and ultimately important to my argument that there is an immanent and real basis of our moral practices and judgments, which can result in a remarkable diversity. Note well that I am not arguing that these dimensions or ways of living are separable from each other. Instead, I see the discussion below highlighting specific features of our ways of living in much the same way that the transparencies in *Gray's Anatomy* bring out the various constitutive systems and structures of the human body and their relationships to one another.

In my explication of this concept "form of life," I want to be very careful not to commit the philosophical mistake of the substantive seeking an object. The human form of life is not a something that stands separate from the activities of humans. Nor do I want to engage in the sort of essentializing moves about which Wittgenstein is so critical. Wittgenstein is not directing our attention to any one particular thing—be it natural or supernatural—and claiming, "Here is *the* feature that makes us human or that is our humanity." Ventures to identify such a feature will always fail, though this does not stop philosophers from trying. Rather, Wittgenstein is directing our attention to what it is that we do and the activities in which we engage. This is Wittgenstein's starting point in his later philosophy, and it is mine in metaethics.

Attending to these two senses of forms of life is closely aligned with John McDowell's work on second nature he develops in *Mind and World*.[7] McDowell focuses on the nature of human subjects and how it is that our sensibilities enable us to have experiences. McDowell directs our attention back to our animal nature. Rationality is a part of this animal nature, and combined with our capacities and sensibilities it produces our second nature. While McDowell develops his account along more explicitly Aristotelian lines, the influence of Wittgenstein is unmistakably implicit. I will develop an explicitly Wittgensteinian approach. Our practical reason or practical wisdom is a matter of our human nature. As our practical reason develops, deepens, and strengthens, this is our second nature. Our second nature is a matter of the dynamic interplay of our capacities, sensibilities, potentialities, education, customs, and initiations into various communities and societies. In other words, second nature is a product of the complex overlapping and crisscrossing of the two senses of forms of life.

Wittgenstein tells us to rotate our examination around our needs, and in this chapter, I ask what we need as an alternative to what moral realism

---

7. McDowell, *Mind and World.*

and antirealism promised but failed to deliver. I will argue that what we need in our world and in our shared ways of living is stability of the sort the Maison à Bordeaux has as a consequence of the relationships among its different elements and materials. In order to make this argument, I will draw heavily from Wittgenstein's *On Certainty*, arguing that what we find there is not an appeal to foundations (as Avrum Stroll argues), but rather something more philosophically radical yet prosaic. As I said in the previous chapter, as much I want to avoid positing philosophical theses, clarity and efficiency dictate that I name my account something. So, I have chosen to name my account "felted contextualism." With its conception of language as inseparable from the world, felted contextualism provides a genuine alternative to realism and antirealism, and opens an interesting avenue for normativity, as I discuss in the following chapter.

NEITHER IMMATERIALIST NOR MATERIALIST

Through his investigations of language, Wittgenstein is showing what is distinctively human about language and about human beings themselves. Such a project must begin with a recognition of the conditions of human life, which will include limitations that are ineliminable. It is human beings—and not minds—who think, feel, use language, and interact with others and their environments. The point perhaps seems so obvious that many would say that it need not even be mentioned. But this is an important reminder in metaethics.

The account of human beings that emerges from Wittgenstein's later writings is very useful for this feminist metaethical endeavor. Feminists have deep reservations about conceptions of human nature and human agency that do not begin with and recognize our being bodied or embodied, for lack of a better expression. Beings who share this form of life are human beings—not Cartesian egos, not a body, and not some odd or mysterious combination of the two. How could a Cartesian ego see the pain in another (once of course others are admitted to existence) and recognize suffering? In this Wittgensteinian view, a Cartesian ego would not be human enough to be capable of using and developing language and participating in the myriad language-games that humans play. Our use of language "is anchored in our way of living and acting" (*RFM* IV § 36). Wittgenstein says:

> The question is: What kind of language-games can someone who is unacquainted with fear eo ipso not play?

> One could say, for example, that he would watch a tragedy without understanding it. And that could be explained this way: When I see someone else in a terrible situation, even when I myself have nothing to fear, I can shudder, shudder out of sympathy. But someone who is unacquainted with fear wouldn't do that. We are afraid along with the other person, even when we have nothing to fear; and it is this which the former cannot do. Just as I grimace when someone else is being hurt. (*RPP* II § 27)

The Cartesian ego may be capable of participating in some form of life, but it doesn't seem to be ours. The Cartesian ego stands alone in many ways, seemingly not communing with others. This lack of participation makes the Cartesian ego incapable of understanding any life other than its own (if even it can understand that).

We can learn certain things only by living with other people and not by observing people from a detached perspective. Anyone whose exposure to human life was only through observation without participation would no more understand human life than he would the life of fish or plants (*RPP* II § 29). Participation is what anchors us in our ways of living, and it this anchor that the Cartesian ego lacks.

Human beings also cannot be understood as their bodies or as material objects. Consider of the following from *Philosophical Investigations*:

> But isn't it absurd to say of a body that it has pain?—And why does one feel an absurdity in that? In what sense is it true that my hand does not feel pain, but I in my hand?
>
> What sort of issue is: Is it the body that feels pain?—How is it to be decided? What makes it plausible to say that it is not the body?—Well, something like this: if someone has a pain in his hand, then the hand does not say so (unless it writes it) and one does not comfort the hand, but the sufferer: one looks into his face. (*PI* § 286)

We feel empathy or pity for the person who is in pain and not the particular body part in question. We usually do not treat another person as we treat a log or some other inanimate object. Rather, we have a tendency to think that there is something more to a person than her body, which is why we comfort a person and not just a particular body part.[8]

8. As I write this, I am acutely aware that in oppressive societies, some people are

There is also a temptation to think that a human being must be some combination of material and immaterial dimensions. On this view, something immaterial like a soul animates the inert material of the human body, making itself manifest in outer behavior. The soul is the inner mysterious entity that provides the animation to the body. In this dualist view, a human being has an odd constitution, and philosophers have spent an inordinate amount of time addressing the nature of this dualism and the terms of interaction. The dualist approach conceives of the mind as the realm of mental processes and entities that are assumed to be like their counterparts in the physical realm. These mental processes become mysterious and hidden in the body. The assumption is that these mental processes have causal powers that are made manifest in outer behavior. For Wittgenstein, this presumption that mental processes must be like physical processes is the first move in the conjuring trick, escaping notice because it seems so innocent (*PI* § 308).[9]

Wittgenstein highlights the connection between one's body and the ascription of psychological predicates. He says, "Only of a living human being and what resembles (behaves like) a living human being can one say: it has sensations; it sees; is blind; hears; is deaf; is conscious or unconscious" (*PI* § 281). And Wittgenstein goes on to say that we do at times apply psychological predicates to inanimate objects such as dolls or teapots in fairy tales, but that this is a secondary usage (*PI* § 282). It is not the case that dolls and teapots can themselves manifest certain behaviors, but that we endow them with these attributes and make them act in certain ways that resemble our behaviors. Wittgenstein is pointing to a conceptual connection between our psychological terms and our behaviors as much as to an empirical connection. Only of those beings capable of certain behaviors do we ascribe certain psychological or experiential predicates. They must be able to manifest them in regular and recognizable ways. As he explicitly says, "The concept of pain is characterized by its particular function in our

---

treated as bodies or material objects and not as human beings. Women are often reduced to their bodies or to an assemblage of body parts in the pornography industry, for example. Many people are shocked when they encounter pornography, in part because it is a disruption of the regular ways in which we think of people. Unfortunately, these sorts of cases are not thought experiments of anomalous instances that Wittgenstein recommends we imagine. Rather, pornography and the sexual objectification of women are so pervasive that they escape notice because they are before our very eyes. I will address just this worry in Chapters 6 and 7.

9. As Wittgenstein so aptly puts it, "It is humiliating to present oneself as an empty tube only inflated by the mind" (*CV*, 13).

life. Pain has *this* position in our life; has *these* connections. (That is to say: we only call 'pain' what has *this* position, *these* connections)" (*Z* §§ 532–33). This is not simply a matter of the regularity and consistency between an individual's psychological state and her actions. These alone are not enough to provide the requisite connections for intelligibility. About the person whose expressions of grief alternated with the ticking of a metronome or a clock, we would say that he is not manifesting a characteristic formation of grief.[10] The connection is very much a matter of an individual's behaviors and their function in our life. How do people respond to an expression of grief? How do my ways of grieving and expressing grief fit together with those of others? How do grieving practices and rituals shape the form of a particular grief?

It might be tempting to think that a materialist approach to thinking would be capable of skirting this inner/outer problem. The materialist substitutes the brain for the immaterial soul or immaterial mental. The distinction is not between immaterial soul/mind and material body but between physical brain and the physical body. The brain, now, is the inner while the body remains the outer. Even with this switch, there is still the issue of how the brain operates and controls the body. Are the intentions of the brain somehow *in* the behavior? A materialist is no less susceptible to Wittgenstein's critique of the distinction between the inner and the outer as they relate to human behavior.

Here it is important to reintroduce what it is we take for granted—what is beyond being justified or unjustified—in human natural history. In regular interactions, I treat others neither as minds only or as bodies only, nor as a composite of the two (as if I essentially engage with your mind/brain accidentally through your body's faculties). I certainly do not treat others as thinking machines. We do not assume that the human-looking people around us are automata. The interactions in our usual course of events make this assumption difficult to maintain (*PI* § 420). Wittgenstein says, "My attitude towards him is an attitude towards a soul. I am not of the *opinion* that he has a soul" (*PI*, 178). On that same page he says, "The human body is the best picture of the human soul." My comportment toward others never questions the humanity of the other. I do not need to convince myself that this person who appears to be human is human. No, that is a matter of certainty and trust. Holding an opinion about something is a matter of deliberation, allowing for the possibility of doubt. Our ways

10. See also *LW* I § 406.

of acting toward each other as human is the sort of certainty that is part of our natural history. That one is a person and not a machine is something that can be accepted without being proven.

There is a very significant objection that can and should be raised at this point concerning the extent of this acknowledgment and recognition of the humanity of others. History and the present both are rife with examples of failures of recognition. There are those who are not taken as fully human because of their race, gender, or class. Where do these failures of recognition fit in with the certainty and stability that I am developing? I owe an examination of just this question, and I will return to it in Chapter 6 in the context of moral understandings. In brief, I will argue that these significant and fundamental failures of recognition and acknowledgment are the appropriate subjects of moral inquiry. This is one instance where metaethics and normative ethics are inseparable, and feminist analyses are especially useful.

FORMS OF LIFE AND NATURAL KINDS

The expressions "form of life" and "forms of life" appear relatively few times in Wittgenstein's writings.[11] Their infrequent appearance ought not to lead a reader to conclude that the concept is relatively unimportant. On the contrary, the concept is quite important, as is evidenced by his use of it in the same section in which he introduces "language-games." He says, "Here the term 'language-game' is meant to bring into prominence the fact that the speaking of a language is part of an activity, or as a form of life" (PI § 23). This connection indicates a central strand in Wittgenstein's thought. Utterances play a role in language-games, but they do not constitute the whole range of possible activities within a language-game. Talking is but one move in a language-game, and it gets its meaning from the rest of our proceedings (OC § 229). Language can never be described or understood in isolation from the world and the world can never be described or understood in isolation from language. Kallenberg notes that language use, because it is performative, cannot be excised from the world of experience. Language does not simply picture the world in a way that

---

11. The expression "form of life" appears in PI in §§ 19, 23, and 241. "Complicated form of life" appears on p. 174 of PI and in § 358 of OC. "Forms of Life" appears on p. 226 of PI and in RFM at VII:47. A variant translation of "facts of living" appears in RPP I § 630.

leaves everything as it is. Rather, language use contributes to the world of experience, making the world what it is.[12]

One way to read Wittgenstein's use of "form of life" is to pick out what biologists call a natural kind. Forms of life are those of natural history: lupine, feline, canine, and human, for example.[13] There is one human form of life having a natural history and is therefore distinct from all other forms of life found in the world. For Wittgenstein, the natural history includes not only what might be called biological dimensions, but social and cultural ones as well. These dimensions produce incredible diversity within this shared form of life.[14]

Wittgenstein links forms of life with natural history by comparing the activities and capacities of human and nonhuman animals. In comparing the various actions, Wittgenstein is not seeking *the* criterion that absolutely distinguishes human living from other forms of living. In no way is Wittgenstein looking for the essence or the hidden commonality that many philosophers have presumed. There is no such essence. Instead, Wittgenstein points toward the differences not in order to demonstrate the deficiencies of other animals, but to clarify what it is that we humans do.[15] Wittgenstein says that "what we are supplying are really remarks on the natural history of human beings; we are not contributing curiosities however, but observations which no one has doubted, but which have escaped remark only because they are always before our eyes" (*PI* § 415). These facts are the sort that our talk passes by, because they are so taken for granted (*RPP* I § 78). As Newton Garver says, "Natural history is just plain fact, differing from natural science in that it involves neither theory nor hypothesis and is accepted without having been proven—hence being, in

---

12. Brad J. Kallenberg, *Ethics as Grammar: Changing the Postmodern Subject* (Notre Dame, Ind.: University of Notre Dame Press, 2001), 185.

13. Newton Garver offers a similar reading. See *This Complicated Form of Life: Essays on Wittgenstein* (Chicago: Open Court Press, 1994). See especially chapter 15, "Form of Life," and chapter 16, "Naturalism and the Transcendental."

14. The biological dimensions will also result in multiplicity and diversity. An excellent example of this involves intersex and transgendered persons. As Anne Fausto-Sterling argues, there are not just two sexes. Rather, there are five. See "The Five Sexes: Why Male and Female Are Not Enough," *Science*, March–April 1993. See also her book *Sexing the Body: Gender Politics and the Construction of Sexuality* (New York: Basic Books, 2000).

15. There will always be a certain asymmetry in these comparisons, because we are human, using languages to make these comparisons. This is inevitable because there is no way to get outside our language system. What matters is the point of these comparisons as well as the uses to which they are put.

its way, beyond being justified or unjustified."[16] I will return to this in greater detail below.

As I mentioned above, Wittgenstein introduces language-games in the context of form of life. He highlights a number of activities linking language and actions. Any and all attempts to sunder language from the world and our activities will fail. He tells us,

> Review the multiplicity of language-games in the following examples, and in others:
> Giving orders, and obeying them—
> Describing the appearance of an object, or giving its measurements—
> Constructing an object from a description (a drawing)—
> Reporting an event—
> Speculating about an event—
> Forming and testing a hypothesis—
> Presenting the results of an experiment in tables and diagrams—
> Making up a story; and reading it—
> Play-acting—
> Singing catches—
> Guessing riddles—
> Making a joke; telling it—
> Solving a problem in practical arithmetic—
> Translating from one language into another—
> Asking, thanking, cursing, greeting, praying. (*PI* § 23)

This list illustrates some of the various uses of languages as well as some of the ways these uses are interwoven with our lives. In § 25, he offers a comparison to animals: "It is sometimes said that animals do not talk because they lack the mental capacity. And this means: 'they do not think, and that is why they do not talk.' But—they simply do not talk. Or to put it better: they do not use language—if we except the most primitive forms of language.—Commanding, questioning, recounting, chatting, are as much a part of our natural history as walking, eating, drinking, playing." The natural history of humans, as well as the natural history of other animals, begins with basic and elemental acts such as the final four in § 25.

---

16. Newton Garver, "Beginning at the Beginning," in *Essays on Wittgenstein and Austrian Philosophy*, ed. Tamás Demeter (Amsterdam: Rodopi, 2004), 143.

As §§ 23 and 25 indicate, human actions, unlike those of other animals, "are soon differentiated and refined though language, so language-games too are a part of natural history."[17] The multiple language-games mentioned in § 23 are the sorts of activities that more obviously involve the use of more developed and refined language. Wittgenstein draws his readers' attention to just such use and mastery of language. Activities such as commanding, chatting, speculating, problem solving, and describing are characteristic bits of the natural history of humans.

To say that the human form of life is a complicated form of life is to say that humans are simultaneously engaged in a number of language-games at any particular time and that these language-games are connected to one another in a multitude of ways. Some language-games might be considered more basic or primitive (crying or pointing, for example). Describing might well require pointing and is necessary for a number of other language-games, such as the drawing and forming of a hypothesis.

Physiognomic language-games are important, especially as they relate to the primitive reactions. These language-games provide a public framework, giving meaning to our talk of private sensations and experiences. It is only through the use of a public language-game that we can describe our private sensations. These public language-games are physiognomic because of their reliance on the natural expressions of one's sensations and emotions. These natural expressions include facial expressions, gestures, bodily movements, and verbal exclamations. In § 225 of *Zettel*, Wittgenstein describes some of these natural expressions:

> "We *see* emotion."—As opposed to what?—We do not see facial contortions and make inferences from them (like a doctor framing a diagnosis) to joy, grief, boredom. We describe a face immediately as sad, radiant, bored, even when we are unable to give any other description of the features.—Grief, one would like to say, is personified in the face.
>
> This belongs to the concept of emotion.

Language is interwoven with the actions and gestures that constitute crying, and these physiognomic language-games often replace and refine these prelinguistic natural expressions. Having or embodying emotions is also part of our human form of life. Consider hope:

17. Garver, "Beginning at the Beginning," 3.

Can only those hope who can talk? Only those who have mastered the use of a language. That is to say, the phenomena of hope are modes of this complicated form of life. (If a concept refers to a character of human handwriting, it has no application to beings that do not write.)

"Grief" describes a pattern which recurs, with different variations, in the weave of our life. If a man's bodily expression of sorrow and of joy alternated, say with the ticking of a clock, here we should not have the characteristic formation of the pattern of sorrow or of the pattern of joy. (*PI*, 174)[18]

The characteristic patterns of sorrow and joy are similarly part of our natural history.

With respect to something as basic as pain, there are rules that govern speakers' use of language, even where the language use is a gesture. Gestures, no less than words, are "intertwined in a net of multifarious relationships" (*RFM* VI § 48). Other gestures, such as covering our ears at loud sounds or flinching when we touch something unexpectedly, are similarly so basic that the best we can do is make note of them. Kallenberg claims that "Wittgenstein called these behaviors 'primitive reactions' in order to emphasize their givenness for functioning of language. One way (and only one way) to think of this connection is to imagine language as going proxy for these other behaviors."[19] This is Wittgenstein's point in § 244 of *Philosophical Investigations* when the interlocutor asks if the word "pain" means crying. Wittgenstein's reply is a denial: a verbal expression can replace crying, but that verbal expression does not describe the pain.

Prelinguistic behavior, such as smiling, grimacing, and pointing, for example, can lead to many language-games. Pointing gestures can lead to naming, shaking one's head to assertions and denials, facial gestures to aesthetical, ethical, and emotional language. As Ackermann notes, "At a more elaborate level, our ability to walk over difficult terrain, sail across lakes, and build primitive supports and structures leads in symbolic language to the sophisticated assertions of politics, work, and other aspects of our daily lives. In the beginning was deed, then language came along to describe and discuss."[20] Language-games extend and refine these behaviors while providing a coherent linguistic framework.

18. See also Z § 469.

19. Kallenberg, *Ethics as Grammar*, 106.

20. Robert Ackermann, *Wittgenstein's City* (Amherst: University of Massachusetts Press, 1988), 56.

Underpinning any language-game is regularity and agreement; without them there is no language. Wittgenstein's interlocutor asks, "So are you saying that human agreement decides what is true or false?" to which Wittgenstein responds, "It is what human beings say that is true or false; and they agree in the language they use. That is not agreement in opinions but in form of life" (*PI* § 241). In order for there to be correctness of any sort, there must be some regular pattern or practices or ways of living to which an action does or does not conform. In the absence of these, it is impossible to speak of correctness. The patterns and practices are not simply shared attitudes, beliefs, or opinions. Rather, they are shared actions, behaviors, and reactions that are not freely chosen. These constitute the deep agreement, which is agreement in form of life. This agreement is not the product of ratiocination and intellectual and intentional assent. It is part of the framework or world that provides a criterion for correctness, meaning, and intelligibility in our lives. The complicated character of our human form of life is a matter of the agreement and regularity that spans the language-games we play. Recognizing these patterns is part of our shared living, which requires a certain degree of regularity. The regularity and the recognition of the regularity are part of the pattern. Where that regularity is lacking, there is no language (*PI* § 207). Thus, we might conclude that there is a human form of life having characteristic bits of natural history that are woven together by the agreement and regularity of our sayings and doings.

MULTIPLE FORMS OF LIFE IN THE HUMAN FORM OF LIFE?

There is another way to understand "form of life" that is different from the way outlined above. Instead of claiming that "form of life" describes a natural history, one can read Wittgenstein as claiming that there are many forms of life within humanity. Forms of life might best be understood as world views, such that a person trained in scientific methodologies may have a form of life that is different from a theologian who rejects scientific explanations. In some ways, even though they inhabit the same physical world, their worlds are different. One may see law-like operations where the other sees God's grace. Yet to another theologian or scientist, God's grace is manifest in the laws of nature. To imagine the language of the scientist, one would have to imagine a world open to examination and inquiry, one susceptible to certain methods of testing and confirmation.

For some theologians, the scientist's attempts of examination and explanation bypass the world. Such theologians might claim that there is no point to scientific inquiry because it attempts to explain the ineffable and incomprehensible.[21] Clearly, it seems that there can be multiple worldviews that arise from backgrounds and training other than academic ones. In this way, "forms of life" indicates the remarkable diversity within human life.

New Orleans, in the context of Hurricane Katrina, provides a more complicated example, one that I will develop in much greater detail in the final chapter. While blacks and whites share a geographic region, in many ways, their lived realities are markedly different. These different realities contribute to very different understandings about the reasons why certain groups of marginalized people—mostly black, poor, elderly, or disabled—were left behind. It makes sense to say that these groups have a different form of life from those of wealthier, white, and able-bodied people. For many blacks, much of the devastation was both a cause and consequence of long-standing structural and institutional inequality and injustice. While blacks saw racism operating in the world, many whites were unable or unwilling to see racist dimensions. Such radically different worldviews, having sharply divergent explanations for what happened in New Orleans, constitute different forms of life in this second sense.

There is nothing contradictory or surprising in these two different ways to read "forms of life." Rather, they are compatible and complementary. Wide cultural variation and divergence from common practice, rather than serving as evidence against there being a range of behaviors common to humankind, actually shows how much we do have in common. When attempting to understand people who are quite different from or enigmatic to us, we appeal to this common behavior of humankind. Wittgenstein asks us to suppose that we come into an unknown country with a language quite strange to us. In this situation, he asks under what circumstances would we say that "the people gave orders, understood them, obeyed them, rebelled against them, and so on? The common behavior of mankind is the system of reference by means of which we interpret an unknown language" (*PI* § 206). The case of another person being a puzzle or enigma to me is radically different from the talking lion not being understandable to me. In the case of an enigmatic person, I do have something to which to appeal to make his or her behavior understandable, namely, the common

21. For a discussion of religion and science as competing worldviews, see Renford Bambrough, "Fools and Heretics," in *Wittgenstein Centenary Essays*, ed. A. Phillips Griffiths (Cambridge: Cambridge University Press, 1991), 239–50.

behavior we share in virtue of our both being human. In the case of the lion, however, there is not sufficient commonality to enable the differences between our forms of life to be bridged.

Wittgenstein himself recognizes that there are cases where the breakdown is more radical. For example, when we come into a strange country with entirely strange traditions and we do have a mastery of their language, we may still not *understand* the people. We cannot find our feet with them (*PI*, 223). Garver's position is that even though they seem so unresolvable, "These breakdowns, however poignant they may be, are contingent and corrigible, since they result from not having learned the practices rather than from not having the capacity to learn them. Therefore they do not connote any difference in form of life."[22] Wide individual and cultural differences reveal the depth and range of the possibilities of this complicated form of life.

The distinction between not having learned a particular practice and not having the capacity to learn a practice is important. Wittgenstein's point is that those members who share a form of life have, on some very fundamental level, similar capacities to learn and participate in practices. That we do share similar capacities means that there will be similar behaviors among humankind. These capacities are characteristic of our form of life, and different forms of life will have different capacities.

RELATIONSHIPS BETWEEN FORMS OF LIFE

What is the relationship between the human form of life and all the diverse forms of life within it? It might be tempting to sunder them, and then show that one has priority. One might make the case that Wittgenstein's use of "primitive" makes it seem as if certain aspects in the human form of life are more basic than others. He explicitly says that "I want to regard man here as an animal; as a primitive being to which one grants instinct but not ratiocination. As a creature in a primitive state. Any logic good enough for a primitive means of communication needs no apology from us. Language did not emerge from some kind of ratiocination" (*OC* § 475). Language develops through our behaviors and acts, some of which are primitive and instinctual. His discussion of pain and crying can be read in support of this interpretation. Similarly, we can also point to the patterns of sorrow and joy mentioned above. Our expressions of joy—on our face—

---

22. Garver, "Beginning at the Beginning," 148.

are language. So, it might seem there is some sort of foundationalism at work.

On the basis of this alleged foundationalism, it might be tempting to conclude that some concepts, especially those connected to primitive reactions in the human form of life, must be the ones that cannot be doubted. This is the tack that Avrum Stroll takes, as I discuss below. These will form the basis for Stroll's claim that Wittgenstein is a foundationalist. Consider Wittgenstein's question: "Could a legislator abolish the concept pain? The basic concepts are interwoven so closely with what is most fundamental to our way of living that they are therefore unassailable" (*LW* II:43). In the ordinariness of our lives, we do not interrogate the concept of pain. People use this concept with enormous regularity and without question in the vast majority of cases. We take note of the exceptions precisely because they do deviate from normal practice. The concept of pain is so easily and regularly used by people that our talk passes it by.

Our pain behavior is a part of our natural history. Our concept of pain is one that we use with certainty. Its certainty is akin neither to hastiness nor superficiality but rather is part of a form of life. By this, Wittgenstein means that he wants "to conceive it as something that lies beyond being justified or unjustified; as it were, as something animal" (*OC* §§ 358–59).

At this point, a critic might object that while the concepts that develop out of primitive reactions (something animal) have stability in the sense of being unassailable in the ordinary course of events (such as is the case with pain), the concepts that develop out of the various forms of life within humanity are arbitrary and variable. The objection might continue that these various forms of life rest on the human form of life. It is possible to pry off the multitude of forms of life or worldviews from the basic human form of life. With this extraction, we are left with a relativism of the sort that entails that there is no grounding for our moral lives. Rather, there is a groundlessness to our moral lives, and the result is a relativism of an extreme sort.

The therapy prescribed here is to remind ourselves that forms of life are sayings and doings, experiences and languages. These sayings and doings, including all the sorts of primitive reactions discussed above, combined with the multiplicity of language-games, combined with the facts or givens of nature, do not cleave into two discrete forms. Rather, they are embedded and enmeshed in our ways of living; they are entwined with each other in multifarious relationships. These enmeshments are our ways of living. It is not possible to draw boundaries between the human form of life and the multitudes within that form, for an analogous reason that we cannot count all the possible language-games we play. It isn't a matter of there being too many, but rather a matter of them being so intertwined that we cannot separate them to count.

The enmeshment and entanglement of ways of living are integral to understanding the nature of stability. In the next section of this chapter, I want to focus more explicitly on certainty; I want to show that certainty—with all its various elements felted—provides the stable context for our moral language games. I will show that certainty is heterogeneous and runs throughout—and not just underneath—our language uses.

THE NATURE OF CERTAINTY

At this point, I owe a more careful description of the various elements that provide stability in the felted world. My aim here is to show that this stability has the character of certainty as Wittgenstein develops the concept in *On Certainty*. In that work, Wittgenstein's immediate target of criticism is G. E. Moore, who, after a promising start in "A Defense of Common Sense," ultimately gave in to the temptations of a Cartesian epistemology. Cartesian foundationalism makes the distinction between certainty and knowledge; Wittgenstein, however, offers a devastating critique of point of view. Wittgenstein's work in *On Certainty*, however, is not simply critical. In the process of identifying Moore's mistakes (as well as those owing to the Cartesian tradition), Wittgenstein develops an account of certainty that according to Avrum Stroll is absolutistic.[23] For Stroll's Wittgenstein, there are some elements of the foundation that are ineliminable and unrevisable. While I agree with Stroll's reading of Wittgenstein's critical project, I disagree with the attribution of an absolutistic foundationalism, even one that is a radical alternative to other forms of foundationalism. Instead, I read *On Certainty* as pointing toward what I identify as felted contextualism, an approach that will be more descriptively accurate as well as more radical than any form of foundationalism.

My objection to Stroll, in part, is that he has Wittgenstein give into the very same philosophical temptation about which he was so deeply critical. Completely independent foundations can have a seductive appeal; they support without being supported. For Stroll, this unsupported base is certainty that undergirds language-games but is not a part of language-games.

---

23. Avrum Stroll, *Moore and Wittgenstein on Certainty* (Oxford: Oxford University Press, 1994).

Stroll's account turns on language-games being distinct from their external supports. Thus Stroll's certainty is a foundation of the sort that Balmond describes as the tabletop. My objection to Stroll's view is that, oddly enough, it locates the conditions for the possibility and intelligibility of language *outside* of language. I want to argue that certainty, with its various elements, provides important structure to and support of language-games not just from below but also throughout. Certainty is part of a language-game in the same way that structural beams, load-bearing walls, and lateral supports are part of the Maison à Bordeaux. These elements both support and are supported by one another. The various constitutive elements of certainty cut across both dimensions of forms of life discussed above. In order to have the stabilist view stand in clear relief, however, I want to briefly focus on the targets of Wittgenstein's criticisms.

ON MOORE, FOUNDATIONS, AND CERTAINTY

Avrum Stroll makes a compelling case for Wittgenstein's regard for Moore's project in "A Defense of Common Sense," as well as for his declining respect for "Proof of the External World."[24] Though Wittgenstein was deeply critical of and delivered devastating blows to Moore's conclusions, he also recognized that Moore was trying to point toward something that was original. The kinds of claims that Moore was making were philosophically important; the problem was Moore's way of understanding their importance. Moore's mistakes, for Wittgenstein, trace back to at least two major errors in Cartesian epistemology.

For Descartes, knowledge is a mental state achieved through a purely intellectual reasoning process. Descartes claims to know, with absolute certainty achieved solely through introspection, that "I think, therefore I am." The cogito is foundational; it is the knowledge claim that supports all other claims to knowledge but is itself not supported. The foundation and that which it supports are of the same kind. Stroll identifies this central tenet of foundationalism as the doctrine of homogenous foundations. Wittgenstein will very clearly reject the homogeneity between that which supports and that which is supported by.

---

24. Michael Kober argues that Wittgenstein was aiming his criticisms more at Norman Malcolm's "Defending Common Sense" than at Moore's work. The upshot of Wittgenstein's criticisms remains the same regardless of the particular target. See Kober, "Certainties of a World Picture: The Epistemological Investigations of On Certainty," in Sluga and Stern, *The Cambridge Companion to Wittgenstein*, 411–41.

Cartesian epistemology tends to conflate knowledge and certainty. When Moore says, "I know that here is one hand,'" he takes himself to be making a genuine claim to knowledge that is no different in kind from "I know that Maine is to the north of Massachusetts." There is a difference in degree of certainty of these two claims, but they are both knowledge claims. For Moore, no one can really doubt such an obvious claim about my hand. And where doubt attaches to the latter claim about the locations of Massachusetts and Maine, the matter can be resolved. For Moore, the certainty of the knowledge claim about my hand is foundational; nothing can shake it.

In Chapter 6, I will focus more explicitly on Wittgenstein's argument that no kind of knowledge is a purely mental state of the sort that Descartes, and then by extension other epistemologists, has taken it to be. For now, Wittgenstein's point can be summarized thusly: "I know that here is one hand" and "I know that Maine is to the north of Massachusetts" have a similar surface grammar. Their clothing makes them look the same (PI, 224). Wittgenstein argues that only the latter, however, is a genuine knowledge claim. This is the sort of claim about which we can demand justification and seek evidence. The former is not such a knowledge claim. It plays an important role but not as a knowledge claim possessing absolute certainty. For Wittgenstein, the two claims are not different in degree but different in kind. The claim about the relationship between Maine and Massachusetts is a knowledge claim, but the claim about my hand is a matter of certainty. Wittgenstein spills a great deal of ink (for him) marking and showing the differences between knowledge and certainty. Unfortunately Moore, trapped in a Cartesian picture, was unable to see this difference, though he did sense its importance. Wittgenstein, not so trapped, was able to see both the difference and the importance.

Stroll argues, correctly I believe, that one of Wittgenstein's innovations is the rejection of the doctrine of homogenous foundations. Wittgenstein's genius is to argue that the foundation is not composed of or constituted by knowledge claims, but rather certainty. The foundation and that which it supports are heterogeneous. Certainty itself is heterogeneous; it comprises various elements. The Cartesian project makes knowledge a product of ratiocination, which entails that certainty too is such a product. Given Wittgenstein's alternative conception of certainty, for him, it is not primarily a product of intellectual processes. For Wittgenstein, certainty is not a product of intellectual processes.

Wittgenstein recognized that the kinds of claims Moore was addressing were important. They were important, in large part, for the very reason that Moore indicated. They were so obvious that they left little room for doubt. The concept of mistake has little application; what would it be like to seriously doubt that this is my hand or to be mistaken about the Earth having existed for a very long time? This sort of doubt just cannot get any real traction in our everyday living.

For Wittgenstein, Moore would have been much better served to assert that "this is my hand and it stands fast for me." The "standing fast for me" can be applied to Moore's propositions. It is not just that I do not doubt my hand or the world, but also that *no one* does in a serious and sustainable way. Wittgenstein argues that Moore's propositions—those that stand fast—are grammatical; they have the appearance of empirical propositions, but they do not play the same role. I will discuss grammar in greater depth in the following chapter. But for here now, grammatical principles have a normative function, whereas empirical propositions are descriptive. Wittgenstein uses the image of the hinge to demonstrate how what stands fast enables other kinds of movement.

Stroll sees in Wittgenstein two original forms of foundationalism, though Stroll argues that Wittgenstein rejects one in favor of the other. With both forms, the foundation stands outside of but supports language-games. Having problematized the doctrine of homogeneous foundations, Wittgenstein's foundation—in both versions—is different in kind from that which it supports. And finally, what stands fast is not a product of reasoning in each version of foundationalism.

To make his case for Wittgenstein's foundationalism, Stroll appeals to Wittgenstein's metaphors: a hinge, rock bottom of convictions, and substratum. These are metaphors for certainty. He says that "it is Wittgenstein's thesis in *On Certainty* that that which stands fast is not subject to justification, proof, the adducing of evidence or doubt and is neither true nor false. Whatever is subject to these ascriptions belong to the language game. But certitude is not so subject, and therefore stands outside the language game."[25] In both versions of Wittgenstein's foundationalism, Stroll argues that certainty stands outside the language-game. It is the base on which the mansion rests.

25. Stroll, *Moore and Wittgenstein on Certainty*, 138.

Given that Wittgenstein was concerned with the propositions Moore claimed to know, Stroll's attribution of propositional certainty to Wittgenstein makes sense. Propositional certitude can be either relative or absolute. Propositions that are beyond doubt in one context may be subject to doubt in another. Wittgenstein's metaphor of the riverbed in *On Certainty*, §§ 96–99, supports this view of the relative certainty of some propositions. Grammatical principles are the riverbed, channeling the flow of empirical propositions. There are times when and conditions under which a piece of that channel may break off and be pulled into the moving water. A statement that was formerly a grammatical principle becomes an empirical proposition, subject to justification, doubt, and the gathering of evidence. Wittgenstein also recognizes that empirical propositions can harden into grammatical principles and begin to play a channeling role. The meaning of empirical propositions and grammatical principles changes when their role and use changes.

The propositions that have absolute certainty, such as "The Earth exists" and "The Earth is very old," are ones that are not subject to revision in any context. These are beyond doubt, and Stroll concludes that "their certitude is absolute."[26] It is important to note with hinge propositions—both the relatively certain and the absolutely certain—that properly speaking they are not propositions because they are neither true nor false, nor are they subject to justification. They are different in kind from empirical propositions. For this reason, Stroll concludes that they do not belong to the language-game though they do provide the external support.

Stroll argues that by the end of *On Certainty*, Wittgenstein's view underwent a significant change, prompting him to abandon propositional foundationalism. What persist are the heterogeneous natures of certainty and that which it supports and the externality of foundation to language-games. Part of the reason for the shift, according to Stroll, is that the temptation to say that hinge propositions can be known is simply too great. Instead, Stroll claims that Wittgenstein conceives of certainty as a mode of acting that stems from our immersion in human living. Stroll reads Wittgenstein as offering a conception of certainty that is something primitive or animal, a matter of acting, and deriving from our rote training. Unlike propositions, these elements are nonsystematic and are not a product of our reasoning or intellection. Wittgenstein, Stroll claims, welds instinct, acting, and training into a conception of what stands fast for us.

26. Ibid.

What is so important for Stroll is that this version of foundationalism is not a product of reason. Certainty of this animal or acting sort is different in kind from that which it supports. Wittgenstein's genius, for Stroll, was to develop an account of human knowledge where the foundations are in no way like knowledge.

Stroll acknowledges that Wittgenstein did not have the opportunity to develop these in any detail. Stroll does develop an account of how instinct, acting, and training might weld themselves into a foundation. Stroll himself undergoes a shift, claiming that it is community that stands fast for us; it is our inherited background of which Wittgenstein spoke (*OC* §§ 94, 162). Stroll discusses three levels of depth of community. The first level is the totality of humans and animals interacting with their behaviors and practices. The totality also includes the physical world and our interactions with and through this world. The second level includes the set of human practices, including our customs and traditions. The third level includes individual practices, such as asserting, questioning, inquiring, and so forth (*OC* § 170–72). It is community, on all three levels, that constitutes the background against which we live, act, and interact. The community provides the necessary presuppositional support for our ways of living and our claims to knowledge.

For my purposes, there is much in Stroll's account that I find compelling and useful. I do see us as fellow travelers, having common cause in the conception of certainty. But I do think it is inaccurate to attribute a foundationalist position to Wittgenstein. The originality of Wittgenstein's treatment of certainty is too radical to be put back into the metaphor of a foundation. Certainty itself is heterogeneous; it has various constitutive elements. So too is the structure that certainty supports. In typical discussions of foundations, especially the Cartesian sort, the homogeneity of the base extends all the way through the superstructure. But Wittgenstein's discussions and characterizations of language-games, with all their included activities, speak to heterogeneity. My concern is that the radical heterogeneity is muted by continuing to use the metaphor of foundation, especially when it comes to morality. Morality is a heterogeneous set of activities. Its end or purpose is not a construction of a system of knowledge in the Cartesian tradition.

My second concern with Stroll's attribution of a foundationalist position to Wittgenstein is that it lends itself to assuming that the structure or mansion of language use can be separated from the base of certainty. In a similar vein as my argument that forms of life cannot be pried from each other, certainty cannot be cleaved from language. In other words, they are felted. All of the various constitutive elements of certainty and language have open and closed over one another. They have fused together to create an enormously dense weave.

My final concern with Stroll's representation of Wittgenstein as an absolutist foundationalist concerns the treatment of hinge propositions. There is a much stronger case to be made for Wittgenstein having included grammatical principles as an element of certitude. By the time a grammatical principle has achieved that status, it isn't really a product of ratiocination or intellection. Rather, it is taken as a given and functions in a way that shows how far removed from doubt it is. The heterogeneity of Wittgenstein's certitude allows for this inclusion. If Stroll really does want to argue for community as standing fast for us, it is not possible to exclude grammar as the element that functions normatively. I will discuss the normative role of grammar in the following chapter.

Stroll does not develop the notion of community very extensively. But his characterization of the levels of community fits well with the two different ways that I have argued Wittgenstein uses the expression "form of life." Our characteristic ways of showing grief and pain stand fast for us. Our methods of calculating and measuring stand fast for us, both as cause and consequence of our doing things uniformly and regularly.

If we think of those of us sharing a natural history as making up a community, there is an important connection to be made to Wittgenstein's account of logical necessity. Wittgenstein begins with a recognition of the radical but related contingency of the world (that it is the way it is) and of us (that we are the ways we are and that we do the things we do). The facts of the world are contingent; they might not have obtained, or at some point they may no longer obtain. But these facts are somehow "constitutive" of mankind. That is, their obtaining is what is responsible for human's nature being what it is.[27] Counting, quantifying, and calculating are activities in which we engage, in large part because of the way the world is. As Wittgenstein says, "Mathematics is, after all, an anthropological phenomenon" (*RFM* V: 26). Logical and mathematical necessity are creations within the dynamic of the contingent but constitutive relation between world and human nature.

27. See Barry Stroud, "Wittgenstein and Logical Necessity," in *Meaning, Understanding, and Practice* (Oxford: Oxford University Press, 2000), 12.

CERTAINTY AND STABILITY CREATED WITHIN HUMAN LIVING

My aim in this chapter has been to provide a positive account of the stability engendered by our ways of living. These ways of living—as humans and as members of particular communities—involve certainty. Much of what constitutes our forms of life escapes our notice because we take it for granted. The certainty and the trust that are part of our everyday living are integral to our human form of life. This certainty and trust are engendered in our sayings and doings, some of which are primitive in the sense discussed by Wittgenstein, and others of which are nuanced because they involve more complicated uses of language.

Our uses of language are very much connected to our forms of life and certainty, providing the stability in our life, though in ways different from what most philosophers might conclude. One might assume that the only way that language can provide the kind of stability my project requires is it involves correspondence to the world. On this view, the grammar of our language is due to correspondence to a reality that is external to and independent of our language use. On this picture, correspondence mediates the gap between language and the world. Returning to the language of architecture and the formal/modern in the introduction, this view limits the structure of language to a bar pattern, where the space between world and language is punctuated by the "regular and monotonous beat of verticals and horizontals" that are correspondence. This correspondence view, I believe, rests on an assumption about the homogeneity of language and purpose. Being heterogeneous, certainty and language will not lend themselves to the monotonous beat.

The deep agreement of a community in the sense of natural history is not untethered and free-floating. It is very much a product and producer of our world, in all its givenness and contingency. Our natural history is part of, responsive to, shaped by, and shaper of the physical world we inhabit. The actions, practices, rules, regularities, reactions, and givens of nature overlap, crisscross, and tangle with one another. This is the felted world.

Our language use shapes the world and the world shapes our language. Grammar, which limits what makes sense, both shapes and is shaped by our human activities. We can transcend neither the world nor language; they make movement within them possible but not movement out of them. Within them, humans engage in activities and practices that grow out of, respond to, and change the conditions of our lives. The stability is also a matter of the constraints that the natural world imposes on us; we live in a world of limits. Stability also comes from the overlapping and crisscrossing of language-games; they are interwoven in more ways than we could possibly count. Stability is also a matter of regularity, uniformity, and complementarity of our actions and practices. Language-games are a part of our natural history, and they both presume and reinforce the trust and certainty on which our shared lives depend.

The expression "language-game" has a tendency to mislead if one is not attentive to the ways in which Wittgenstein develops the concept. "Game" makes it seem as if they are playful or unimportant. "Language" has a tendency to be taken as "linguistic" or "verbal." The dominant picture is that language is something that we humans impose on the world of brute fact. To be correct, our language must represent or correspond to that reality. And if one believes that the function of language is to represent objects in the world and there are no such moral objects, "moral language-games" could seem devoid of content in a way that science is not. "Moral language-games" could be taken to mean "verbal expressions of our preferences or attitudes" that, without the grounding of science, can become free-floating and transient. And this, to many, would be a quite inadequate description of what we are doing when involved in moral activities. It certainly would to me. But clearly Wittgenstein is not defining language-games as a set of verbal moves, because he is denying the deeper claim on which such a view rests, namely, that language-games sit atop from and are separable from the world.

The practices and shared attitudes and behaviors are different in kind from real or material objects. The word "practice" is also freighted with its own connotations. In this case, the temptation is to take practices to be social conventions in the sense of shared attitudes and behaviors, which are different in kind from real objects in the world. Like language-games, they are taken to rest atop the natural world and to have a separable existence. There seems to be no way in the absence of a neologism to avoid the freighted meanings of these terms. My tendency is to use them interchangeably, acknowledging the potential risk for misunderstanding my use of them.

Language-games are not optional; it is not the case that someone can choose not to play any language-games. It is true that people can opt out some particular language-games, but even here there are constraints. The language-games of morality are not optional. Even though I may choose no longer to identify with or believe in certain moral judgments and concepts, I myself have little control over the fact that others treat me as a moral being. Others will continue to interact and treat me in morally relevant ways. Morality is inescapable within our shared ways of living. Morality is an integral dimension or weave in our complicated forms of life. What does morality comprise? This may seem an odd question to many. Unknowingly invoking a Wittgensteinian imperative, they may exhort us to look and see all the different things we do that we call morality. We make judgments and recommendations, offer evaluations of others' actions and attitudes, follow rules, offer help to someone without even thinking, engage in disagreement and puzzle about what we think we should do, make claims to knowledge, extend sympathy and empathy, and recognize and respond to the suffering of others. We do all of this and more. These activities may really differ from one another in some significant ways, and they may be in tension with one another. Others are very similar and bear a striking likeness to one another. These activities, we might say, bear a family resemblance to one another. Taken together, these activities constitute what I will call the language-games of morality. These language-games, like all others, depend on grammar.

Moral language-games are practical. They do not have any one purpose, but rather an extended family of purposes. Under the umbrella of morality, we engage in myriad activities, some of which tightly overlap while others are more loosely associated. Some of the activities are so basic that we fail to notice them, while others seem bigger than life. In some cases we are trying to resolve a conflict (perhaps disagreeing about what would count as a resolution), while in others we are taking responsibility or assigning blame. Sometimes we are expressing concern for another's actions and their consequences, trying to remain respectful but all the while believing she is making a colossal mistake. In yet other language games, we are trying to repair damage from mistakes we have made. These are just some of the innumerable moral activities in which we regularly engage.

CONCLUSION

Having tied logical and mathematical necessity to natural history, there is good reason to revisit the question of normativity and necessity. My aim in the next chapter will be to provide an account of necessity or grammar, as I will use the term, that recognizes a radical contingency and can provide an account of authority that can vanquish certain forms of conventionalism and relativism.

5 NORMATIVITY AND GRAMMAR

Compare the solution of philosophical problems with the fairy tale gift that seems magical
in the enchanted castle and if it is looked at in daylight is nothing but an ordinary
bit of iron (or something of the sort).
—WITTGENSTEIN, *CULTURE AND VALUE*, 13

We say: "If you really follow the rule in multiplying, it MUST come out the same."
Now, when this is merely the slightly hysterical style of university talk, we have no need to be
particularly interested. It is however the expression of an attitude towards the technique of
multiplying, which comes out everywhere in our lives. The emphasis of the "must"
corresponds only to the inexorability of this attitude, not merely towards the technique of
calculating, but also towards innumerable related practices.
—WITTGENSTEIN, *ZETTEL*, § 299

If we reframe our inquiries along the lines I have been suggesting—
rejecting a world/language dualism, shifting the focus away from an ontological conception of moral properties, rejecting the metaphysical theses
of realism and antirealism, and challenging the context independence of
necessity—and instead start from a felted stable world of practices and
language-games as I described in the previous chapter, then we have different ways to frame questions about normativity. I will argue that normativity has its life in practices and language-games, which make up our
shared felted world. It is only within practices that the distinction between
correctness and incorrectness can be drawn. As we saw in Chapter 3, the
philosophical theses of realism and antirealism, with their shared reliance
on a world/language divide, could not provide any standard of correctness.

Practices are shared and communal, and they are the context of our
meaningful living. All the things a realist would claim as real or given—
humans, animals, conventions, mores, and so forth—are all elements enmeshed within practices. And it is only in the world of practices that
individuals come to have identities and act in meaningful ways. It is within
practices that we can speak of rule following and normativity, because it is
only in this context that we develop a second nature.

What makes something a practice or gives a practice its shape or structure is grammar. In the absence of grammar, there is no practice. In this chapter, I focus on grammar—what it is, how it functions, what roles it plays in our practices, and how it is exercised—as an alternative way to understand normativity and normative authority. Grammar plays a special role in creating any standard of correctness. Grammar, as I shall develop the concept, plays an ineliminable and ubiquitous role in our lives. It is that which creates the musts, shoulds, and oughts that exert an authority over us and from which we act. Normative status is not something inherent or essential in a particular property or proposition, but rather is conferred through our ways of living.

While this may all seem quite mysterious and occult at first glance, this grammatical account demystifies and makes normativity common and ordinary. Grammar is not something that stands over and above us, but rather it flows around us and we move through it in all sorts of ways. Grammar is perhaps best understood as both a process and a product, a dynamic that has vitality because it is a matter of our human use. This, I argue, is the best way to understand normativity and normative authority.

We are born into a world having inescapable normative dimensions, into which individuals are quickly enmeshed. We are enmeshed in all sorts of relations and constraints. One type of relation in which we are enmeshed immediately is with a caregiver or teacher. Our focus is productively turned to the relationship between teachers and students, and how immature individuals come to be able to do certain things, as well as to hold shared attitudes. This, I submit, is the key to understanding how grammar functions normatively and how we can act out of recognition of normative authority. How is it that individuals come to feel the pull of grammar and start to act in ways that are in accordance with grammar and yet avoid the competing pulls of determinism (we have no choice) and voluntarism (we have unrestricted choice)? The answer is quite simple and rather unglamorous: education, training, mastery of a technique, and competency. Wittgenstein treats these questions most explicitly in the *Remarks on the Foundation of Mathematics*, *Philosophical Investigations*, and *On Certainty*. While Wittgenstein's examples initially appear simple, the insights that we gain from looking at a mathematical example such as "add two" are illuminating for moral rules and commands. Of course, there are important differences between different areas of discourse and the degrees to which there is flexibility in the requirements for uniformity and sameness, and one is wise to attend to these carefully.

Normativity is a participatory dynamic, and normative authority comes to have a hold on us through our participation in normative activities and relations. But note that by "participatory" I include not just human interactions, but also the context in which these interactions occur. The world, in all its dimensions and givenness, is a participant in normative relations. This I offer as a warning to guard against the tendency to reinscribe the world/language dualism and view normativity as something projected onto the world from without.

I begin this chapter with a discussion of the dual nature of grammar; it is both arbitrary and nonarbitrary. Given the nature of the world as I discussed in the previous chapter, this should not be surprising.

THE DUAL CHARACTER OF GRAMMAR

"Grammar" is a deceptively complex concept. At times, Wittgenstein claims to be using it in its ordinary sense, meaning the subject matter that treats of the correct construction of sentences. At other times, he uses the term in an uncommon way to uncommon ends. Using Wittgenstein's comparison of language games to other games, grammar plays the same role as rules that govern games like Monopoly, chess, or my all-time favorite, kickball. The rules that govern a game are distinct from the particular moves themselves. Rules, however, are not simply regulative; they are constitutive of the game itself. If the rules of chess were to change such that a bishop could move orthogonally and pawns in zigzag patterns, then this would no longer be the game of chess. It would be a new, different game. So too does grammar constitute an area of activity or practice. Grammar is what makes a move possible in addition to providing the standard against which to judge the permissibility or meaningfulness of a particular move. Thus, for Wittgenstein, grammar plays a normative role in a very fundamental way.

Normative status is not something inherent or essential in some special way in a particular proposition, but rather is something that we confer through our ways of living. As I discussed in Chapter 3, Wittgenstein launched a devastating series of criticisms at any account of necessity that assumed it was intrinsic to any property or proposition. Wittgenstein's approach to logical and metaphysical necessity is to reject the claim that the rules or laws function as genuine propositions in the sense of being true or false, or by picking out or corresponding with logical and mathematical objects. Not only are necessary propositions not statements about necessary states of affairs, they are not propositions at all. Rather they reflect the "rules of logical syntax" that determine whether a particular combination is meaningful. While Wittgenstein exchanged the expression "rules of logical syntax" with "grammar," he carried this normativist view through his writings. Grammar is the basis for our sense of necessity and impossibility, and this includes logical necessity just as much as what is termed metaphysical necessity. Garver reminds us of Wittgenstein's remark that *Essence* is expressed by grammar (*PI* § 371) and writes that "Essence, necessity, and impossibility are modal features of the human experience."[1]

The dual character of grammar continues the discussion of felted contextualism and certainty begun in the previous chapter. This dual nature shows that grammar is neither absolute in the sense of being unchanging or simply given nor relative in the sense of being a matter of voluntary choice. It is conventional in a very deep and inescapable sense. Quite important, grammar is autonomous; it neither reflects the essence of reality nor is it simply a product of human nature. The arbitrary and nonarbitrary dimensions of grammar are similarly enmeshed and entangled. It is not possible to separate these dimensions, as will become evident below.

THE ARBITRARINESS OF GRAMMAR

Grammar's arbitrariness guards against the propensity to reach absolutistic conclusions about our life and our concepts. In an interesting and illuminating treatment of grammar's dual nature, Michael Forster advances what he calls a diversity thesis.[2] Grammar is arbitrary in the sense that there are alternatives to what Forster identifies as six areas of grammar. For each of these, there are alternative grammatical principles that result in similar but alternative concepts. Wittgenstein, in Forster's view, is profoundly interested in the possibility of these alternative grammars that result in different norms of representation, none of which has a greater claim to rightness, correctness, or truthfulness than any other. Consider the following six areas of grammar and alternatives to them:

1. Formal logic: double negation as meaningless or repetition of simple negation (*PI* § 554)

1. Newton Garver, "Philosophy as Grammar," in Sluga and Stern, *The Cambridge Companion to Wittgenstein*, 160.

29 Michael Forster, *Wittgenstein on the Arbitrariness of Grammar* (Princeton: Princeton University Press, 2004).

2. Mathematics: people who count to five (*RPP* I § 295) and people for whom $2 \times 2 = 5$ (*PI*, 226)

3. Necessary propositions: recognizing a reddish green (*Z* § 362)

4. Ostensive definitions: color classification of four primary colors plus black and white (*Z* § 331)

5. Criteria: two distinct concepts for pain, one of which is tied to a criterion of bodily damage and the other to a criterion like a stomachache (and associated with a lack of sympathy) (*Z* § 380)

6. Apparent empirical propositions: people who believe in the biblical creation story and those who do not (*OC* § 336).[3]

These alternative grammars, in their constitutive role, will create different concepts, meanings, senses, and norms.

Another way that grammar is arbitrary is in the sense of not being justified. It is not possible to justify one grammar over an alternative one. Wittgenstein asks what such a justification for one over the other would have to be. One could offer two candidates to provide justification, but neither is sustainable. First, one might argue that a principle of Grammar A is justified because A is true in virtue of the meanings of the terms used to articulate the principle.[4] Necessary propositions, however, make up our norms of representation that constitute the meaning of our words. Our rules of inference are such a norm of representation, and they determine the meaning of logical constants. Given that norms constitute meanings, it is misguided to speak of the truth of the norm being a matter of the meaning of their constituents. This attempt puts the cart before the horse.

The second attempt to justify grammar appeals to facts or reality. Grammar A is justified because it gets the facts right by being a true/accurate mirror of reality. But Wittgenstein explicitly states, "The rules of grammar cannot be justified by shewing that their application makes a representation agree with reality" (*PG* I § 134). Necessary propositions are not mirrors of necessary states of affairs or objects, and therefore talk of accurate representations of such affairs or objects is nonsensical. This was the subject of discussion in Chapter 3. At issue is what would count as corresponding or tallying with the facts, as Wittgenstein says in *On Certainty*, § 199. In order to answer these questions, one already has to assume much that cannot be justified on the basis of correspondence. Once again, we encounter the difficulty of placing the cart before the horse.

3. Ibid., 22–23.
4. Ibid., 31.

Grammatical principles are arbitrary in still another sense. They are neither true nor false, correct nor incorrect. Grammatical principles are not and *cannot* be subject to evaluation by a single standard that is not language dependent. Grammatical principles are antecedent to *any* judgments made within a language-game. This is connected with Wittgenstein's rejection of realism due to its inability to provide any criterion or standard for correctness. The hope in appealing to such a language-independent standard is that it could provide the ultimate justification, dispelling any doubts about what is correct or true. Such a standard would remove any arbitrariness. Holding out for such a standard is a vestige of the world/language dualism. The expectation was that this context-independent standard could then be applied from a similarly language-independent vantage point. Neither of these expectations is able to be met.

The demand for a language-independent vantage point from which to apply a standard is also a carryover from the world/language split. This demand is unmeetable because it requires that there be a gap between world and language, such that one would be able to escape into a language-free zone. As I have been arguing, language permeates, penetrates, infuses the world all the way up and down; it does not sit on the world. The world permeates our language just as thoroughly. Language and language use are inseparable from other aspects of the world. There is an innumerable number of vantage points from within this stable felted world, but it is only within this context that one can make judgments or apply standards.

An example will help to illuminate the depth and character of grammar's arbitrariness, as well as to point us to some of the nonarbitrary dimensions. Wittgenstein asks us to consider the procedure for weighing a piece of cheese in order to fix a price (*PI* § 142). In this case, one of the givens with which we must work is that pieces of cheese do not shrink or expand spontaneously. Our grammar of weighing is tied to this given, such that if items did just suddenly increase or decrease in size, then our practices of weighing would become pointless. If we did place a piece of cheese on a scale and it offered various readings, our first inclination would be to check whether the scale is in the proper working order. Echoing Sherlock Holmes, only after eliminating all the possibilities do we accept what we have taken to be impossible in the normal workings of our lives: cheese spontaneously expands and contracts in its weight. This is one instance in which the arbitrariness and nonarbitrariness of grammar exist simultaneously.

Now consider one group of people who measured with rigid rulers and produced certain results and another group that used elastic rulers. As much as we rigid-ruler people might want to exclaim, "But that isn't *really* measuring!" it is not truth in the sense of correspondence or rightness that licenses us to do so (by measuring, we mean measuring like *this*). Our way of measuring conflicts with theirs, and the practical purposes served by each are different.[5] I will develop this point below.

Wittgenstein seems to delight in highlighting grammar's arbitrariness. His later writings are riddled with questions about the givenness or correctness of our concepts. He writes, "I want to say: an education quite different from ours might also be the foundation for different concepts" (*Z* § 387). A number of times he asks his readers to imagine very different societies or people who calculate, reason, or measure in radically different ways from our own. The point of such imaginings, Oswald Hanfling claims, is to disabuse readers of the belief that these must be the absolutely rights ones.[6] Wittgenstein issues a challenge: "let him imagine certain very general facts of nature to be different from what we are used to, and the formation of concepts different from the usual ones will become intelligible to him" (*PI*, 230). Wittgenstein says that our view that our concepts *must* be the rights one is so strong that the only way we can see alternatives is if "life would run on differently" (*Z* § 388). And this is precisely what Wittgenstein challenges us to imagine. He aims to show or shock us into seeing that the concepts we have are not absolute; they could be otherwise were our ways of living different. They could be different were the world different or our faculties radically different. From this recognition, however, it does not follow that our concepts are untethered, even the more basic ones. The point I want to emphasize is that even though they are not absolute in the sense of being unchanging or forever given, they certainly are not willy-nilly or capable of changing in the blink of an eye. There is an enormous stability of a heterogeneous sort that staves off an anything-goes conclusion.

THE NONARBITRARINESS OF GRAMMAR

Grammar's arbitrariness is only part of the story. Grammar is nonarbitrary in several important regards. Grammar is nonarbitrary in the sense of our

5. As Wittgenstein himself notes, a shopkeeper might employ this alternative way of measuring to treat customers differently (*RFM* I: 5).

6. Oswald Hanfling, *Wittgenstein and the Human Form of Life* (New York: Routledge, 2002), 4.

being in the world in ways that are heavily constrained. We cannot simply adopt whatever particular grammar we desire, nor can any sentence serve a grammatical role. Forster discusses several constraints that preclude the easy casting off and adoption of grammatical principles or norms of representation. These concerns help to resist the pull of surface conventionalism and voluntarism.

There are those constraints that are a matter of human nature or human capacities, as discussed in the previous chapter. Humans share perceptual and cognitive capacities within a range. We have certain primitive reactions. For example, we have certain responses and reactions to fear (*PG* I § 68). We express certain emotions and recognize them in others. We see, for example, someone else's pain. We respond to others without gathering evidence that they are human. In many instances, we act without reflection; we act with a certainty that is akin to me showing certainty about the door by opening it. Humans are also creatures who are capable of following rules and characterizing our behavior in normative terms. Human nature, as discussed earlier, does limit the norms of representation we can accept. The person who is unfamiliar with fear will not be able to make sense of nor meaningfully interact with those of us who are acquainted with fear. We cannot find our feet with him, and most likely he cannot with us.

There are also constraints that are a matter of our social practices, traditions, and customs. Wittgenstein tells us to "compare a concept with a style of painting. For is even our style of painting arbitrary? Can we choose one at pleasure? (The Egyptian for instance)" (*PI,* 230). Forster also includes in this category of constraints the sort that Wittgenstein discusses in *On Certainty* concerning our worldview as the inherited background (§ 68). But important too, even our laws of inference compel (or constrain) us in ways not dissimilar to other laws. Our laws of inference mean that we *must* reach certain conclusions or do certain things. If we accept modus ponens and are confronted with both a conditional statement and the antecedent, we must infer the consequent. If we do not, then we have not understood modus ponens and we have made a mistake. Not correctly following the rules of logical inference means that we get into "conflict with society; and also with other practical consequences" (*RFM* I § 116). The strength of the social practice, custom, or tradition of logical inference is great. Forster claims that "it is a consequence of [Wittgenstein's] famous rule following argument that grammar is of its very essence a product of ongoing social practice."[7] This is a very different account of the strength of normativity and normative authority from the one that a more traditional account of logical necessity advances. Instead, it is something in which we participate in myriad ways. I will return to this below.

The final set of constraints that Forster discusses concerns the transformation of empirical statements into grammatical ones. It is important to note that something becomes a rule or standard by its use. A rule is a standard when it is employed as such. This is why the status of particular propositions can change. Empirical propositions harden into grammatical ones. In their normative role, these grammatical principles channel other empirical and descriptive propositions (*OC* § 96).[8]

Wittgenstein argues against the view that at will we can turn what appear to be empirical sentences into grammatical ones. This constraint mitigates voluntarism. A sentence, in order to be grammatical, must be meaningful. A grammatical sentence, on Forster's reading, is meaningful if it has both employment and application in our lives.[9] Forster lays out five considerations this employment and application approach has for meaning. These he presents in order of increasing strength. I am primarily concerned with developing the last three.

1. Meaning does not consist in a kind of object: "You think of meaning as a thing of the same kind as the word, though also different from the word. Here the word, there the meaning. The money and the cow that you can buy with it. (But contrast: money and its use)" (*PI* § 120).

2. Meaning consists in the function or form of words in a language. This involves conformity to grammatical rules: "Compare the meaning of a

---

7. Forster, *Wittgenstein on the Arbitrariness of Grammar*, 68. These sorts of constraints can also be understood as framework conditions, described by Hans-Johann Glock. See the entry "framework" in *A Wittgenstein Dictionary* (Oxford: Blackwell, 1996).

8. Every branch of inquiry has a history of transformation of empirical propositions into grammatical ones. Einstein's initial recognition of the difficulties and limitations of Newtonian physics produced a whole new set of grammatical propositions that radically reframed the field of physics.

In my book *Oppression and Responsibility: A Wittgensteinian Approach to Social Practices and Moral Theory* (University Park: Penn State University Press, 2002), I focus on the grammar of oppressive practices, particularly the ways in which beliefs about marginalized and oppressed people come to function grammatically. These grammatical propositions then serve as justification for all sorts of violations of justice and equality. Many of these grammatical propositions have been challenged on multiple fronts to good effect, removing much of their normative force. The reality, however, is that it is a constant struggle to jettison oppressive grammatical propositions, because they are so adaptable, much like a virus.

9. Forster, *Wittgenstein on the Arbitrariness of Grammar*, 70.

word with the 'function' of an official. And 'different meanings' with 'different functions'" (*OC* § 64).

3. Meaning is a function in language that involves the achievement of practical purposes: "Knowledge in mathematics: Here one has to keep reminding oneself of the unimportance of 'inner process' or 'state' and ask 'Why should it be important? What does it matter to me?' What is interesting is how we *use* mathematical propositions" (*OC* § 38).

4. Meaning consists of a form of words' practical function in an enduring practice: "Is what is called 'obeying a rule' something that it would be possible for only *one* man to do, and to do only *once* in his life?—This is of course a note on the grammar of the expression 'to obey a rule'" (*PI* § 199).

5. Meaning consists of the form of words' practical function in an enduring social practice: "Could there be arithmetic without agreement on the part of calculators? Could there only be one human being who calculated? Could there only be one who followed a rule? Are these questions like, say, 'Can one man alone engage in commerce?'" (*RFM* VI § 45).

The achievement of practical purposes is significant with respect to the meaning of our concepts. This is certainly the case with our concepts of measuring and weighing. These concepts enable us to do things, to achieve practical purposes. Some of the things that mathematics enables us to do include determining how many people attended an event and estimating how much gasoline is left in the tank. There is nothing mysterious about practical considerations and their connections to what we should do. We are aware of all sorts of practical considerations, in all sorts of unproblematic ways, that present no troubles or mysteries about recognizing and acting out of them. If I see water spewing all over the floor from a broken pipe, practical considerations prompt me to shut off the water valve. I must shut off the valve if I want to stop the water flow. Practical purposes are centrally important to the language-games we play; in fact, they are the whole point.

The enduring practice consideration is inseparable from Wittgenstein's rejection of a view that a concept or thought is privately expressive but publicly inexpressible. Not only is the requisite uniformity missing in the private language such that we cannot speak of sameness or correctness, but we cannot even name the object in the first place. In the absence of being able to identify *this sensation* or name *this* (it could be nothing), there is no way to talk intelligibly about obeying a rule. Obeying a rule already requires some degree of normativity, because that is what enables us to judge that a rule has been followed correctly or in the same way. Private language, Wittgenstein might well have said, cannot have a normative element, and therefore it cannot be a language.

While Forster uses the expression enduring "social practice," I prefer just to use the term "practice."[10] My concern is that the expression "social practice" may pull one back into the world/language dualism by assuming that the sociality is separate and different in kind from the other conditions that constitute our world. It might prompt us to give in to the temptation to untangle the fibers in order to get to a neatly knit row. I prefer to say that grammar is a product of our felted world. It is a matter of certainty, what stands fast for us, and community agreement in actions and attitudes. There is also the temptation to contrast social practices with private practices in the sense of private discussed just above. So to avoid all this baggage and potential for slippage, I prefer simply to speak of practices. A practice, as I have been using the term, is an overlapping and crisscrossing of physical objects, givens and regularities of nature, behaviors, actions, and shared attitudes. Some practices that Wittgenstein mentions, such as commerce, are highly integrated and complex, while others are more basic or general, such as description.[11] All practices have an inescapable and ineliminable normative element, because they involve grammar and are formulated and played within the felted world. In the absence of normativity, we cannot speak of language and practice.

Grammatical principles are inextricably bound up with empirical regularities, and though often removed from the regular traffic of doubt, they are not necessarily untouchable or unrevisable. Without empirical regularity, grammatical principles become meaningless but not false. If massive confusion about 25 x 25 became standard, then calculating would lose its point. Calculating has a point and serves a practical purpose. Judgments of measurement become meaningless if rulers are elastic. Having said this, Wittgenstein does argue that grammatical principles can change

10. There are those who argue that a practice need not be social, in the sense of shared, in order to be a practice. See, for example, G. P. Baker and P. M. S. Hacker, *Wittgenstein: Rules, Grammar, and Necessity* (Oxford: Blackwell, 1986). This, however, is not my view.

11. Theodore Schatzki makes this distinction between integrated and what he calls dispersed practices in *Social Practices: A Wittgensteinian Approach to Human Activity and the Social* (Cambridge: Cambridge University Press, 1996). For a complementary account, see also Todd May, *Our Practices, Our Selves: Or, What It Means to Be Human* (University Park: Penn State University Press, 2001). See also my book *Oppression and Responsibility*.

when they are challenged on multiple sides. The change is never whole-sale, and much must remain stable in order for any transformation to occur.[12]

One other additional way to see the connections between the arbitrary and nonarbitrary dimensions of grammar is in the establishing of internal relations between concepts. Internal relations are a matter of and are only possible within the stable world, where the various elements are related to each other in felted ways. Keeping in mind what Wittgenstein said about essence being expressed by grammar, and the ways in which metaphysics often masks grammar, we ought to focus closely on the meaning and use of concepts and how concepts are related to one another. Internal relations are those in which the relation is constitutive of the relata. Internal relations are "creatures of our practice, since they are effected by the way we identify things."[13] This includes our calling 144—and no other number—the square of 12. It also includes our calling only unmarried men bache-lors. This means that I am committed to and more strongly *must* accept that bachelors are unmarried men. If I use the term to talk about married men, then I am not using the concept correctly.

DEEP AGREEMENT AND STABILITY BUT NOT VOLUNTARISM

Wittgenstein's examples of alternative ways of counting, measuring and calculating, at first glance, seem to lend weight to the claim that our adop-tion of certain practices and standards is a matter of choice. We could have chosen differently, but we have not. Thus, there does seem to be some weight behind the charge that Wittgenstein's approach is a form of radical conventionalism or, as Michael Dummet calls it, "full-blooded convention-alism."[14] These conventions appear to us as intelligible practices. The elas-tic-ruler users get different results from us, but yet we can conceive of a world in which their activities made sense, even if we think it foolish or misguided. They choose to do things in *that* way while we choose to do it *this* way.

But can we really understand these elastic-ruler users and their activi-ties? Can we understand the woodsellers Wittgenstein introduces who sell

---

12. Newtonian physics is just such an example. It isn't regarded as wrong but rather as having a more limited scope of application.

13. See the entry "internal relations" in Glock, *A Wittgenstein Dictionary*.

14. Michael Dummett, "Wittgenstein's Philosophy of Mathematics," *Philosophical Review* 68 (1959): 324.

wood by the area covered (with no attention to height) rather than by a cubic measure? At first glance, it seems that we can. We can imagine that the woodsellers simply have an alternative price-fixing plan, and for whatever reasons, they have decided that area matters more than volume. Do these people differ from us only in that they have chosen and accepted different conventions, or do their ways of living differ far more radically? Initially it seems that the former is a better description of how the alternatives differ. The latter, however, is more accurate. In one of the most insightful treatments of this question, Barry Stroud rejects Dummet's conclusion, arguing that Wittgenstein's position is not a form of conventionalism of this sort.[15]

The initial appearance of intelligibility is misleading, according to Stroud; on closer examination, it disappears. When the alternative begins to appear intelligible, it is at the expense of the intelligibility of our ways of doing things. So, as much as we might like to say that the woodsellers simply have a different pricing schema, this is not so. About the woodsellers and their ways of living, Stroud says:

> Surely they would have to believe that a one-by-six-inch board all of a sudden increased in size or quantity when it was turned from resting on its one-inch edge to resting on its six-inch side. And what would the relation between quantity and weight possibly be for such people? A man could buy as much wood as he could possibly lift, only to find, upon dropping it, that he had just lifted more wood than he could possibly lift. Or is there more wood, but the same weight? Or perhaps these people do not understand the expressions "more" or "less" at all. . . . And do these people think of themselves as shrinking when they shift from standing on both feet to standing on one?[16]

Our initial understanding of these alternatives dissolves when confronted with the depth and degree of the differences of beliefs and orientation in the world. It is not just this one particular practice that differs, but rather a significant portion of how they act and what they believe. They treat the beam standing on its one-inch edge as worth less or as a different size from a beam standing on its six-inch edge. Wittgenstein shows that when

---

15. Stroud, "Wittgenstein and Logical Necessity."
16. Ibid., 10.

you look at the particular practice of price fixing by woodsellers, for example, you'll see the intense imbrication of the nature of the beings engaged in this practice, givens of the world, and certainty. These practices are both deeply contingent and arbitrary but just as deeply stable.

Of course the overwhelming pull here is to say, "BUT THEY ARE WRONG!!" though this is precisely the conclusion that we must resist. We must resist the temptation to say that our ways are the correct ones and their ways incorrect. The pull should direct us to consider the contingency of our own practices. Their way of doing these things, no more than ours, is contingent. It is not only contingent that we infer in this particular way, but also that we infer at all. From this dual level of contingency, however, it does not follow that we are free to decide and adopt just any set of practices. There are significant constraints on what we can and cannot choose to do, and these constraints are vital in understanding our moral practices in their same dual contingency.

These constraints endemic to our world and our ways of living limit the meanings and sense we can make. But it is a mistake to say then that everything is already determined, as some forms of conventionalism imply. Thus, the position I advocate avoids the determinism that burdens many forms of conventionalism. To say that there are limits carries no implication that only certain moves can be made. To return to Wittgenstein's image of the rails laid out to infinity, the steps are not already taken. We must take them. We have to take a step, but it is not fixed in advance which step it will be, and it can't be just any step and still count as correct or intelligible.

The felted world is a world of practices, comprising various elements. This felted contextualism does not presume a world/language divide, but rather maintains that practices have a depth that goes all the way down into what most people simply call the natural world. My position is that our world is not one part natural and one part social, but rather is a shared world where these are intermingled and tangled, resulting in ways of acting and conventions that are inescapably bound together.[17] Practices do go all the way through the world, involving the interaction among human animals, nonhuman animals, the physical environment, and what we might call facts of nature or regularities. The arbitrariness and nonarbitrariness runs all the way through our world. The deep agreement that results

17. For a complementary analysis in philosophy of science, see Rouse, *How Scientific Practices Matter.*

from these interactions is a matter of convention, but in a way very different from explicit and voluntary agreement. So, my position is that morality and moral matters are stable in the sense that they—like logic, mathematics, and science—are inseparable from the context, which I have identified as the felted world. Just as important, I am committed to a certain contingency: we are the creatures we are, we do the things we do, the world is the way it is, and all these things are contingent.[18] They could be otherwise, and may well be otherwise if certain things about us and our capacities or givens or facts of nature were radically altered. But from this it does not follow that we can simply reach any agreement we want, or that we can cast off whatever aspects or dimensions of living in our shared world that we do not like. For this reason, my position does not easily fit with the ways that the labels "conventionalism" and "relativism" are used. In place of these terms, I shall use the terms "felted contextualism" and "stabilism." In Chapter 7, I will show how different stabilism is from various forms of relativism.

THE HOLD AND AUTHORITY OF GRAMMAR

As I discussed in Chapter 2, there is good reason to be suspicious of the linkage of normative authority to causal efficacy in motivating action. Linking these requires that causal efficacy be a property that some reasons or some objects possess, which then exerts some sort of motivational force. In addition to the metaphysical challenges this view presents, there is an epistemological problem as well: how, exactly, and by what faculty, are we supposed to recognize this property? Mysteries abound against this backdrop. J. L. Mackie, as a typical antirealist, claims that these mysteries provide sufficient justification to reject the claim that there could be anything like objective moral reasons. Against the world/language dualism, not only do the objective moral reasons look fishy, but any form of normative authority looks just as dodgy.

It is tempting to assume that normativity is a kind of causality. We often talk about the motivating force of normativity. Normativity causes one to have a reason for action; normativity provides a motivation to act. The motivation may be sufficient or it may be insufficient, but regardless it

18. As I noted, felting can be a matter of degree, tighter or looser, denser or thinner. In many ways, the degree of felting is itself a matter of the various elements and their relations—the yarn, the water temperature, the amount of lanolin, time in the water, agitation, and so forth.

does have some motivating power. This view locates normativity in objects, in much the same way that the MAN located causality in an already determinate object. But Joseph Rouse has provided a compelling argument for reframing discussions of causality away from determinate causes and equally determinate effects to the intra-active phenomena in which these objects and relations obtain. If normativity is a kind of causality and causality is not located in already-determinate objects, then we should not expect normativity to be located in such objects.

Having rejected the world/language distinction and offered instead a conception of the world as felted and stable, the categories of objectivist and subjectivist are terribly inadequate to explain normative authority. Rejecting these categories, however, in no way entails a rejection of the concept of normative authority. It requires that we reconceive the category and our expectations for normative authority. I propose understanding normative authority in terms of grammar and necessity. If we take anything from Wittgenstein's treatment of necessity, it is the rejection of the view that we need some sort of metaphysical justification for necessity. The laws of inference lay down rules; they do not describe a reality. The musts and shoulds of logic are normative but not causal. Given the temptation to re-inflate necessity with metaphysical baggage, I prefer to use the expression "lived mustness" instead.[19] This expression highlights the ways grammar's normativity is created and maintained by our actions, uses, and practices within this shared world.

This account of lived mustness will be neither objectivist nor subjectivist, but will be able to meet the requirements initially offered in Chapter 2. The requirements as originally stated are in regular type, while my revisions are in italic. Briefly stated, those requirements are:

1. There is a course of action that must be (*but the origin and nature of the must isn't what we think*).
2. Humans can see the rightness (*or the mustness or necessity*) of this course (*not some special quality, but rather the ability to recognize practical considerations*).
3. Humans can act out of/for the sake of this rightness (*with understanding, and not as some weird causal property*).

---

19. This expression is Meredith Williams's. See *Wittgenstein, Mind, and Meaning* (New York: Routledge, 1999), especially chapter 6, "Rules, Community, and the Individual."

By meeting these requirements, I show that our moral judgments, rules, prescriptions, and reasons carry an authority that is an important component of the stability of our moral lives. This authority is much a matter of our taking on a second nature, developing a second nature, and seeing that certain things must be the case.

Saying that normative authority is a participatory dynamic entails that we do share responsibility for the content of our normative judgments, good and bad. This was my concern in *Oppression and Responsibility;* namely, how those of us who are privileged in various ways have responsibility for the maintenance of oppressive systems, entities that exist in the context in which particular acts have their meaning. We are all teachers and learners, transmitters of judgments, and wielders of normative authority. Our focus is productively turned to how immature members of a community both come to be able to do certain things and hold shared attitudes. This, I submit, is the key to understanding how grammar functions normatively and how individuals become members of communities (all the while recognizing that communities can have boundaries and that there are disagreements between communities).

What we need to do, I submit, is pay attention to education and the moral dimensions of all forms of education. Moral education is yet another of the practical concerns that drops out of contemporary metaethics. While it seems as if it is just assumed that we can recognize moral considerations within a situation (however you define them), it requires training and sensitivity that in no way are simply given or that one simply possesses. I start this section by examining how we learn to look in a direction, to count and to measure; I intend to highlight both the context in which these activities have their lives and the ways that individuals come to recognize and act in concert with the pull of grammar. This will meet the three requirements stated above: that there be a course of action that must be, and that we not only recognize it but also act for the sake of it.

SOME EXAMPLES OF DEEP AGREEMENT, CONTINGENCY, AND NORMATIVITY: LOOKING, COUNTING, AND MEASURING

Let's start with some actions that function grammatically. If I say to someone, "Look over there," and I point, how does that person know where to look? Out straight from my finger or at a right angle from my finger or up along my arm? The answer, we would all say, is out straight from my finger. How do I know this? Well, I might be inclined to say that I just do.

No one ever gave me a finger-pointing tutorial, but yet without hesitation I look in a certain direction. I would be willing to go so far as to say that I have looked correctly. Finger pointing can be done with a quite confined context (I point to a word on a piece of paper) or it can be done in a wide-open space, such as when I point to a tree in a field to indicate where a fence might be built. In the latter case, me saying, "Look over here" while gesturing with my finger, can be more or less exact. But it would be incorrect for a person to look in the direction from my finger up my arm. To that person, no one would hesitate to say, "You are looking in the wrong direction. Really, you are looking incorrectly." The finger pointing tells us where we *should* look, and we are inclined to do so. The action becomes so ingrained that we cannot imagine doing it otherwise.

Counting is a rule-governed activity, and no one here would deny that there are correct ways to count and incorrect ways to count. Counting plays such a basic and stabilizing role in our lives that it is inconceivable to us that our way of counting may be just one among many. Consider this long quotation from Wittgenstein:

> We should presumably not call it "counting" if everyone said the numbers one after the other *anyhow;* but of course it is not simply a question of a name. For what we call "counting" is an important part of our life's activities. Counting and calculating are not— e.g.—simply a pastime. Counting (and that means: counting like this) is a technique that is employed daily in the most various operations of our lives. And that is why we learn to count as we do: with endless practice, with merciless exactitude; that is why it is inexorably insisted that we shall all say "two" after "one," "three" after "two" and so on.—"But is this counting only a *use,* then; isn't there also some truth corresponding to this sequence?" The *truth* is that counting has proved to pay.—"Then do you want to say that 'being true' means: being usable (or useful)?"—No, not that; but that it can't be said of the series of natural numbers—any more than of our language—that it is true, but: that it is usable, and, above all, *it is used.* (RFM I: 4)

There are several important points raised here. First, Wittgenstein denies that truth is the appropriate category for numbers. There is nothing to which our numbers truthfully correspond. There is no Platonic realm of numbers. The conflicts that would arise between our ways of counting and the random method are not conflicts about truth. Rather, they are conflicts of practical purposes. What interests me here is the notion of counting as a technique "employed daily in the most various operations of our lives." Counting becomes second nature to us—so deeply ingrained—that it recedes into the background, though it is an activity in which we engage in myriad ways. Repetition and endless practice aim to engender a skill that one can exercise without conscious thought and without hesitation or error. We learn the order of numbers as we use them. Training is complete, in a sense, when the student is no longer able to countenance the possibility that there may be other forms of counting. That is why we mean counting like *this* when we talk about counting. In saying that counting is part of our life's activities, we cannot imagine alternate ways of counting because the life activities in which these alternatives exist would be so vastly different from ours that they would not be intelligible to us. But note here that we are not precluded in principle from alternate modes of counting, but precluded in practice and practical purposes.

As another example of deep agreement and contingency, consider our practices of measuring, which really are a family of activities for a family of practical purposes. Large parts of the world use metric measurement while others use inches and feet. While the results produced are different in a sense (I measured 2.54 centimeters while you measured 1 inch), in another sense they are the same measurement. The length measured is equal, though we express this in different terms. The technique used by both is the same. But note well that the correctness of the measurement is not a matter of human agreement in the sense of reaching a consensus. All of us agreeing that thirteen inches is the equivalent of one foot will not make it the case that a foot is thirteen inches. Measurements are possible only where there is agreement that is broader, deeper, and antecedent to any agreement by consensus. With respect to measuring, the accord involves the actions and techniques of measurement as well as the instruments we use. We use rigid rulers to measure length; we do not use elastic ones. There is consensus about how to take measurements. When measuring the entire length of something, we start from one terminus and end at the other. We also must agree that there are termini. We usually lay the ruler or measuring tape alongside the object to be measured. We pull the tape taut as well. If in measuring length I start or end at arbitrary points, I will not produce a useable result. The agreement that produces sameness in measuring results is so far in the background that it escapes notice and does not seem to play a role. That agreement is much a matter of the techniques becoming second nature to us. It is also a matter of our sharing affective attitudes toward our action. The agreement that undergirds our measuring and counting has so receded into the background or is so taken for granted that it really is not a matter of our conscious choice any more. It's really not voluntary.

In the course of our initiation into our forms of life in both senses as I developed in the previous chapter, we acquire totalities of judgments, systems of verification, and hosts of beliefs. This is another way of saying that we develop a second nature. We have a second nature about all these sorts of practical activities and also about moral ones. All these activities involve shaping our abilities and sensibilities so that we can *do* things. Second nature also means that we have developed the ability to see and act from the lived mustness. According to Wittgenstein, when we first come to believe anything, what we believe is a whole system of propositions and not just single propositions (*OC* § 141). And these systems or totalities of judgments are acquired by means of observation and instruction. Wittgenstein intentionally does not say that one "learns" these systems (*OC* § 279). But while one does not "learn" whole systems, one does learn to do particular things. For example, we learn to make judgments and recognize that *this is* judging while *that is* describing (*OC* § 129). But even our practice of making empirical judgments, for example, relies on our having been taught judgments and their connection with other judgments. A totality of judgments is made plausible to us (*OC* § 140).

To become a competent participant in a language-game, one must be trained in following the rules of the game. An important element in this training is the use of what Sabina Lovibond names coercion but what at this point I would call rational suasion.[20] This rational suasion is exercised both by individuals and the public community as a whole. One way to understand the function of coercion in language training is to consider what Quine calls the "pull toward objectivity."[21] This pull is a socializing process whereby children or immature members of a linguistic community are brought to see things in the same way as other members of the community. Every individual is subjected to this pull by those who already

---

20. Lovibond, *Realism and Imagination in Ethics.* "Coercion" is a morally laden word and so I do not want to make use of it in cases where the actions of people do not have any direct or obvious moral implications. I want to reserve coercion and its moral implications for when there are elements of moral blameworthiness involved.

21. It is Lovibond who introduces this comparison between language training and the pull toward objectivity, discussed by W. V. O. Quine, *Word and Object* (Cambridge, Mass.: The MIT Press, 1960).

speak a language. In order to competently use certain words, such as "square" or "red," there needs to be a conformity in our responses such that we all say "square" in the presence of the same surfaces. And further, our response will still be "square" even though the shape may vary given our particular position relative to the surface. The competent speaker is one who can, independently of the prodding or supervising of another, appropriately respond to the stimulations.

In order for there to exist such a "pull toward objectivity" there must be certain relations or forces that would exert such a pull. To be in a position to exert a pull over others, one must be in a position of authority. It is only possible to talk about following a rule where there exists a seat of authority from which we can find out if *this* counts as following the rule.

Wittgenstein asks, "So is this it: I must recognize certain authorities in order to make judgments at all?" (*OC* § 493). If we maintain that a discourse can be objective, then when we make judgments within that particular discourse, we are aiming to say something that is correct. In our pursuit of correctness we recognize that certain people possess sound judgment with respect to the relevant subject matter.[22] Those people who have been so positioned and recognized as possessing sound judgment have been accorded a certain intellectual authority. Certain persons, in virtue of their position as parents and teachers are accorded intellectual authority. Structured institutions such as universities are also taken as possessing intellectual authority. The child learns by believing the adult, and further, Wittgenstein says, "I learned an enormous amount and accepted it on human authority, and then I found some things confirmed or disconfirmed by my own experience" (*OC* § 161). Understanding what counts as confirmation and knowing how to go about it in particular instances depends on my already having accepted and participated in a wide range of practices with their constitutive grammars, beliefs, and judgments.

The "pull toward objectivity" has a material basis. The goal of training is to instill and maintain both the normativity and uniformity of practices. This involves the use of material means. We influence others through praise and encouragement as well as by criticism. Depending on how well a child is able to count, for example, either I let him go on his way or I hold him back (*PI* § 208). Material expression can be given to our judgments, and the expressions can range from material suasion in the sense of giving praise and rewards for things done correctly, to more coercive

---

22. Lovibond, *Realism and Imagination in Ethics*, 64.

means where a person may be reprimanded or punished for saying or doing some thing. Many laws, from the laws of inference to the norms of human behavior, are social laws that are enforced by human agency. Flouting laws results in the imposition of material and intellectual penalties. Sanctions are brought to bear on those who seek to act, think, or talk in ways that are deviant.[23] One runs into conflict and consequences when one deviates from common practice (*RFM* I § 116).

Those people and institutions that have intellectual authority will exercise "the pull toward objectivity." This "pull" works in such a way that when we first began to believe anything, what we believe is not a single proposition but a whole host of propositions. This socializing process or "pull" eliminates individuals' peculiarities of judgments. The end results are people who subscribe to a totality of judgments by taking on a second nature.

These worldviews or systems acquired by us and others allow our correct following of a rule to be acknowledged. And further, according to Wittgenstein, "I did not get my picture of the world by satisfying myself of its correctness; nor do I have it because I am satisfied of its correctness. No: it is the inherited background against which I distinguish between true and false" (*OC* § 94). Questions of correctness, truth or falsity, or justification can only meaningfully be asked by someone within a system. The system is the felted world with all its grammatical complexities and relationships. It provides the ground and makes possible the very conditions for asking and answering such questions.

With respect to learning to count and to take measurements, the rules have authority in virtue of their being applied in the same way. Their authority is in their application and their use, rather than in some intrinsic or inherent property. Lived mustness means that rules, norms, and normative authority are all created and maintained by our actions, uses, and practices within this shared world. Authority always requires a context; its exercise is always in a context. Authority is not a property of an object or a rule or a convention, but rather a participatory and shared dynamic. Because of our living in the world we do, normative authority is an ongoing activity.

Normative authority compels immature or new members of a community to act the same and do so with a certain shared attitude, through learning from and acting with other members of the community, as Wittgenstein's examples of counting and measuring illustrate.[24] In learning

23. Ibid., 64.

24. Foucault's work on power is useful in understanding how individuals are brought into membership in communities, as I note here and discuss in *Oppression and Responsibility*. Developing a more robust account of power is beyond the scope of this present work. For

proofs in algebra or geometry, a student becomes convinced of something; he realizes that it must be like that. As Wittgenstein says,

> The "must" shews that he has gone in a circle.
> "It must be so" means that this outcome has been defined as essential to the process.
> This *must* shews that he has adopted a concept. (*RFM* VI: 7–8)

In understanding the equation "2 + 2" the student really does not have a choice about reaching the answer "four," given that he wants to make sense and be intelligible to others, especially his teachers. Nothing that contravenes this conclusion will count as an intelligible or correct usage; "2 + 3 = 4" is nonsensical.

With the adoption of concepts comes the ability to self-regulate one's behavior. As Jose Medina so aptly puts the matter, "through training processes, our behavior becomes, not causally determinate, but normatively structured."[25] The normative authority initially exercised by the teacher over the student slowly becomes shared. As the student progresses and is able to "go on in the same way" when confronted with a series of numbers, for example; the student regulates his own behavior and begins to exert normatively authority over and with others.

The discussion of training and initiation shows how we come to see these musts as a matter of course; it also shows that we act out of understanding of them. The aim of training is not simply mechanical behavioral regularities but also normatively structured behavior. Part of education and training is to inculcate shared normative attitudes and the ability to recognize and act on reasons. There is nothing particularly mysterious about this. There is no magical moment when something is turned into a reason. As McDowell notes, "The demands of reason are essentially such that a human upbringing can open a human's eyes to them."[26] Recognition and motivation are fundamentally connected. The motivating force of these oughts and shoulds resides in the actions themselves; they do not somehow mysteriously reside in the rules understood in a realist or antirealist way. The rules provide reasons, and it is the nature of the reasons to be motivating. This, Wittgenstein might have said, is a grammatical point.

---

an excellent treatment of the issue of power, see Wendy Lynne Lee, "The Sound of Little Hummingbird Wings: A Wittgensteinian Investigation of Forms of Life as Forms of Power," *Feminist Studies* 25, no. 2 (1999): 409–26.

25. Medina, *The Unity of Wittgenstein's Philosophy*, 159.
26. McDowell, *Mind and World*, 92.

The reasons are not causes in the sense, however, that Harman talks about a physical event causing an observation. This is an important point, and it is one I develop in the following chapter.

Training and education are the keys in understanding how normative force gets a grip on us. We are no longer able to even conceive of alternatives. We take on certain ways of doing things as second nature such that we can no longer countenance alternatives. Each of us exercises this authority and exerts various pulls. This grounds normativity of rules in a very real way. We don't project it onto the world, nor does the world force it on us.

I would like to return to the three considerations raised at the beginning of this section about there being courses of actions that must be, and that we can recognize and act from them. Grammar has its life and its arbitrary and nonarbitrary dimensions in the stability it creates in the felted world. Grammar is autonomous in the sense of being neither reducible to nor determined by the natural world understood in a realist way that requires total and absolute separation from language and human agency. Grammar is immanent; it structures and infuses all practices and their various constitutive elements. Like the Maison à Bordeaux, the stability is a matter of relationships between the various elements of the felted world, including us humans. The mistake, I claim, is to attempt to sunder these elements, and locate the musts and the shoulds—the normativity—in one particular element or set of elements. Instead, my claim is that the musts and shoulds cannot be sundered from this complicated interaction. Grammatical rules are conventional in this sense but not in the sense of being the result of conscious and voluntary decision and choice. In its constitutive role, grammar creates the relationship between concepts such as we see in identity and in analytic truths, for example. "H_2O is water" expresses a grammatical rule, not a deep metaphysical truth that is disconnected from human life and living.

The next chapter continues this discussion of grammar in a number of ways, especially as it relates to understanding, rule following, and the offering of reasons and justifications. In order to follow a rule correctly or to use a concept correctly, one must not only act in accordance or act in a uniform manner, but rather one must act also for the sake of the rule or act with understanding. This understanding will itself rest and rely on myriad elements.

How can I understand a proposition now, if it is for analysis to shew what I really
understand?—Here there sneaks in the idea of understanding as a special mental process.
—WITTGENSTEIN, *ZETTEL*, § 445

We are trying to get hold of the mental process of understanding which seems to be
hidden behind those coarser and therefore more readily visible accompaniments. But we do
not succeed; or, rather, it does not get as far as a real attempt. For even supposing
I had found something that happened in all those cases of understanding,—
why should it be the understanding? And how can the process of understanding have been
hidden, when I said "Now I understand" because I understood?! And if I say it is hidden—then
how do I know what I have to look for? I am in a muddle.
—WITTGENSTEIN, *PHILOSOPHICAL INVESTIGATIONS*, § 153

As I have been arguing throughout this book, at least one set of debates in
metaethics has been overly concerned with the metaphysical and epistemological status of moral *properties*. As I have attempted to show throughout, this focus is overly narrow, and it brackets as unimportant or as
philosophically uninteresting all that I argue makes morality what it is. It
certainly casts aside everything that makes moral inquiry understood in a
fairly narrow sense: as the acting on moral reasons or in recognition of
moral features as possible. So, too, does this narrow focus cast aside much
of what makes it possible to justify moral claims to knowledge. Consider
Wittgenstein's warning about mice and rags:

> If I am inclined to suppose that a mouse has come into being by
> spontaneous generation out of grey rags and dust, I shall do well
> to examine those rags carefully to see how a mouse may have
> hidden in them, how it may have got there and so on. But if I am
> convinced that a mouse cannot come into being from these
> things, then this investigation will perhaps be superfluous.

> But first we learn to understand what it is that opposes such
> an examination of details in philosophy. (*PI* § 52)

As Cora Diamond so succinctly explains, Wittgenstein's point is "to show
that philosophers miss the details, the rags, that a philosophical mouse
comes out of, because something has led them to think that no mouse *can*
come out of *that.*"[1] Our lack of attention to these rags and details prompts
us to undertake quixotic philosophical tasks, to chase philosophical mice.
We never will be satisfied with a solution to the problems we generate,
especially when that "solution" is anything less than suavely sophisticated
and exceedingly abstract. But for Wittgenstein and for me, philosophy in
general and metaethics in particular ought to start with the rags and end
with the rags. It is far from glamorous, but it is the best way to avoid
philosophical fantasies.

The particular philosophical mouse with which I am concerned in this
chapter is moral knowledge. Given the dominance of certain forms of philosophical naturalism predicated on the nature/normativity dualism, moral
knowledge seems to have the character of knowledge manqué. The wan-
nabe status of moral knowledge is a consequence of the increasing imbalance between rationality and reasonableness. Stephen Toulmin chronicles
this development in *Return to Reason*. He says,

> For the last four hundred years, the ideas of "reasonableness" and
> "rationality"—closely related in Antiquity—were separated, as an
> outcome of the emphasis that seventeenth-century natural philos-
> ophers placed on formal deductive techniques. . . . Mathematical
> techniques have had such prestige in our discipline-oriented uni-
> versities that they continued to entrench themselves well into the
> twentieth century. They were especially influential in the aca-
> demic world of the United States, where the need for rational cal-
> culations to be complemented by reasonable judgments about
> their relevance to particular real-life human situations faded, for
> the time being, into the background.[2]

---

1. Diamond, *The Realistic Spirit*, 47.
2. Stephen Toulmin, *Return to Reason* (Cambridge, Mass.: Harvard University Press,
2001), 204.

The enthronement of rationality, Toulmin shows, was a consequence of a desire to discover or create new certainty as theological and religious authority eroded. Over time, the "rationalist agenda" became institutionalized, so familiar perhaps that it now escapes notice. Toulmin traces the effects of the demands for the rationality of formal theories and calculations along with the expectations for value neutrality on development of disciplines such as economics, sociology, and psychology. As a student of Wittgenstein, the need to focus critically on the practice of philosophy is obvious to Toulmin. He sees in Wittgenstein a remedy to the problem of rationalization and its costs to practical tasks. He says, "If Rene Descartes is a symbolic figure marking the beginning of the Modern Age, we may take Ludwig Wittgenstein as marking its end."[3] The fullest expression of Wittgenstein's blend of intellectual and manual skills, for Toulmin, is seen in the home he designed for his sister Margaret Stonborough. Like Toulmin, I see huge potential in Wittgenstein for redressing this imbalance and restoring reason to a more prominent place in our thinking and living, particularly with respect to the moral dimensions of our lives.

As I discussed in the second chapter, the debates between Gilbert Harman and Nicholas Sturgeon are shaped by shared assumptions about causation, observation, confirmation, and explanation. Their shared expectation is that moral properties—if they are real—must cause our moral observations and confirm our moral theory; that theory in turn explains the observation in question. The expectation is that this must be a gap-free circle. Explanation is understood in terms of demonstrating causation; we understand something when we can trace how something came about. The satisfaction of these demands produces knowledge that is both empirical and propositional. It is a kind of theoretical knowledge that leaves behind any of its practical dimensions.

Along with this picture comes another about practical reason. Here, practical reason is seen as a capacity that humans possess. This faculty, when supplied with good data and when in proper running order, produces good reasons for actions. The exercise of reason produces a mental entity—a reason—that acts as an efficient cause of action. Action is the outer effect of the inner cause.[4]

---

3. Ibid., 206.
4. This expectation helps make sense of the influence that cognitive science has come to have in moral psychology.

These two pictures—one that focuses on the causes of observations and subsequent explanation of moral properties and the other on reasons as the cause and explanation for behavior—are deeply problematic. There is a tendency to assimilate reasons to causes, and this is certainly the case in the picture just described. I do not, however, want to reinscribe the world/ language divide by adhering to a sharp distinction between reasons and causes. Reasons and causes, however, have very different aims and play very different roles in our lives, as I intend to make clear.

Starting points always matter. Any moral theory that does not begin with recognition that moral agents are embodied human beings in a multitude of relations has already traveled halfway down a wrong path. Add to this a conception of normative reasons as generated by these abstract individuals and you have arrived at the land of false universalizations of a very oppressive sort. One must also begin with a recognition of the diversity within human lives, and see it not as a problem to be overcome, but as a given.

My rejection of both moral realism and antirealism and my advancement of felted contextualism require a shift in our understanding of what has traditionally come under the umbrella of moral epistemology. The different metaphysics of morals I present requires a different approach to moral reason and moral knowledge. Focusing on certainty, stability, and the practices and language-games that both constitute and grow out of this certainty lands squarely in the realm of practical reason, that little realm that seems like the Model T in this age of the Turbo suv of theoretical rationality. Like many feminists, I am suspicious of this elevation of rationality over reason, and elsewhere I reject the view that practical reason is best understood as a facility or set of capacities possessed by individuals.[5] Instead, I argue that practical reason is irreducibly social; it is possible only within language, which is itself necessarily public and shared. Practical reason or practical wisdom is part of our second nature that we develop by playing multiple language-games that comprise our complicated form of life. In addition, I argue that the emphasis in moral epistemology on causation and explanation reflects an empiricist bias and is misplaced with respect to moral understanding. My aim, instead, is to highlight the roles of reasons and justifications in our moral understandings. They are what

5. See Peg O'Connor, "The Stability of Rationality," in *Oppression and Responsibility*. There is a long history of essentialist approaches to rationality and reasons that have justified the oppression of various peoples.

make our actions intelligible to others, and they show the significance of our actions.

Knowing how to follow rules, providing justifications, and correctly using concepts are activities that just do not fit into traditional epistemology. These, along with a host of basic abilities and competencies, are the philosophical rags. And how could knowledge come from *that*? While one might object that Kant is deeply concerned with knowing how to follow the Categorical Imperative, for example, I respond that the conditions under which Kant imagines us to engage in moral inquiry are quite different from our actual conditions. Furthermore, it is not clear exactly how one learns how to apply the Categorical Imperative. Our Reason may be innate, but the ability to apply the Imperative is not. It requires an enormous stage setting and a host of rudimentary skills in order to undertake the task that Kant sets for us. This stage setting, along with how we come to be able to follow rules, is often neglected in metaethics.

Conceiving reasons and justifications in relation to practices effects a significant change in our expectations for moral knowledge or understandings. For Wittgenstein, it is a category mistake to say that we can know Moore's common-sense propositions. Instead, we should say that those propositions are certain and stand fast for us. They function grammatically, constituting language-games and regulating the moves within them. Additionally, other features of the world and our ways of living stand fast for us and provide stability. This distinction between certainty and knowledge prompts me to jettison the expression "moral epistemology" in terms of "moral understandings."

Knowledge of the propositional sort is but a small subset of what I will include in the category of moral understandings. Understanding is not a mental state but rather a matter of acting. Learning practical judgments and then learning how to make them, applying moral concepts, following rules, offering justifications for actions, making assessments, and assigning responsibility are some of the activities that must be included in this more robust account. And finally, this Wittgensteinian approach addresses concerns that feminists have about the relationship between metaethics and normative ethics (in its most extreme form, the worry is that there really is not one that matters). By changing the subject matter and dealing with the philosophical rags, we can create a feminist metaethics that has indissoluble links to normative ethics. This is particularly evident with respect to limitations in recognition and acknowledgment.

AYER'S LEGACY, QUEER PROPERTIES, AND PRACTICAL EXPERTISE

A. J. Ayer set the course of much of twentieth-century moral epistemology, claiming that "sentences which simply express moral judgments do not say anything. They are pure expressions of feeling and as such do not come under the category of truth and falsehood. They are unverifiable for the same reason as a cry of pain or a word of a command is unverifiable—because they do not express genuine propositions."[6] Genuine propositions, in Ayer's view, are empirical propositions. Any other kind, even if it has the clothing of an empirical proposition, is not genuine. Moral propositions are not "about" anything real in the world that has the capacity to make beliefs true or verifiable or justified.

Ayer's view is that moral knowledge is a category mistake; it is not a possibility. The emphasis on propositions, verification, and truth consistently appears in treatments of moral knowledge, and this of course starts from and leads back to questions about the metaphysics and foundations of morals. But note what Ayer takes for granted: that moral knowledge is propositional. Why should we accept this as our starting point in moral epistemology? This starting point makes sense when we are operating with certain metaphysical assumptions. My work up to this point has been to reject these metaphysical assumptions and to change the subject of metaethics. I have been arguing for an alternative conception of the grounding of our moral living. We do not need foundations as they typically have been conceived (independently existing sui generis properties or moral properties as natural kinds nor abstract universal principles) but rather something far more mundane and prosaic. We need stability, and this stability has a heterogeneous nature (unlike foundations). Practices make up an enormous amount of this stability, as do certainty and framework conditions of the sort Wittgenstein discusses in *On Certainty*.

Reading *On Certainty* as a sustained response to and improvement of Moore's attempt to refute the skeptic about knowledge reveals one of Wittgenstein's distinctive strategies. In this case, his strategy is to deny precisely that which provides skepticism with some purchase, making it seem initially plausible. Julia Annas, in an essay focused on Mackie's use of the Forms in his argument about the epistemological problems that moral facts present, adopts a strategy that resonates with my Wittgensteinian account.[7] Annas, like Wittgenstein, targets the assumptions that make

---

6. A. J. Ayer, *Language, Truth, and Logic* (New York: Dover, 1952), 108–9.
7. Annas, "Moral Knowledge as Practical Knowledge," 236–56.

skepticism about moral knowledge seem initially plausible. We can rightly be skeptical of some particular claims to moral knowledge, but this does not license us to be skeptical about the possibility of any moral knowledge.[8] The biggest assumption is that normativity is different in kind from nature. Normativity is tied to the purported causal powers of these queer properties.[9] Accessibility to values is different in kind from our access to empirical matters. But all these claims, Annas argues, are made by fiat more than anything else. As I discussed in Chapters 3 and 4, there are compelling grounds to reject the nature/normativity dualism and instead conceive the world as felted.

Annas rejects Mackie's depiction of the Forms, claiming that Mackie's notion of intuition is a product of empiricist assumptions. Plato's model for knowledge, Annas argues, is practical expertise. Practical expertise is a matter of understanding; it is the ways in which we use our minds to think about and beyond experiences. Understanding is a web of abilities and competencies that, among other things, enables us to see similarities and resemblances between experiences. Understanding is a matter of thinking through our beliefs and aiming at unifying them.[10] Practical expertise can be taught, and so our attention is rightly focused on education, as I discussed in the previous chapter. And furthermore, understanding as practical expertise requires that people be able to provide an account of what they are doing, which is another way to say that understanding involves justifications. Annas argues that coming to understand a form is really a matter of coming to have and exercise practical knowledge. Understanding a form is not a theoretical matter but a practical one. Practical knowledge is the appropriate model for moral knowledge, and only with a deflationary account does it become easier to see how normativity is not queer in the ways that Mackie suggests. Is there anything metaphysically suspect in a car mechanic saying to her assistant that she ought to proceed in such a manner in order to make the repair correctly?[11]

Reconceiving moral knowledge in these deflated practical terms highlights the importance of Wittgenstein's conception of understanding and its relationship to training, mastery of a technique, and ability (PI §150).

8. Ibid., 253.
9. Ibid., 238.
10. Cf. ibid.
11. Annas makes the claim that Mackie's concerns about the motivating power of allegedly objective properties produces an argument that calls all practical knowledge into question. Surely this is not an outcome that Mackie would embrace.

Moral understandings are not theoretical, nor are they simply propositional. They are deeply social and practical, necessarily public and shared.[12] Only embodied and engaged persons make and show moral understandings in what we say and do. Wittgenstein's treatment of knowledge in *On Certainty* turns our attention back to the often-neglected importance of knowing how. In fact, one could argue that knowing how underpins knowing that, thus underscoring the importance of practical reason. A moral-understandings approach resists the tendency to make morality primarily a matter of knowledge, where knowledge is understood in an empiricist/ verificationist way. Moral understandings involve both knowledge and certainty, proposition and practicality, in a very fundamental way. These are all matters of acknowledgment and recognition.

UNDERSTANDING: NOT A MENTAL STATE

Understandings is the broader category I prefer to use. Knowledge and certainty constitute understandings and belong within the felted world in different though related ways. Certainty belongs to the givenness and the lived mustness while knowledge belongs within particular language and practices. Certainty and knowledge are inseparable; knowledge is possible only where there is certainty.

As Wittgenstein uses the term, knowledge is best understood in terms of moves made within a language-game, and whether these moves are correct or are in accordance with the rules of the game. While I can make knowledge claims from within a game (this is the only place from which any claims to knowledge can be made), I cannot make knowledge claims about the system itself. I may well be able to isolate certain parts of the system for criticism, but at no point can I call the entire system into question. Any attempt to do so gives away the very grounds such criticism requires.

Wittgenstein cautions us against claiming that we know grammatical principles, including the laws of logical and mathematical necessity. This is a great philosophical temptation that we must avoid. We can be certain of them, but we do not know them. Grammatical principles provide an

---

12. I am not denying that empirical knowledge plays important roles in our moral understandings. That would be ridiculous. Empirical knowledge is integral in our assessments of situations, recognition of various features of situations, and choosing a particular course of action over others. But I am denying that it is the primary component or the defining feature (or both) of moral understandings.

important condition for making any claim to knowledge, without themselves being known.

As I argued in Chapter 4, language-games (and their constitutive grammar) are fused right into the fabric of the world. As opposed to saying that we can know grammatical principles (which would require that they themselves be justified), Wittgenstein says that we are better served to say that they stand fast for us. We are certain of them, but we do not know them. But here it is important to recall that Wittgenstein says to use a concept without justification is not to use it without right. Plenty of the concepts that we regularly use every day, with no hesitation or in anticipation of justification, are those that have receded into a background, now playing a grammatical or normative role. Their function changes.

With respect to a grammatical statement such as "You should not commit murder," most of us would say, "I know that." But this way of speaking lends itself to confusion once you start scratching its surface. In response to the question that can always be asked, "How do you know it?" you might cite all sorts of authorities, be they religious, parental, or legal. But this knowledge is thin, in a certain sense. It does not really seem akin to the common-sense ways that we speak of knowing something. I know the formula that $E = mc^2$ on one level, but on another level of understanding, I cannot do much right with it. I know it in a way that has little practical implication and application. There is so much that comes before and must already be in place in order to legitimately claim knowledge of this law of physics.

Like counting, measuring, and judging the same, morality is employed within the various operations of our lives to serve practical purposes. As we learn to follow rules and apply moral concepts correctly, we see that lived mustness; we see that we must reach certain conclusions or act in certain ways. When we come to see this, grammatical principles become motivating. These principles do not *cause* me to act, but I see that I must act in this way to achieve practical purposes and to remain intelligible to others. Thus, meaning, use, rule following, understanding, and normativity are inextricably linked.

To follow a rule correctly or to use a concept correctly, one must do so for a reason. To put it in a slightly different manner, correct rule following involves not simply acting in accordance with a rule, but also acting for the sake of the rule. This is not to deny that a rule may be cited as part of a reason for acting, but Wittgenstein notes that correct rule following requires more than regularity and uniformity. As discussed in the previous chapter, mere regularity is not normative. Normativity is created and exercised in the context of a dynamic that has its origin in the context of an instructional relationship. Wittgenstein says:

> If one of a pair of chimpanzees once scratched the figure | -- | in the earth and thereupon the other the series | -- | | -- | etc., the first would not have given a rule nor would the other be following it, whatever else went on at the same time in the mind of the two of them.
>
> If however there were observed, e.g., the phenomenon of a kind of instruction, of shewing how and of imitation, of lucky and misfiring attempts, of reward and punishment and the like; if at length the one who had been so trained put figures which he had never seen before one after another in sequence as in the first example, then we should probably say that the one chimpanzee was writing rules down, and the other was following them. (*RFM* VI:42)

Absent this training, there is no normativity and no rule following.

Agreement plays a fundamental role in all rule following. But what does agreement look like in these cases? This mistake, Wittgenstein would say, is to assume that one first learns the concept of agreement and then learns to obey a rule. Rather, Wittgenstein asserts, one learns "the meaning of agreement by learning how to follow rules" (*RFM* VII:39). It is not the case that the concepts of sameness and agreement strike us as intuitively obvious, but rather they are concepts we learn to use correctly through a variety of techniques. A child may learn the concept of sameness, for example, by learning to play the card game Go Fish. The concept of sameness is one of the most basic and useful concepts in our repertoire.

Judging cases alike, recognizing certain differences as salient, making generalizations, recognizing certain facts or considerations as relevant, ranking competing demands, adjudicating conflict, and assigning responsibilities are all actions that we employ in every domain of inquiry. Each of these skills has a prosaic and perhaps even unimpressive beginning in learning to follow rules. As these skills become more nuanced, they are what makes our form of life complicated and enable us to navigate these complexities.[13]

---

13. Many of these skills are discussed in Anthony Weston's *A 21st Century Ethical Toolbox*

Agreement recedes so far into the background that it is no longer part of the justification but now functions as a condition for justification. Agreement of this sort plays a very different role from the agreement that may be made or given in response to a question. We regularly do not appeal to the agreement of humans to affirm identity (*RFM* VI: 406). Of course there may be cases where one challenges a particular identity claim or the ascription of a color predicate or a psychological predicate. In cases such as these, particular reasons can play a justificatory role and have traction against this broader background of agreement. This agreement is part of the certainty I identified in Chapter 4. It is one of the stabilizing forces in what Wittgenstein calls this complicated form of life. It is only against this background that we can speak of normativity and rule following.

The concepts of normativity, training, knowledge, and understanding are inextricably linked in my account. As I discussed in the previous chapter, normativity is dynamic and relational. In explaining the instruction "add two," the teacher is not attempting to create a causal link between a student's mental state and the external world, but rather to inculcate a shared normative stance in addition to creating uniformity and regularity. Wittgenstein offers numerous arguments against the view that understanding is a matter of having the right or correct interpretation in my mind's eye. Moreover, we should not assume that the right formula or interpretation causes us to act. Understanding and claims to knowledge are matters of ability in acting and in providing "compelling grounds" (*OC* § 243). These compelling grounds are neither something I encounter in the contents of my own mind nor are they solely decided by me. Justifications can take many different forms, and someone must already know what the acceptable forms are.

Grammar is that which provides the structure or shape to a language-game or practice, and so it will set the parameters of justification. These parameters are a product of the complex interplay of grammar's dual nature and all the elements of our world that provide stability. Oftentimes in justifying a particular action, we appeal to a concept or a broader rule. But justifications ring hollow when they are unaccompanied by an understanding of what a rule requires or what is a correct use of a concept. Such an attempted justification lacks traction in knowledge and understanding. How do we come to possess these?

(Oxford: Oxford University Press, 2001). This text is notable in that it foregrounds these fundamentally important skills and tools that may help us think more creatively and productively in relation to the most deeply entrenched moral disagreements.

As I stated above, knowledge is a kind of understanding. More specifically, knowledge is a set of sustained abilities in which and through which
someone shows understanding. When someone understands something,
be it a mathematical axiom, a law of inference, a scientific formula, or a
moral principle, then one can *do* something with it in a correct way. That
is to say, one can show that she understands by how she acts. There is
an ineliminable practicality to knowledge in all these different domains.
Knowledge—even the most abstract and theoretical—can never totally
shake its practical roots. How do I understand counting? Well, I can list
all the numbers and I can, in response to the request to "bring five red
apples," show my understanding by bringing the correct number of the
correct items. Knowing how to count is a sustained ability, which entails
that in any situation, I mostly do the right thing. Of course there are times
when I make mistakes, such as losing my place or repeating a number,
but this happening occasionally does not weigh against my knowing how
to count. If it happens often enough, then that may well weigh against my
carefulness and responsibility, but no one would challenge my ability to
count. But always making mistakes or making the same mistake repeatedly will be taken as evidence of my being unable to count.

As an example of how we come to apply concepts, consider our use of
psychological predicates. Children often learn to use psychological predicates in the context of playing with toys such as dolls and stuffed animals.
Most children feel no hesitation in ascribing emotions or mental states to
their toys. In many ways, children treat their toys as their friends. They
acknowledge and recognize their toys not unlike how they recognize other
children. The repertoire of children's abilities to recognize others expands.
While this is a mundane example, this basic sort of recognition is crucial
for much more complicated activities, including offering justifications. We
only justify our actions to those whom we recognize. I turn to this next.

ACKNOWLEDGMENT AND RECOGNITION

As I discussed in Chapter 4, one of Wittgenstein's concerns is to draw our
attention to what is distinctive about us and the language we use, as opposed to other sentient beings. Wittgenstein's intent, as I have argued, is
to highlight some of the features of the contexts in which we use language,
and the context is what I have called the felted world or the stable world.
Our world is a world of limits, and limitations are endemic to our ways of
living. This Wittgensteinian account that I have been building argues for

an alternative way to conceive the elements that provide the requisite stability for our playing moral language-games. Human beings—not Cartesian egos, not a body, and not some odd or mysterious combination of the two—are part of this felted world. This is an important starting point and recognition that often is neglected.

Returning to a discussion in Chapter 4 concerning forms of life, Wittgenstein reminds us of the importance of awareness and recognition of and responsiveness to others, all of which he might have called characteristic bits of natural history. I think it is reasonable to include these in the category of primitive reactions. Robert Hannaford considers this awareness, combined with our concerns, capacities, and attitudes as part of our moral anatomy.[14] Using language in certain ways is characteristic of humans, enabling us to create and engage in all practices, including moral ones. This natural history provides the certainty and stability necessary for some of the most basic actions of living as well as for the more complicated activities. This I take to be Wittgenstein's point when he says, "Instinct comes first, reasoning second. Not until there is a language-game are there reasons" (*RPP* II § 689).

On this view, no radical break separates what we are from what we do. The fact that we are embodied is crucial to understanding the nature of morality. Morality is created and maintained through humans' interactions with one another, other beings, and the physical and social environments. Morality can be understood as a complicated, not fully circumscribable set of human social practices made possible with language.[15] Moral agents are beings who can do certain things, such as recognize the suffering of others, take and assign moral responsibility, offer justifications for their beliefs and actions, recognize expectations and demands that others might have on us, and engage in moral disagreements. We can apply moral concepts and evaluations in order to figure out what we should do. We can abstract and universalize the right as much as we can quantify and qualify the good. We can do all of these things, but we must recognize that these rest on our being able to do some other very basic and mundane things. Collectively, these make up our moral understandings. Moral inquiry is much broader than recent metaethics concedes and is concerned with much more than the adjudication of conflict. All these activities are forms

14. Robert V. Hannaford, *Moral Anatomy and Moral Reasoning* (Lawrence: University Press of Kansas, 1993).

15. On this understanding of the origins and grounding of morality, the demand for "independence existence" of moral properties or features from humans is nonsensical.

of moral inquiry that take embodied humanity for granted and all are kinds of awareness of and responsiveness to others.

Wittgenstein says that "the human body is the best picture of the human soul" (*PI*, 178). In saying this, Wittgenstein has more than one target in his sights, which is typical of his approach in philosophy. When confronted with an apparent dualism, he challenges the oherence of each side. His position is neither immaterialist nor materialist as traditionally understood. On the immaterialist/soul side, his criticism is directed at a Cartesian view that self/subject is an immaterial thinking substance distinct from material body. Such a view of personhood is profoundly alienating. We are not in the world as immaterial objects. Rather, we are material beings who do certain things. In this way, all the talk of mental processes and psychological states are bankrupt if we cannot in some sense *see* those entities. When we neglect or banish the body from our psychological talk or from our talk about what it means to be a person, we have given up the grounds of sense and intelligibility.

Alessandra Tanesini offers an illuminating reading of Wittgenstein concept of the human soul offered primarily in *Philosophical Investigations,* and points to some of the ways this has great potential for feminist development. The soul, for Wittgenstein, is not a religious concept. Nor is the soul a property of a human body or an entity that is somehow contained within a body. Rather, as Tanesini claims, "To be a human being, to have a human soul, is to have the life of a human being. . . . Wittgenstein also points out that, in order to treat others as human beings, we do not need first to ascertain whether they have a soul. Quite the contrary, it is impossible to acquire a human soul unless one is first treated as having one."[16] This approach cedes no ground in which skepticism could take hold. Skepticism is almost impossible to maintain in the face of others; quite literally in the faces of others, Wittgenstein might say. We see emotions in others; we see on their faces what they are feeling. This is not an epistemological problem about my knowing what you are feeling, but rather a condition of our living in which people recognize and acknowledge others.

Being human is a matter of being treated as such. As material, embodied creatures, interdependence with other humans, acknowledgment, and recognition are the preconditions for autonomy and independence. These are the conditions in which we live and engage with others as moral, political, and epistemological agents. They are centrally important but often neglected.

16. Tanesini, *Wittgenstein,* 91.

Through our interactions with others, we come to develop what can be called a physiognomic literacy. That is, we learn how to read each other's bodily expressions.[17] We come to understand that certain expressions convey grief, while others amusement. We even come to recognize that in some instances, these expressions can be crossed or poignantly juxtaposed. The person who finds herself first laughing and suddenly crying is not an anomaly. But we become experienced in reading these expressions, in part by attending to their context. We can understand displays of emotions in the weave of our lives. These competencies are essential in our knowing our way around in the world. The person who lacks these skills is often noticeable, and we who do possess these skills often have a hard time finding our feet in our interactions with him.

While Wittgenstein is warning against banishing the material body from the understanding of personhood, there is a danger of the pendulum swinging too far in the materialist direction. Given all the emphasis on behavior, what work does "the soul" or "the mental" do in explaining human behavior? In positing the mental, aren't we really spinning an ornamental knob? As devastating as Wittgenstein's critique is against the immaterialist, so too is his critique against materialism. Humans are not just bodies or physical objects, and they are different from machines. It is not brains that think; nothing that a brain could do would constitute thinking. Wittgenstein says, "What a lot of things a man must do in order for us to say he *thinks*" (*RPP* I § 563). Humans think in and through our behaviors, and our thinking is seen in our behavior.[18]

ACKNOWLEDGMENT AND JUSTIFICATION

One of the main ways that we respond with recognition to others and engage with them is by answering the questions that people often ask

17. See *PI* I § 285, where Wittgenstein says, "Think of the recognition of facial expression. Or of the description of facial expressions—which does not consist in giving the measurements of the face. Think, too, how one can imitate a man's face without seeing one's own in a mirror."

18. Writing at a time when the potential for thinking or calculating machines was just beginning to be imagined, Wittgenstein is very clear in his arguments against computers' thinking or understanding. These are things that humans do. This is a conceptual point. To speak of computers as thinking is to make a category mistake. In a Kantian way, computers can act in accordance with rules (in the form of programs) but they do not follow rules. Following rules is a matter of manifesting understanding in our behavior. Even computers that can perform more sophisticated operations in accordance with more complex programs are still not thinking. In the case of the computer acting in accordance with a rule, the normative dimension is missing. And the normative dimension is inseparable from rule following. Wittgenstein might also say that our interactions with such computers or thinking

about our actions and behaviors, often along the lines of "Why did you x?" Asking and answering this Why question are forms of moral inquiry. These questions can be answered in several ways, depending on whether one involves reasons or causes, which are often conflated. Reasons provide justifications, while causes provide explanations. The request for justification and the request for explanation look alike, but they belong to different games and play different roles in our lives. Explanation aims at producing causal chains that can be discovered/established/verified on the basis of evidence. Consider the question "Why did you stop to help the person who had fallen down?" You might offer a big complicated tale of how your momentum stopped or how you offered your arm as a steadying force to help that person up to her feet. These causal explanations might be given in great detail, yet they may well pass the Why question right by. Even if I understand a chain of causes, I may still not understand your action.

Perhaps sensing my confusion, you cite a particular volition as a cause of your action. The assumption is that the volition—a mental entity—has causal powers that are made manifest in outer behavior. Introspection is important; each of us assumes that she can become aware of our reasons as causes "seen from the inside," as Wittgenstein says (BB, 15). The expectation is that one can explain her behavior by demonstrating the reason that caused it. On this view, introspection is supposed to guarantee that one can grasp the mechanism behind the action.

This, you assume, will answer my question in a satisfactory way. For Wittgenstein, this presumption that mental processes must be like physical processes is the first move in the conjuring trick, escaping notice because it seems so innocent (PI § 308). I may meet this response with skepticism, because volition is exactly the sort of thing that evidence cannot prove. Causes are supposed to be determined on the basis of evidence. But evidence, or more accurately, the conditions for anything to count as evidence, is missing in this picture of volitional action. No amount of introspection can provide the possibility for correctness in ascertaining the cause of an action. The naming of this volition is an idle ceremony. The baptismal naming act, identifying *this* as the volition, is not possible.[19]

---

machines would be quite different from our interactions and responses to humans. We might not recognize and acknowledge them in the same way.

19. Such a naming requires an enormous stage setting that is absent in this case. It is not simply a matter of the requisite consistency missing. See Meredith Williams, "Wittgenstein on Representations, Privileged Objects, and Private Languages," in *Wittgenstein, Mind, and Meaning*, 19–22.

No causal explanation is helpful to me in understanding the action. Something more than a description of the (alleged) causal connections is necessary for practical understanding.

Reasons, on the other hand, aim to produce not causal chains for explanation but rather justifications. Returning to my question, "Why did you stop to help the person who had fallen down?" note that you do not find it necessary to say, "Well, first I needed to ascertain whether she was a human or not and then whether she was capable of feeling pain." These things are taken for granted; they stand fast as certainty. No, instead you may provide reasons that help to make the action intelligible to me. You may say that you saw the person suffering or heard a shout of pain that was instantly recognizable. You may have seen the difficulty she was experiencing when trying to stand up. These things, you might say, were instantly obvious. There were no inferences needed, nor were there any special sensory perceptions involved.[20] You offer these things unproblematically in the attempt to make your action fit with other actions and behaviors within practices.

Reasons are neither simply first-person avowals nor third-person statements. Rather they are interesting hybrids that play particular roles in our language-games. Third-person statements can be verified, and when the conditions for verification are met, we can talk about truth and falsity. First-person avowals differ from third-person statements in a significant way. Unlike third-person statements, first-person avowals do not allow for verification in the ways that empirical statements do. The reference for truth is different.[21] With the offering of reasons, there is a dual reference to truthfulness and to significance. The truthfulness can be understood in terms of my sincerity (I can marshal evidence for it), but the significance is not solely or even primarily in reference to me. Reasons do have a very public character and play a very public role in our language-games.

In advancing a reason in our moral language-games, a person is not simply reporting something about her interior or mental life, but rather is saying something about her very public actions. A reason expresses a relationship among me and my action and the broader community of

20. In a case such as this, Mackie's contention that there must be some special faculty to apprehend moral states of affairs—and Harman's claim that one's moral judgments are understood by reference to a person's set of moral beliefs—seems to miss the ordinary dimensions of a moral action. There is nothing metaphysically odd standing over and above our practices. There just are our practices.

21. There are grammatical differences between avowals and empirical statements. They have different grammars and therefore different references to truth.

which I am a part. In offering her reason, she is offering her justification for an act, advancing a way to see the significance of the act in our ways of living. She is showing how her action fits with or hangs together with others. As a public and shared undertaking, justification is a fundamentally interactive process; it can never be a purely private affair. No one can offer a purely private justification for reasons analogous to those concerning the impossibility of a private language and a rule's having been followed only on one occasion. It is more than a matter of the requisite consistency and regularity missing—its sociality is absent. The grammar of justification makes it nonsensical.

There are three important features of justifications to highlight. The first is that justification is only possible within a language-game or set of practices. In other words, justifications are language-game dependent in that that they are grounded in a language-game. What people accept as a justification is shown by how they think and live (*PI* § 325). Justification is a particular activity or set of activities that can be offered only because people are engaged in a complicated array or nexus of activities and practices. The normativity of grammar within a practice sets the parameters of what will count as an acceptable justification. The dependence of justification on language-games and shared activities necessarily puts constraints on the degree to which justifications can be abstracted. This limits the transferability and application of justifications among language-games. Such transfers and applications may require qualification and adaptation. The key insight is that there is no possibility of a justification that is language-game independent because the grounds are missing.

The second feature is that justification as showing significance is always in relation to others. Significance is not determined by a particular individual, but rather is based on acknowledgment of others (*OC* § 378). The grounds for significance are shared; these grounds are created and maintained by our shared ways of living. Justification, then, involves not only showing the significance of an action in connection with other actions, but also establishing and recognizing connections to other people. A request for a justification is a demand for responsibility to other particular individuals and to a broader community. Thus, reason and responsibility are fused in interesting ways.

The third feature to note about justifications is that they must always come to an end. If a justification did not come to an end, then it would not be a justification (*OC* § 485).[22] An infinite regress of reasons as justifications cannot do the work that we demand of justifications; they do not and cannot make our actions intelligible to others and cannot show the significance of an action by showing its connections to others. At some point, the justification needs to end when my spade hits bedrock. But to use something without justification is not to use it without right (*OC* § 212). The issue, of course, is what is the bedrock. My argument is that all the elements and their relationships of the stable felted world play this role. The felted world involves both forms of life, interlocking, overlapping, and mutually constituting and stabilizing each other. Our natural history, primitive reactions, moral anatomy, language-games, and grammar all act as the bedrock. It is a mistake to locate this bedrock in any one place or any one particular element in isolation from the others. The bedrock is our shared ways of living in a shared material world.[23]

THE LIMITS OF ACKNOWLEDGMENT AND RECOGNITION

One criticism that is often lobbed at metaethics is that it really does seem a separate enterprise from normative ethics. But the shift I am hoping to effect makes it much more difficult to sunder the two. In the most general sense, I am arguing that certainty and stability are matters of action ("in the beginning was deed," to quote Wittgenstein quoting Goethe) and that certainty is a kind of moral understanding. More concretely, consider my discussion above concerning recognition and acknowledgment of the humanity of others. Even if we take all Wittgenstein's points to heart that "the human body is the best picture of the human soul," there is still the very real danger for oppressed people, that their bodies are taken to define them. History and the present are both replete with examples of people being defined by their bodies. Isn't it the case that some groups of people are seen as little more than bodies or that their bodies reveal characters or traits of their souls? Margaret Urban Walker raises just this question, stating that, what happens is that "when people respond to the blackness, the femaleness, the Semitic or wizened appearance, the physical deformity or

22. See also *OC* §§ 192 and 204.

23. Paul Johnston, in *Wittgenstein and Moral Philosophy* (New York: Routledge, 1989), has a similar understanding of the justificatory role of reasons and the requirement that they come to an end. We disagree on the location of the bedrock that serves as the end. Johnston locates it in the individual, and I locate it in our shared ways of living.

so on, instead of to the person, there prejudice gets its grip."[24] Instead of human beings, we have the pathetic (the starving in Africa), the unindividuated (Islamic), the horrifying (concentration camp survivors), and the needy (homeless in the United States). The personhood of each member of these groups is unrecognized by those of us who construct these groups through our representations.

So doesn't this present a fundamental challenge to the notions of certainty and trust that I have been arguing provide a great degree of our stability in "our complicated form of life"? Isn't my position vulnerable to the charge that the moral system I have described is one that is predicated on the exclusion of some by others? This would mean that the stability is really predicated on a lack of acknowledgment and recognition, and therefore it is not really stable (or it is stable but it is exactly the sort of stability we should challenge).

The treatment of blacks by whites in the United States, especially prior to the Civil War but by no means only then (as I will discuss in the following chapter with respect to Hurricane Katrina), is a paradigm case of the nearly wholesale denial of humanity and dignity. Frederick Douglass's 1852 speech "What to the Slave Is the Fourth of July," delivered in Rochester, New York, to the Rochester Ladies' Antislavery Society, details some of the atrocities whites perpetrated against blacks.[25] This speech is a rhetorical masterpiece, beginning with a paean to the Founding Fathers of the nation, extolling their wisdom in drafting and signing the Declaration of Independence. Douglass refers to "your nation" and "your fathers," signaling even to the least attentive listener that his speech will take a very profound turn.

The part of Douglass's speech that is particularly interesting and relevant to my concerns here has to do with the forms of acknowledgment and recognition of blacks' humanity. Douglass condemns the perverse paradox that this recognition takes. Quoting at length, Douglass says:

> Must I undertake to prove that the slave is a man? The point is conceded already. Nobody doubts it. The slaveholders themselves acknowledge it in the enactment of laws for their government.

---

24. See Walker, *Moral Understandings*, 21; see also chapter 8, "Unnecessary Identities: Representational Practices and Moral Recognition."

25. Frederick Douglass, "What to the Slave Is the Fourth of July," retrieved from the Frederick Douglass archives, http://www.douglassarchives.org/doug_a1o.htm, on May 9, 2006.

> They acknowledge it when they punish disobedience on the part
> of the slave. There are seventy-two crimes in the state of Virginia,
> which, if committed by a black man (no matter how ignorant he
> be), subject him to the punishment of death; while only two of
> the same crimes will subject a white man to the like punishment.
> What is this but an acknowledgment that a slave is a moral, intel-
> lectual, and responsible being? The manhood of the slave is con-
> ceded. It is admitted in the fact that Southern statute books are
> covered with enactments forbidding, under severe fines and pen-
> alties, the teaching of the slave to read or write. When you can
> point to any such laws, in reference to the beasts of the field, then
> I may consent to argue the manhood of the slave. When the dogs
> in your streets, when the fowls of the air, when the cattle on your
> hills, when the fish of the sea, and the reptiles that crawl, shall be
> unable to distinguish the slave from a brute, there I will argue
> with you that a slave is a man![26]

Douglass directs his listeners' attention to what he calls the great sin of
America, the fundamental contradiction on which the United States is
founded. The simultaneous acknowledgment and denial of blacks' humanity by whites is fused into the cornerstone of the country. Slavery, as
an institution upheld by social, legal, and religious institutions and practices, excluded blacks' participation in some of the activities that are part
of our complicated form of life (reading and writing) while forcing them
into others (farming and building). This simultaneous acknowledgment
and denial was a stabilizing factor in the institution of slavery.

Not only does Douglass not undertake a proof to show whites that
blacks are human, but he would see no need to prove to blacks what they
already know. Douglass was unwilling to grant that this was something
that stood in need of proof. For Douglass, that was certain; it was beyond
doubt and had no need for justification. Blacks recognized and acknowledged their own humanity in their relationships, connections, and communities.

> For the present, it is enough to affirm the equal manhood of the
> Negro race. Is it not astonishing that, while we are ploughing,
> planting and reaping, using all kinds of mechanical tools, erecting

26. Ibid., ¶ 40.

houses, constructing bridges . . . reading, writing and ciphering, acting as clerks, merchants, and secretaries . . . while we are engaged in all matter of enterprises common to other men . . . living, moving, acting, thinking, planning, living in families as husbands, wives, and children, and above all, confessing and worshipping the Christian's God, and looking hopefully for life and immortality beyond the grave, we are called upon to prove that we are men![27]

As much as the those with economic, social, political, and religious power and privilege attempt to deny the humanity of others, that denial can never be complete. Those with privilege, even as they exert an enormous control over the lived realities of those whom they enslave and oppress, do not have the power to confer or deny the humanity of others. No matter how brutally violent the means employed to sever and destroy relationships, they could never fully succeed.[28]

Douglass ends his speech on an uplifting note, after having graphically described some of the horrors that slaves face everyday. By directing his listeners' attention to the inherent tension of slavery and democracy within the United States, Douglass points at the same time to that which might be the source of moral and political transformation. He shows that the material needed for transformation of the system of slavery is presently ready at hand in the form of the Declaration of Independence and the Constitution. His audience in Rochester was there to celebrate these principles, and Douglass makes it very clear that he cannot and will not celebrate them so long as they remain limited in scope to white men and are used in any way to justify the enslavement of blacks. Douglass clearly understands his audience and uses the very moral and political concepts that it holds so dear. Because they understand the concepts and principles, they can come to see the contradiction in limiting equality and liberty to a select population. Douglass rightly places the burden to justify this exclusion and inhumane treatment not just on those whites who are slave owners, but also on all whites.[29]

27. Ibid., ¶ 41.

28. For an interesting account of the ways that mothering practices in African American communities developed in response to these realities as a means to ensure well-being and create community, see Patricia Hill Collins's "Black Motherhood," in *Black Feminist Thought: Knowledge, Consciousness, and the Politics of Empowerment* (New York: Routledge, 1991), 115–37.

29. See Albert Taylor Bledsoe's *An Essay on Liberty and Freedom* (Philadelphia: J. B. Lip-

CONCLUSION

Douglass's speech, by my reckoning, is a form of moral inquiry. He was seeking shared moral understandings about the moral atrocity that was slavery. He appealed to moral concepts that had a currency but were restricted in ways that were both unjustified and contradictory. The understandings he was engendering were predicated on acknowledgment and recognition. His speech also points toward questions that still resonate today, especially about the role of justification and power. Who can ask whom for a justification? How do some people, by virtue of having certain kinds of power, not have to offer justifications for their actions? Good questions, which belong equally to normative ethics and metaethics. These are exactly the sorts of questions that feminists have been asking and must

---

pincott, 1856), especially chapter 3, "The Argument from the Scriptures," for a defense of the moral permissibility of slavery. Taylor argues that slavery is not always and everywhere wrong, and rests his scriptural argument primarily in the Old Testament. His argument is a *quasi-reductio ad absurdum*. God sanctioned slavery among the Hebrews. Abraham was the friend of God and the father of the chosen. Abraham had slaves. Could we imagine that Abraham lived his life in great sin? Bledsoe also points to passages in which slaves are described as property that could be sold and passed on as inheritance. His argument from the New Testament is that because there is no explicit disapprobation of slavery, then it cannot be a sin against God. If it were, why would the Gospels be silent on the issue? Bledsoe also invokes Saint Paul's exhortation that all men stay in the station into which Providence has placed them.

Bledsoe is careful to argue that it is only in some cases that slavery is justified and that the enslavement of Africans is one of those cases. The enslavement of civilized men is not. Bledsoe also claims that the Old Testament provides justification for not returning some slaves to their master while others must be returned. Slaves from heathens were not to be returned, but slaves who escaped from Hebrews were to be returned. Bledsoe was responding to the Fugitive Slave Act: African slaves belong to the category of slaves that must be returned, which is just as much a consequence of the goodness and civilized nature of the masters as it is about the nature of the slave. The upshot of Bledsoe's arguments is that slaves in many ways are better off under slavery than they would be left to their own devices. If slaves were to be free, they would wreak great havoc on the social fabric because they are so unsuited to lives of freedom and liberty.

While it might be tempting to relegate Bledsoe's view to the dustbin of history and argue that his views would not be well received today, Confederate Reprint Press recently has reissued *An Essay on Liberty and Freedom*. The ad copy for the book reads,

> Was Southern slavery at odds with true liberty? To the contrary, the author clearly shows in this outstanding treatise that Southern slavery as it existed in the Nineteenth Century went a long way toward preserving the fragile social order by denying liberty to those who were as yet unprepared to make proper use of it. This book also demonstrates that the agenda of the Abolitionist movement of the mid-1860s was to utterly destroy constitutional government and to substitute a lawless egalitarianism (slavery for all) in its place.

A quick Google search indicates that Bledsoe's views are still receiving favorable airplay and that many of the sentiments he expresses are still not uncommon.

continue to ask. These questions are fundamentally about the conditions for moral understandings and how we can expand those conditions. Moral understandings really are prosaic and quotidian. But they are centrally important to how we live and order our lives. So much of moral understandings are matters of certainty and stability—the very things that to many philosophers appear uninteresting and unimportant. To them these are the rags.

In the next chapter, I address the topics of moral disagreement and relativity, continuing with the issues of racism and oppression as they shaped responses to Hurricane Katrina. As much as the entrenched disagreements between slavery advocates and abolitionists have economic and political dimensions, so too do the events surrounding Katrina. But these are, at rock bottom, moral disagreements; they are disagreements about humanity, dignity, justice, rights, and entitlements that belong to our concept of humanity. That chapter will show that the felted stable world of practices, one that is deeply relative in the ways I discuss in Chapters 4 and 5, provides everything we need to preserve an account of objectivity that helps to transform disagreements and generate and meet obligations of justice, for example, without the need for moral absolutes or foundations.

"It is as if our concepts involved a scaffolding of facts."
That would presumably mean: If you imagine certain facts otherwise, describe them
otherwise, than the way they are, then you can no longer imagine the application of certain
concepts, because the rules for their application have no analogue in the new
circumstances.—So what I am saying comes to this: A law is given for human beings,
and a jurisprudent may well be capable of drawing consequences for any case that ordinarily
comes his way; thus the law evidently has its use, makes sense. Nevertheless its validity
presupposes all sorts of things, and if the being that he is to judge is quite deviant
from ordinary human beings, then, e.g., the decision whether he has done a deed with evil
intent will become not difficult but (simply) impossible.
—WITTGENSTEIN, *ZETTEL*, § 350

Here *once more* there is needed a step like the one taken in relativity theory.
—WITTGENSTEIN, *ON CERTAINTY*, § 305

Admittedly, the final chapter in a book on metaethics is perhaps an odd place to ask about the point of morality. Shouldn't that have come sooner? Nevertheless, I ask it here in the context of a discussion of relativism and moral disagreement. One significant assumption that regularly appears in otherwise very different positions is that the point of morality is to adjudicate conflict. Morality has its source in conflict and discord. One need look no further than Thomas Hobbes to see one of the clearest and frankest expositions of this view. This same assumption extends to contemporary moral theorists as well. David Wong, a moral relativist, claims that the principal point of morality is to regulate and adjudicate conflict.[1] Gilbert Harman claims that morality is a bargaining system about conflicting affective attitudes. Morality represents a compromise between people of different powers and resources.[2] On this view, while many conflicts and

1. David Wong, *Moral Relativity* (Berkeley and Los Angeles: University of California Press, 1984).
2. Gilbert Harman and Judith Jarvis Thomson, *Moral Relativism and Moral Objectivity* (New York: Blackwell, 1996), 20, 24.

disagreements can be adjudicated by our morality, there are some disagreements that are so entrenched and longstanding that no rational resolution is possible. Fundamental moral disagreements are those that
continue to remain even where there are shared beliefs about all the facts
and properties at issue. It is something about the nature of the subject as
well as the nature of the disagreement that make these disagreements
incapable of resolution. The existence of these conflicts and disagreements
is taken as evidence for metaethical relativism.

Interestingly enough, even some moral realists, such as David Brink,
claim that there are some fundamental moral disagreements and problems of incommensurability.[3] If anything were supposed to be able to resolve these fundamental disagreements, it would be moral facts having
the sort of independence from human agency to ensure objectivity. But
apparently not.

Many people take the existence of longstanding or fundamental disagreements to be a very undesirable state of affairs, and they seek to resolve these disagreements by appealing to forms of moral absolutism and
foundationalism. The expectation here is that disagreements can (and
must) be resolved. The problem may be that the disputants have not yet
recognized or accepted the right absolutes or foundations. Appeals to absolutes and foundations have serious repercussions for meta-, normative,
and applied ethics. This is something that feminists have understood for
quite some time. Lest anyone doubt whether the concepts of absolutes and
foundations still have currency, consider some recent events. The German
cardinal Joseph Ratzinger, in a homily delivered at a mass on April 18,
2005, prior to the conclave to elect a successor to Pope John Paul II,
warned against the threats to the church and the next pontiff. Ratzinger
asserted that the fundamental truths of the Roman Catholic Church are
under attack from various quarters, citing marxism, liberalism, atheism,
and agnosticism, along with "radical individualism" and "vague religious
mysticism." He directed particular warnings against relativism. He said,
"Having a clear faith, based on the creed of the church, is often labeled
today as a fundamentalism. Whereas relativism, which is letting oneself
be tossed and 'swept along by every wind of teaching' looks like the only
attitude acceptable to today's standards. We are moving toward a dictator-
ship of relativism which does not recognize anything as for certain and

3. David Brink, *Moral Realism and the Foundation of Ethics* (Cambridge: Cambridge
University Press, 1989).

which has as its highest goal one's own ego and one's own desires."[4] Perhaps heeding these warnings, the conclave elected Ratzinger pope; he is now Pope Benedict XVI.

The picture Ratzinger paints is clear and unambiguous: There are the fundamental truths of the Roman Catholic Church that serve as the absolute foundation on which our religious and moral beliefs ought to rest. Deny any one of these foundational truths and you unleash the devastatingly destructive force of relativism in the world. Anarchy is the result. The only remedy is to embrace the truths of the Catholic Church, according to Ratzinger.[5]

Feminists are often charged as some of the most effective agents of this destructive force. Most often delivered in the same dire and dour manner of the cardinal, we know well these moral indictments and the ways that they are intended to silence and intimidate. They are also intended to shape public opinion by trading off various fears and anxieties. If these fears and anxieties can easily come home to roost in one persona, so much the better. For many neoconservative Catholics and fundamentalist Christians (who might come under the cardinal's umbrella of sects), that person is the feminist or the homosexual, any left-leaning Democrat, or anyone who rejects absolutism.[6] One need look no further than the 2004 presidential election in the United States in order to see the specter of the "dangerous feminist lesbian."

According to exit polls and the subsequent election results, feminists and other left-leaning groups posed a threat to the safety and well-being of the United States that is greater than combined threats posed by Al-Qaeda and by a president who has gotten us into a war in Iraq while giving huge tax cuts to the wealthy, overseeing an economy hemorrhaging union and living-wage jobs resulting in even more people lacking health insurance, underfunding education, and attempting to privatize Social Security. That a large number of people perceive feminists and others in this way is the only way that I can make sense of the fact that more than two out of ten people were willing to put all these other concerns to the side and vote on

4. "Cardinal Warns About Dangers to Church," New York Times, April 18, 2005.

5. The increase in religious fundamentalism in the United States provides many examples of appeals to absolute moral foundations, usually derived from the Bible, which is taken to be the literal word of God. While there has been much common cause made between the Catholic Church and fundamentalist denominations, there are still many significant sources of tension.

6. The specter of moral relativism shows up on the Web pages of both the Christian Coalition (http://www.cc.org) and Focus on the Family (http://www.family.org).

what was successfully packaged as "moral issues," that is, gay marriage and abortion. In the rhetoric of the 2004 presidential election, war, poverty, and the contraction of civil and political rights were not seen as moral issues.[7]

From the global stage of Saint Peter's Square to your state legislature debating marriage as a foundation of our society to your local pharmacist deciding what prescriptions violate moral and religious beliefs, the language of foundations and absolutes is shaping our lived realities in very tangible and immediate ways. As feminists, we have commitments to changing realities so that they are less oppressive not just for women, but for all those who are oppressed and marginalized. Of course the irony in all this is that all the feminists I know are as wary of the form of relativism espoused by the pope as anyone. This is just the sort of relativism that precludes any real meaningful and effective transformations of entrenched moral disagreements. Such moral disagreements, many of us note, are located against structural injustices and oppressions, as I shall discuss below. Feminists, in making moral recommendations and judgments, want our judgments to stick; we want them to be weighty enough to stay put. But we do not want absolutes as endorsed by the pope and others of the same ilk. We've already borne the weight of those absolutes. We find ourselves needing a ground from which we can make our moral judgments, a ground that simply cannot be dismissed as insufficient or lacking in depth and solidity. What we need is stability of a sort that is neither absolutist nor relativist. In order to see this stability, however, we need to alter our starting supposition about the point of morality and not assume that it has only one purpose or point.

The starting point in this work is that agreement—and not disagreement—is the source of morality.[8] Large-scale and deep agreement in action and conventions makes up the stability of the felted world of practices. As I have been arguing throughout, this context and what I called the philosophical rags in the previous chapter are precisely that which escapes

---

7. It is interesting to note that the Christian Coalition understands gays and lesbians who challenge, under the Fourteenth Amendment, gay-marriage bans or laws that define marriage as a union between a man and a woman as subverting democracy by using the courts to advance the homosexual agenda by legalizing gay marriage. I would argue that the courts in the U.S. system are an important part of our democratic government, because we have three separate branches of government that are meant to check and balance one another.

8. Stuart Hampshire chides the moral theorist who would look for "an underlying harmony and unity behind the facts of moral experience." See *Morality and Conflict* (Cambridge, Mass.: Harvard University Press, 1983), 155.

notice because they seem unimportant or preliminary to any important discussion. The tendency is to brush them aside as philosophically uninteresting. Instead, I submit that these background conditions and this context are integral to disagreement, while at the very same time providing us with everything we need to transform disagreements and conflicts.

This different starting point pushes me to follow Wittgenstein's recommendation to take the step that is made in relativity theory. The step is actually more of a two-step. The first part is to reject the expectation that absolute judgments are even possible, because they presume a context-independent perspective. The second part is to reconceive the nature of the framework or context to which judgments are relative. The two-step process results in a rejection of both absolutism and relativism. In their place, I offer stabilism, which allows for an account of objectivity that comes without the baggage of absolutism. My stabilist view will also allow for greater diversity and pluralism but without the untethered quality of anything-goes relativism that accompanies surface conventionalism. This stabilist position follows from the felted contextualism discussed in the previous chapters.

Continuing the discussion from the previous chapter, moral disagreements are not so much theoretical problems in epistemology, nor ontological problems. Rather, they are a series of practical problems requiring embodied and practical solutions. This account will also provide a curative for the tendency Wittgenstein notes in his "Lecture on Ethics." In seeking meaning and value, we humans hurl ourselves against the bars of the cage, seeking transcendent meaning and value and objective absolutes beyond the bounds of our finitude and limitations. Instead, I argue that our moral frameworks and language-games provide everything we need just because—and not despite the fact that—they are all pervasive, inescapable, and ineliminable. They are embedded, connected, and overlapping with other frameworks that are part of the felted stability but yet are flexible and dynamic.

The example that exemplifies my felted and stabilist position concerns the federal government's response to Hurricane Katrina and its aftermath. In the context of this discussion, I will briefly show some of the ways that Hurricane Katrina has a felted character. Blacks and whites held radically different views about the federal government's response. Of course there are competing claims to justice, fairness, equal treatment, and impartiality, and some make these in the hopes of identifying what we ought to be doing for hurricane victims. These are competing descriptive and, more important, prescriptive claims that indicate a very deep moral disagreement, structured within a particular context.

I begin this chapter with an examination of C. L. Stevenson's account of ethical disagreement. While there are more elaborate and refined versions of noncognitivist and subjectivist positions, I chose Stevenson's because his so neatly and easily displays some of the dominant assumptions about the nature of ethical disagreement (opposing attitudes or affective responses) and the means for resolution that appear in the more sophisticated forms. Having highlighted those assumptions, I move to a discussion of the moral relativism and moral absolutism offered by Gilbert Harman. Harman's characterization of relativism centers on a reading of Einstein's theory of relativity; he makes the argument that moral judgments are relative in the way that judgments about simultaneity and mass are relative to a particular spatiotemporal framework. These two accounts are intended to serve as a contrast to my stabilist model. While at first glance it may appear that Harman's relativism and my stabilist position are similar, there is significant difference with respect to the nature and composition of the frameworks. At issue, once again, is the relationship between world and language, as I discussed in Chapter 3. Neither Stevenson's nor Harman's account is sufficient to the task of addressing the ways in which some of the most deeply entrenched disagreements in U.S. culture have their life against a background of oppressive and structural injustice, and as such they cannot offer any resources for transforming these states of affairs. In the context of a discussion of Hurricane Katrina, I show how our moral concepts, in particular our obligations of justice, are generated in our stable felted world of practices. This stabilist account reveals some of the ways that meta-, normative, and practical ethics are intertwined.

STEVENSON ON ETHICAL DISAGREEMENT

In both *Ethics and Language* (1944) and *Facts and Values* (1963), C. L. Stevenson explores the nature of ethical disagreement and agreement.[9] He asks whether ethical agreement and disagreement are analogous to the

---

9. C. L. Stevenson, *Ethics and Language* (New Haven: Yale University Press, 1944), and *Facts and Values: Studies in Ethical Analysis* (New Haven: Yale University Press, 1963).

agreement and disagreement found in natural sciences, differing only with respect to the relevant subject matter.[10] His approach is to focus on ethical disagreement and treat the positive term "agreement" by implication.[11] Stevenson begins his examination of the nature of ethical disagreement by drawing a distinction between disagreement in belief and disagreement in attitude. Disagreement in belief is the kind of disagreement that occurs in science, biography, and history, for example. Disagreements in belief are, according to Stevenson, fundamentally concerned with how matters are truthfully to be described and explained.[12] For this reason, disagreement in belief has epistemic standing. Disagreement in belief involves beliefs, both of which cannot be true.[13] Evidence can be offered for positions, and one can revise her position and belief in light of further information. Resolution of a disagreement in belief depends on a certain good faith on the part of both disputants to let themselves be guided by the facts.

Disagreement in attitude involves the opposition of attitudes, wants, preferences, or purposes.[14] Unlike beliefs, attitudes are not the kinds of things answerable to truth and falsity. For this reason, disagreement in attitude has no epistemic standing. Dispositions of being for and against something are in conflict. Disagreement in attitude involves attitudes, both of which cannot be satisfied.[15] The assumption is that the attitudes in question are absolutely or fundamentally opposed, such that one of them can be satisfied only if the other is not. Stevenson's assumption is that disagreement in attitudes allows for no middle ground; one is either for (pro) or one is against (con).

Disagreements in attitude occur wherever one individual or group of individuals has a favorable attitude toward something and another individual or group has an unfavorable attitude toward it.[16] Mr. A, for example, may favor a particular restaurant while Mr. B does not like it.[17] Mr. and Mrs. Smith disagree in attitude over whom to invite to their party. Mrs. Smith wants to cultivate more highbrow friends, while Mr. Smith is loyal

10. Stevenson, *Ethics and Language*, 2.
11. Ibid.
12. Ibid.
13. Stevenson, *Facts and Values*, 2.
14. Stevenson, *Ethics and Language*, 3.
15. Stevenson, *Facts and Values*, 2.
16. Ibid., 1.
17. Stevenson, *Ethics and Language*, 2.

to his old poker-playing buddies. A workers' union is for higher wages but the management is against them.[18] In these disagreements, each person or group is trying to redirect the attitudes of the other. For such redirection, it must be taken for granted that each is willing to revise her or their opinions in light of what the other has to say.[19] The degree to which one tries to redirect the attitudes of the other and the degree to which one is willing to change her attitude depends on the particular situation in question. A and B, for example, are trying to choose a restaurant. At some point, either A or B must be willing to make a concession on the choice of a restaurant, because without it, they might end up not having dinner together. In the case of management and union, the degrees and conditions under which one tries to redirect the attitudes and is willing to make concessions will be radically different from those in the case of A and B due to the level of the stakes.

Ethical disagreement, according to Stevenson, involves disagreement in both belief and attitude. Disagreement in attitude is taken as the distinguishing feature of ethical disagreement for two reasons:

1. Disagreement in attitude determines what beliefs are relevant to the argument.
2. Ethical disagreement terminates when disagreement in attitude terminates.[20]

For a belief to count as relevant, it must be one that is likely to lead one side or another to a change in attitude.

It is interesting to note that in *Ethics and Language,* Stevenson maintained that the causal relation between beliefs and attitudes is reciprocal. Having certain beliefs may cause one to have certain attitudes, and the possession of attitudes will affect what beliefs one holds to be true. Later, in *Facts and Values,* however, Stevenson removes the reciprocity. Attitudes, to a large extent, are a function of our beliefs; changes in attitudes are a consequence of changes in belief. When we see that someone has changed her attitudes, we can assume she did so because her beliefs changed. But changes in beliefs do not guarantee that there will be an accompanying change in attitudes.[21] Moreover, our attitudes do not affect what beliefs we hold to be true.

18. Stevenson, *Facts and Values,* 4.
19. Stevenson, *Ethics and Language,* 2.
20. Ibid., 14–15; Stevenson, *Facts and Values,* 4–5.
21. Stevenson, *Facts and Values,* 6.

The methods of science may be one mode of inquiry or argument capable of resolving disagreement about matters of attitude. Disagreement in value rests on disagreement in belief, and, according to Stevenson, scientific methods are the only rational methods for resolving disagreement in belief.[22] The methods of science will be successful and effective only to the extent to which agreement in belief can cause agreement in attitude. The problem, as Stevenson sees it, is that agreement in attitude does not always follow from agreement in belief. Science will be unable to mediate or resolve cases where the disputants share a set of beliefs about the situation but yet still have divergent attitudes. In cases such as these, Stevenson's conclusion is that "the purely intellectual methods of science, and, indeed, *all* methods of reasoning, may be insufficient to settle disputes about value."[23] The methods remaining available to us in such disputes are nonrational,[24] such as impassioned oratories or persuasive speeches. Disagreement loses its rational character and becomes solely a matter of competing and conflicting attitudes.

Thus for Stevenson, there may a class of disagreements that cannot be rationally resolved. There may be "resolution" in the sense of a forced conversion or capitulation, but this is different in kind from what we expect in science. This clearly indicates that the source of the "problem" is the affectional attitudes that produce and then reinforce a kind of recalcitrance.

At this point I will make several preliminary comments to mark some significant ways in which my felted stabilist account will differ from Stevenson's. These differences will be amplified later in this chapter.

First, Stevenson's arrival in the realm of fundamental disagreements is a consequence of the fact/value distinction, a first cousin to the world/language dichotomy. Attitudes, preferences, and desires all belong on the language and value side of the divide. By removing the reciprocity between beliefs and attitudes, Stevenson underscores their allegedly separate existence, something that had been assumed in the first place. Fundamental disagreements, then, are inevitable due to their very nature.

Second, the disputants in Stevenson's account—Mr. A. and Mr. B., Mr. and Mrs. Smith, the trade union and management—are individuals or groups of individuals each having their own sets of beliefs and attitudes. These individuals are separate and isolated in their possession of beliefs

22. Ibid.
23. Ibid., 8.
24. Ibid.

and attitudes. A dispute occurs when some attitude in one person's set comes into conflict with an attitude belonging to some other person. Notably missing from Stevenson's account is any explicit treatment of the nature, social location, and relative power or powerlessness of the disputants. It seems as if the disputants all stand on equal footing. My view begins with the presumption that those people involved in moral disputes have social histories and occupy social positions within structures of oppression and privilege. People have systems of beliefs, judgments, attitudes, and concepts that have a social public genesis. These systems of beliefs are not privately constructed solely out of the contents of our own minds.

Third, it is important to recognize that, with the possible exception of the union/management conflict, the examples used by Stevenson don't really seem to involve moral issues or problems that matter. In which restaurant to eat seems more a matter of taste (literally?) and less of morality. Choosing a restaurant may be a moral issue if a particular restaurant has horrible working conditions or is known for condoning sexual harassment of the wait staff. But nevertheless, it does seem that differences in morality cut deeper or go beyond differences in taste, and we are inclined to say that we can have better or worse answers or resolutions to these conflicts. Something more is at stake in moral disagreements than just taste.

Fourth, in Stevenson's account, the participants in an ethical disagreement are each trying to redirect the attitudes of the other. Such a redirection of attitude may or may not require a change in beliefs on the part of the disputants. The redirection that these attitudes are to take is in the direction of convergence. In other words, each individual will come to have the same attitude of being either for or against something. Implicit in this account is the claim that agreement (the absence of disagreement) is the norm and that disagreement is a failure of or a threat to the internal coherence that certain views of morality seem to demand. My stabilist view rejects this normative assumption and maintains that difference and even or especially disagreement plays an important and transformative role in our everyday life. Given the complexity and diversity within our form of life and among different forms of life, it would be misguided to assume that total agreement among all humans is the desired state of affairs. Such "agreement" may be a consequence of immoral and unjust exercises of power.

GILBERT HARMAN'S NATURALISM AND RELATIVISM

The world/language dichotomy undergirds Gilbert Harman's relativism, producing a category of fundamental moral disagreements that are in principle incapable of resolution. Harman offers characterizations of a naturalist approach to ethics and what he calls autonomous ethics. The difference between them, he claims, really does come down to the relationship between science and ethics. Harman uses the term naturalism in a fairly straightforward sense. By a naturalist approach to ethics, Harman means an "approach to ethics that is . . . dominated by a concern with the place of values in the natural world."[25] Naturalism need not lead to a naturalistic reduction in the sense that moral judgments can be analyzed or reduced to factual statements of the sort compatible with a scientific worldview. Mackie's rejection of moral properties as metaphysically queer is an instance of the sort of naturalism with which Harman is concerned. A naturalist approach holds that our scientific conception of the world has no room for entities of this sort. Because moral properties do not fit with our scientific conceptions of the world, a naturalist approach to ethics most inevitably tends toward relativism. Unlike Stevenson's view, Harman's relativism does leave room for some type of moral truth and cognitivism.

Given his metaphysical commitments, Harman's definition of moral relativism is unsurprising. For Harman, moral relativism must be conceived as an issue about objectivity and not as an issue of truth.[26] Harman compares moral relativity to Einstein's theory of relativity in physics. Following Einstein, Harman claims that there is no such thing as absolute mass or absolute simultaneity. There is no uniform or absolute answer to the question of whether two events are simultaneous. There is no objectively privileged absolute spatiotemporal framework. Within framework A the two events may be simultaneous, while in framework B they are not. As Harman explains it:

> A relativist about motion supposes that there are various possible spatiotemporal frameworks, none of which is objectively privileged, even though one might be specially salient to a given observer, for example, the framework in which the observer is at rest

25. Gilbert Harman, "Is There a Single True Morality?" in *Moral Relativism: A Reader*, ed. Paul K. Moser and Thomas L. Carson (New York: Oxford University Press, 2001), 165–84, 167.

26. Harman and Thomson, *Moral Relativism and Moral Objectivity*, 43.

(or the framework in which the Earth is at rest, or the solar system . . .). The moral relativist supposes that there are various moral frameworks from which moral issues can be judged and that none of these frameworks is objectively privileged, even though one might be specially salient to a given person: for example, the moral framework relevantly associated with that person's values.[27]

Moral relativism claims that there is no such thing as objectively absolute good, absolute right, or absolute justice; there is only what is good, right, or just in relation to this or that moral framework. As Harman claims, "what someone takes to be absolute rightness is only rightness in relation to (a system of moral coordinates determined by) that person's values."[28] Something's being good or right is relative to a set of values or moral standards or a certain moral point of view. In effect, what is morally right in one moral framework can be morally wrong in another. There is no moral framework that is objectively privileged as the one true morality.[29] Some frameworks may matter more to people or have some special sort of claim on an individual, but this status has nothing to do with their being objectively privileged.

Harman contrasts a naturalist approach to ethics with what he calls an "autonomous ethics" approach. This autonomous approach "allows us to pursue ethics internally."[30] By this, Harman means that attention to scientific accommodation is not the primary concern, though science is not irrelevant. The main question of ethics is not the naturalistic state of values and obligations. Rather, when we do ethics internally, "We begin with our initial moral beliefs and search for general principles. Our initial opinions can be changed to some extent so as to come into agreement with appealing general principles and our beliefs about the facts, but an important aspect of the appeal of such principles will be the way in which they account for what we already accept."[31] Harman claims that the autonomous approach to ethics tends—though not always—to presume moral absolutism.

27. Ibid., 41–42.
28. Ibid., 18.
29. Ibid., 3.
30. Harman, "Is There a Single True Morality?" 167.
31. Ibid., 168. This seems an odd characterization of doing "ethics internally." It would have been more apt and accurate to say, "doing ethics in a circular manner."

Harman offers several different descriptions of moral absolutism. As we see from his definition of moral relativism above, moral absolutism involves objectively absolute rightness, goodness, and justice. Moral absolutism is the thesis that there are basic demands that apply to all moral agents. He also characterizes absolutism as "a view about moral reasons people have to do things and to want or hope for things. I will understand a belief about absolute values to be a belief that there are things that everyone has a reason to hope or wish for. To say that there is a moral law that applies to everyone is, I hereby stipulate, to say that everyone has sufficient reasons to follow that law."[32] Elsewhere he says that moral absolutism holds that there is a single true morality.[33]

While "moral absolutism" is an expression that does not have much currency in contemporary metaethics, "moral rationalism" does. In most cases, moral rationalism is a version of moral foundationalism and tends toward deontological approaches. In its most generic sense, moral rationalism attempts to link basic or universal moral principles, rules, and demands to rationality. Bernard Gert, for example, argues that there are ten basic rules that one can reject only on the pains of irrationality.[34] Alan Gewirth attempts to demonstrate the necessary truth of what he identifies as the Principle of Generic Consistency.[35] These rationalist approaches seem consistent with the characterizations Harman offers of moral absolutism. While I will not focus on these particular forms of moral rationalism because they will take me too far afield, I do want to focus on problems that are associated with the relationship between universal rules and the reasons they issue.[36]

For the most part, I agree with Harman's characterization of moral absolutism. The lure and seductive force of absolute objective values can be hard to resist; they offer the great promise of rightness, truth, or goodness. These, we hope and expect, would be able to adjudicate conflicts and enable us to speak of moral progress. But on the other hand, moral absolutism comes with a high cost: there is perhaps little room for disagreement with or dissent from these absolutes; they require a certain allegiance. If you deny one of the basic values or undergirding principles,

---

32. Ibid., 171.
33. Harman and Thomson, *Moral Relativism and Moral Objectivity*, 5.
34. Bernard Gert, *The Moral Rules* (New York: Harper and Row, 1966).
35. Alan Gewirth, *Reason and Morality* (Chicago: University of Chicago Press, 1978).
36. Robert Arrington, in *Rationalism, Realism, and Relativism: Perspectives in Contemporary Moral Epistemology* (Ithaca, N.Y.: Cornell University Press, 1988), offers an excellent explication and critique of these two forms of moral rationalism.

then you have provided the grounds for questioning your rationality. This high cost may make relativism seem the more attractive option. Relativism allows us to invoke and make use of concepts such as right and truth and claims to moral knowledge in a more scaled-down version. But here too is a high cost: are we willing to grant that there are conflicts that are in principle incapable of resolution? And do these scaled-down versions of rightness and truth come with their own costs?

Neither moral absolutism nor moral relativism seems particularly attractive. Each of these is wrong and misguided, however, in interesting and productive ways for the alternative that I offer below. Their respective inadequacies trace back to two important presuppositions that relativism and absolutism share: the world/language divide and the idea that morality's chief point (and perhaps origin) is the adjudication of conflict.

With respect to moral absolutism, each of its formulations has problems. What would make a framework true? Is there anything that could make a framework true or rest on some absolute justification? And even if we grant that frameworks can be true or false, there is the problem of perspective. From where—and it would have to be outside of this framework—could one ascertain its truth? Furthermore, what is the criterion or standard of truth? Frameworks provide standards and criteria, so what could possibly play the role of truth criterion in this case? The appeals to truth and ultimate justification will fail.

Regarding absolutism in the form of a universal law or rule, one problem with universal laws is their high level of abstraction. As Wittgenstein argues in *Philosophical Investigations*, the more abstract the law, the greater its indeterminacy. One can rightly and productively ask whether a universal law can provide what it promises when it is burdened by this indeterminacy. When anything can be made to be in accordance with or in conflict with a rule, the concept of correctness becomes incoherent and useless. The very attempt to achieve transcendence from the contingent becomes self-defeating; there is no way for it to shake its origins.

For the moral absolutist, the universal law cannot be a generalization, because generalizations are contingent and subject to change, and that which is subject to change is not absolute. While it is accurate to say that laws and rules provide us reasons, there is something awry in the ways that the absolutist conceives the ways that laws issue reasons and how these reasons come to have a hold on us. This is the question of normativity, as I discussed in Chapter 5. If universal laws are indeterminate, it follows that the reasons they issue will also be indeterminate. How could these indeterminate reasons come to have a sufficient hold on all of us? One of the central issues here is how reasons come to have a hold on us at all. Their hold is not subject-matter dependent, nor is it a matter of some special property of reasons. Rather, reasons have a hold on us because of their use, and their use is always a matter of context.

One should also interrogate the origin of these universal laws, rules, or demands. If it is our reason, as Kant suggests, then any denial of it or even of one of its particular prescriptions is a matter of irrationality. Universal laws are supposed to generate and give all of us reasons to act in certain ways or to hope for certain things. For the absolutist, if we do not see these reasons as sufficient and compelling, then we are acting irrationally in this particular case or we are irrational in a more global sense.

The failure of absolutism in its various guises may point us back in the direction of context and frameworks. The key, of course, is the nature of the frameworks. It seems to me that Harman, as a naturalist, is willing to acknowledge Einstein's relativity all the while recognizing that people cannot simply at will and voluntarily cast off and pick up spatiotemporal frameworks. We do not choose to be in the framework of the Earth or the solar system, for example.

For Harman, spatiotemporal frameworks are very different in kind from moral frameworks. Spatiotemporal frameworks involve physical and natural considerations that are independent of humans and their theorizing, which is precisely what the world/language dualism initially requires and then subsequently confirms. On the other hand, Harman might that claim attitudes, values, and conventions constitute our moral frameworks. Unlike the coordinates one finds in the natural world for our scientific theories and hypotheses, moral coordinates have no independent existence. They are dependent on and thus relative to humans in a way that natural properties are not. They are strictly human creations. For Harman, the frameworks differ not simply in terms of the subject of inquiry but rather in their very nature. A certain materiality is missing with moral frameworks. Harman's relativism rests on a not unfamiliar distinction between a content sense of objectivity and a methodological sense. I will discuss these two senses in the following section.

As Harman describes them, moral frameworks seem unanchored in a certain way. Given his naturalism, combined with his moral antirealism and what I have called surface conventionalism, it appears that there can be gaps between these freestanding frameworks. As a consequence of the world/language divide, it seems as if Harman's frameworks sit atop the natural base. While we are always within a spatiotemporal framework, the same is not true of moral frameworks. Each framework is oriented around a person's or group's moral coordinates, as Harman claims. There may be compelling reasons within each of these frameworks, but the absence of an objectively privileged or true framework entails that there cannot be reasons or demands that are incumbent on all of us. No framework could possibly provide sufficient reasons to everyone because the requisite moral coordinates are missing or not shared. The existence of these gaps lends weight to the conclusion that there are at least some fundamental moral disagreements that are incapable of resolution and transformation.

Thus, for both the absolutist and relativist, there are unbridgeable chasms. These tremendous gaps create disagreements and conflicts that are in principle incapable of resolution. In different though related ways, absolutism and relativism challenge the possibility of any grounding being adequate. One way to understand relativism is that it denies that there is any ground other than our beliefs, attitudes, or social conventions. But these are variable; they are relative to a particular context. Contexts and frameworks have boundaries, and once one crosses them, those reasons are no longer telling. Between these different contexts, there is no shared ground. The existence of widely divergent worldviews and moral beliefs, often called descriptive or cultural relativism, provides evidence for a form of metaethical relativism. And so, however hard we may try to engage with others, the engagement is not possible where there can be no shared ground. The relativists must accept that, in principle, there just are some disagreements that just cannot be resolved.

With the absolutist we have a different form of the problem. The grounds for the absolutist are the absolute truths, rules, laws, or demands. For the absolutist, disagreements become unbridgeable in practice as op-posed to in principle. The absolutist supposes that all disagreements are in principle resolvable, but in practice, some people act irrationally. These are just the sorts of cases Wittgenstein might be warning us against when he says,

> Where two principles really do meet which cannot be reconciled with one another, then each man declares the other a fool and heretic.
>
> I said I would "combat" the other man,—but wouldn't I give him *reasons*? Certainly; but how far do they go? At the end of the

reasons comes *persuasion*. (Think what happens when the missionaries convert the natives.) (*OC* §§ 611–12)

This is the same point at which we left the discussion of Stevenson. Any accord that is coerced and not freely given may not rightly or accurately belong in the category of rational.

Nothing but the absolutes can function as a ground for the absolutist, and the absolutes cannot function as a ground for relativists. The starting points—that the point of morality is to adjudicate conflict and that there is a sharp divide between both world and nature and language and normativity—make it come to pass that certain problems and disagreements either will not (the absolutist) or cannot (the relativist) be resolved, reinforcing our belief that they were incapable of resolution in the first place. We fail to see that the lack of shared conditions or grounds is neither inevitable nor unavoidable; it may very well be a consequence of our ways of being in the world. It may well be a consequence of how we conceive the world and both morality and its purposes.

STABILITY, RELATIVITY, AND OBJECTIVITY

In much the same way that health is something more or greater than the absence of disease and illness, and peace is more than the absence of war, morality is more than the absence of disagreement and conflict. While one of the things morality does is regulate and adjudicate conflict, morality is also constitutive and productive of our lives and identities. Even if it were the case that moral disagreements—even those regarded as fundamental—were resolved, we would still need and want morality. We would not be the kind of creatures we are if we did not participate in the myriad practices that belong under the umbrella of morality. That is to say, being moral by participating in moral language-games is one of the things that we as humans do. Morality and moral practices are integral to "this complicated form of life," as I discussed in Chapter 4.

In invoking the comparison to Einstein's theory of relativity and arguing against absolutism, Harman must agree that there must always be a spatiotemporal framework and that one can never be outside it. Though the judgments may vary from framework to framework, the physics and the rules are always the same. This is the commonality; it is one of the conditions for physics. Harman admits that there are some universal features in both spatiotemporal and moral frameworks. He says:

There will be universal truths about moralities just as there are universal truths about spatio-temporal frameworks. Perhaps all spatio-temporal frameworks must admit of motion and rest. And perhaps all moralities have some rules against killing, harm, and deception. The existence of universal features of spatio-temporal frameworks is compatible with and even required by Einstein's Theory of Relativity and the existence of universal features of morality is compatible with moral relativism.[37]

Harman's expectation for universality for moral frameworks is in the form of principles, not in any of the other elements that make up moral frameworks. In the case of physics, there is more to the framework than the rules. Harman's mistake is in his conception of moral frameworks and their constitutive elements.

Now the question for me is what, if anything, can play the role of the ineliminable and untranscendable framework. Questions of frameworks and contexts have been central in this work. My endeavor has been to problematize a naturalist view of the world that privileges science and what it accommodates and countenances as real. I have also been concerned to dispute certain forms of antirealism that impute too much causal and determining power to our language. In short, I have challenged the plausibility and adequacy of a philosophical thesis that presumes a world/language divide. The answer to the question of what could play the role of an ineliminable framework, I submit, is the stable felted world that I have been describing throughout this work. This world is neither realist/naturalist nor antirealist/surface conventionalist. In its place, I have offered a description of what I have called the stable felted world, which is just that which we cannot transcend, and it is the only context in which we can make sense of morality and normativity. This framework comprises forms of life in the two senses I discuss in Chapter 4. There is what I identified as the human form of life—marked off but not without blurry borders—that involves using language in the ways we do toward the ends we have. There are also multiple forms of life within the human form of life. These two, however, are not separable; they are parts of the same whole. These expressions pick out different dimensions of the whole. Forms of life, in both senses, are the inescapable context.

37. Harman and Thomson, *Moral Relativism and Moral Objectivity*, 9n3.

As my discussions about the arbitrariness and nonarbitrariness of grammar should make clear, there is a deep contingency and stability about everything and in every form of inquiry in our lives and world. But this does not imply that we can at will change these matters. Nor does it entail that we can move from framework to framework as we please. While it is true in a sense that we can move between some spatiotemporal frameworks with ease and a bit of athleticism, when, for example, jumping from the moving train to the platform, we cannot simply just move away from the spatiotemporal framework of the planet Earth or the solar system. Our location in these is not a matter of choice. These frameworks do provide limitations. Similarly, I cannot of my own free will jump from the human form of life to the form of life of a lion or dog. Furthermore, there are also constraints imposed by myriad factors—some grammatical and others more practical—that preclude my moving from one form of life to another. The language-games we play and the frameworks we inhabit are not matters of free will and voluntary choice.

Harman, in his treatment of relativism, understands the defining issue as objectivity and not truth. I follow his lead and argue for an account of objectivity that is fully compatible with the felted contextualism I have developed. This will involve a different sense of objectivity that begins with a rejection of the twin theses of realism and antirealism as I discuss in Chapter 3.

There are at least two senses of objectivity that concern us. The first is a content sense, which is bound up with issues of scientific realism. According to Helen Longino, "Objectivity is bound up with questions about the truth and referential character of scientific theories, that is, with issues of scientific realism. In this sense to attribute objectivity to science is to claim that the view provided by science is an accurate description of the facts of the natural world as they are; it is a correct view of the objects to be found in the world and of their relations with each other."[38] Scientific realism is understood as the doctrine that scientific theories should be understood as putative descriptions of real phenomena. These real phenomena, which are the objects of investigation and knowledge, include unobservable ("theoretical") entities such as atoms, neutrinos, and electromagnetic fields, as well as observable phenomena. Scientific theories describe reality, and reality is prior to and hence independent of thought.

---

38. Helen Longino, *Science as Social Knowledge: Values and Objectivity in Scientific Inquiry* (Princeton: Princeton University Press, 1990), 62.

This content sense of objectivity presumes not only that there are real and independent objects, but also, perhaps more important, that these objects can and *must* play certain causal and determining roles.[39] Given the critique of realism I offer in Chapter 3, it is not at all clear that any object could play these roles. This holds equally true for both natural objects and moral objects.

The second sense of objectivity Longino identifies is methodological. In this sense, objectivity has to do with the modes of inquiry, and to attribute this sense of objectivity to science "is to claim that the view provided by science is one achieved by reliance upon nonarbitrary and nonsubjective criteria for developing, accepting, and rejecting the hypotheses and theories that make up the view."[40] It is typically thought that the content sense of objectivity dictates the methodological sense. Longino shifts this typical order of attention and argues that methodological objectivity points toward a way of conceptualizing content objectivity, rather than the latter dictating the former. While I very much agree with Longino's shift in attention, her approach ultimately does rely on the world/language dualism that I have been rejecting throughout this work. Longino's work is useful in generating an account of objectivity that ties the two senses together in a way that is consistent with the felted world that I have been describing.

Objectivity is a matter of the elements of the felted world. Like normativity, objectivity needs to be deflated and deontologized. Harman's primary concern is objectivity as an ontological issue a la scientific realism. As was the case with necessity, the assumption is that any connection, contact, or dependence of human agency compromises objectivity. Given my description of the stable felted world of practices, there is no reason to assume that content dictates the method, nor is there reason to assume that the method will reveal content that is separate from the method. Rather, objectivity in a felted sense will have a dynamic relational character. As I will show below, objectivity is deeply connected to responsibility. With respect to moral principles, concepts, and rules, these are not responsible to reality (understood in a realist sense) in terms of correspondence but rather responsible to a felted reality in terms of their meanings, uses, and roles in our lives.[41]

---

39. Objectivity is about independently existing objects, that is, objects of scientific realism. The picture here is that these are the sorts of objects that have and confer objectivity. In this sense, objective standards are those having this particular "aboutness" to them.

40. Longino, *Science as Social Knowledge*, 62.

41. In Chapter 3, I discuss the different "aboutnesses" of mathematical and empirical propositions and the different ways that they are responsible to reality.

OBJECTIVITY AND RESPONSIBILITY

What worries me about absolutist and realist accounts of rules, normativity, and rule following is the way in which human agency is obscured, often to detrimental effect. Our hope is that such a standard would be able to provide the answer to a conflict or disagreement. But this approach obscures the origin and history of rules, making them appear to have lives and meanings outside of our shared ways of living. This expectation seems to obscure the role that we play in maintaining disagreements when rules clash. It is almost as if the clashes are not between real living humans anymore, but rather between rules. And this, I submit, is the origin of many moral and political problems. Rules are not the origins of our conflicts, nor are they the hindrances to the transformation of our disagreements: we are. And here we arrive at questions of responsibility.

Lisa Heldke and Stephen Kellert offer a definition of objectivity as responsibility.[42] They explicitly state that their definition is neutral with respect to controversies over realism while avoiding dogmatic antirealism. Because my deflationary program rejects both dogmatic realism and antirealism and reshapes the context of inquiry as the felted world, I see much in their definition of objectivity that is complementary. While their definition conceives objectivity as a property of inquiry (along the lines of the methodological sense of Longino), it does not seem to subscribe to a complete distinction from the content sense, given how they describe the context of inquiry and its participants. Heldke and Kellert assert, "inquiry is marked by objectivity to the extent that its participants acknowledge, fulfill, and expand responsibility to the context of inquiry."[43] They use very intentionally a broad definition of inquiry as any and all processes that are used to generate, evaluate, and communicate knowledge. For me, the interesting and compatible shift is the description of the context of inquiry. For Heldke and Kellert, the context includes all those who participate in the inquiry, and participation is not limited to those who are inquiring, but also includes those inquired into and those to whom the results of the inquiry are conveyed. They claim that "objectivity, when conceived as responsibility, emphasizes relationships among the members of the inquiring context, while de-emphasizing the rigidity and even the importance of the roles of subject, object, and public."[44] They actively resist the labels of

42. Lisa M. Heldke and Stephen H. Kellert, "Objectivity as Responsibility," *Metaphilosophy* 26, no. 4 (1995): 360–78.

43. Ibid., 362.

44. Ibid., 364.

"subject" and "object" because it is possible that a person or an object may be playing more than one role in a context of inquiry.

As I have been arguing throughout this work, the context of moral inquiry is our stable felted world. In the world conceived this way, everything and everyone participates in practices. This is not to say that everything and everyone participates in the same way, but it is to say that nothing stands outside these practices. That is to say, along the lines of Heldke and Kellert, they are part of the context of inquiry. Thus, our lines of responsibility run in numerous directions within this context, though not equally or evenly so in all directions.

Responsibility is a matter of responsibility to other members and participants of the inquiry as well as responsibility for actions and judgments. Both of these senses are compatible with a more expansive notion of responsibility, one that focuses not only on particular actions and judgments, but also the broader conditions and contexts that make such acts possible and meaningful. This is another way to say that we have responsibility to and for the context of inquiry.

Heldke and Kellert's approach shows that objectivity is not a state of affairs or a property of some objects but rather an ongoing achievement. Objectivity increases when responsibilities are met and expanded on. One important responsibility is to meet the demands placed by their relationships or to justify why they decide not to meet these demands. Justifications take very different forms depending on the nature or subject of the inquiry. The terms of acceptable justification belong to the grammar of the practices, but this does not mean that grammar is in principle exempt from similar demands of responsibility.

Heldke and Kellert provocatively clam that objectivity requires expanding the network of responsibilities within a context of inquiry. This entails two related activities: seeking additional perspectives that will contribute to the success of an inquiry project and transforming that project by incorporating concerns that cannot presently be accommodated by the project's configuration. This is a very significant demand; it points to the way that any inquiry that is meant to be a closed rigid process cannot be objective. The absence of other perspectives or the silencing or ignoring of concerns signals that the process of inquiry has been made less objective.[45] My intent in the following discussion is to illustrate these more abstract points through a discussion of Hurricane Katrina.

45. This last point resonates with Longino's work on the methodological sense of objectivity. For Longino, an inquiry is objective to the degree that it satisfies four criteria. First, there must be recognized avenues for the expression and presentation of criticism of the reasoning, evidence, and method of science. In science, these avenues most often include

OBJECTIVITY, RESPONSIBILITY, OBLIGATIONS OF JUSTICE, AND HURRICANE KATRINA

Saying that all norms, standards, and normative authority are creations of a participatory dynamic entails that we share responsibility for the content of our normative judgments, good and bad. It also means that we have responsibility for the maintenance of the context in which rules have their application and meaning. It means that we as individuals and as members of groups have responsibilities for how and under what conditions and to what degree we exercise our normative authority. The questions about Hurricane Katrina and what we should do are not theoretical ones in need of theoretical solutions. Rather, they are practical. Once again, this may seem too plebian and prosaic. The felted world gives us plenty of material and opportunities to see commonality and to forge connections. This is that to which we must appeal and must make use. It is also that to which we appeal in arguing that some perspectives, positions, and practices are better than others.

Hurricane Katrina is itself a set of phenomena of the felted world. Consider the following poll results. According to a Washington Post/ABC poll, three out of four whites doubted that the federal government would have responded more quickly if more of the victims had been white and wealthier. Three out of four blacks believed federal aid would have come sooner had the victims been white and affluent. Another ABC poll showed that seven out of ten African Americans believed New Orleans would have had better flood protection and emergency preparedness resources had it been wealthier and more predominantly white, rather than largely poor and African American. Fewer than three out of ten whites agreed.[46]

The vastly different opinions of whites and blacks about Hurricane Katrina, its aftereffects, and the response of the federal government point

---

forums, journals, and conferences.

Second, there must be shared standards of criticism that can be invoked by the community. These shared standards are what give particular criticisms their bite. These can include "both substantive principles and epistemic, as well as social, values" (Longino, *Science as Social Knowledge*, 76).

Third, the community must be responsive to such criticisms. Criticism accomplishes little when it falls on deaf ears or if the only uptake of criticism is in the form of lip service. The scientific community as a whole must change in response to critical discussions.

Fourth, there must be an equality of intellectual authority within the community. Two points must be made here. The first is concerned with equality among qualified practitioners. The people must share intellectual authority equally. The second point concerns the exclusion of certain viewpoints. Some viewpoints have traditionally been privileged, and the exclusion of others has been at times overt and at other times subtle.

46. ABC News/*Washington Post*, September 12, 2005, http://abcnews.go.com/politics/pollvault/story?id = 1117357.

toward very different understandings of the problems. These differing understandings may well spring from very different lived realities. While the hurricane was a weather event, it is important not to understand it simply as a natural event. Here again, the temptation is to segregate human activity and agency from the natural world that every so often blows its lid.[47] With this view, we humans need to simply withstand these periodic outbursts and then get back to the business of living. This is a simplistic view, of course, and I am not ascribing it to all and even only white people. There was no small degree of suffering and loss for many white people, especially those who were poor, elderly, or disabled. But for the whites who were able to organize their own evacuation and make plans in advance, and who had adequate layers of financial safety and security (including adequate homeowners insurance), their experience was very different from those who were not as well-off. For many, that simply was not an option. Sharing a geographic area does not entail that people share a material lived reality.

Much of the flooding in the Gulf Coast is directly traceable to human actions. Channeling the Mississippi River via levees caused sediment to deposit in the gulf rather than along the coast, which would build up wetland areas. Dredging the channels weakened the ecosystem. Coastal drilling had rapidly accelerated the erosion of areas of wetlands along the coast. Since 1930, Louisiana lost coastal marshlands equivalent to the acreage of the state of Delaware.[48]

Well before the screaming winds and the surging waters, much of the population of the Gulf Coast was living in perilous conditions. Extreme poverty for a family of four in the Gulf Coast is defined as earning $9,675 or less. In Louisiana, 13 percent of children live in extreme poverty, while 12 percent of Mississippi's children live in extreme poverty. Alabama's children fare a bit better at 8 percent living in extreme poverty. In the same region, the average self-sufficiency wage for a family of four is $38,680. Nearly 25 percent of children in these three states live well below that level.[49]

New Orleans's population is at least two-thirds African American, 27 percent of which lives below the poverty level. Most people living in poverty do not own a car and lack reliable transportation in the best of times.

---

47. Nature is a woman, subject to all sorts of tempestuous emotional tantrums. This is supposed to help us make sense of these events.

48. See Douglas Brinkley's *The Great Deluge: Hurricane Katrina, New Orleans, and the Mississippi Gulf Coast* (New York: William Morrow, 2006), 8–10.

49. See National Center for Children in Poverty, Columbia University, http://www.nccp-.org/publications/pub_622.html.

They also rarely have credit cards and bank accounts. Pawnshops and check-cashing businesses are far more common than banks. Most residents rent rather than own their homes. Housing options are limited, and rents account for a disproportionate amount of living expenses.

Poverty is deeply entwined with public health crises. People living in poverty experience food insecurity. That is to say, they do not have regular access to good nutritious food. Lacking health insurance, preventative health care is not possible. Living in homes that may have significant mold problems, lead paint, asbestos, and other toxins contributes to the overall inferior health of poor people.

Blacks, the poor, the elderly, and the disabled were the ones who were left behind when the hurricane hit, though many have commented that they had already been left behind before. For example, the educational infrastructure of areas with concentrated poverty is extremely tenuous. Students and teachers both suffer. In New Orleans, for example, blacks constitute 96 percent of the public school student population. Of the sixty thousand students within the system, ten thousand have been suspended and one thousand expelled. Nearly half of New Orleans's high school students fail to graduate.[50] With earning potential strongly correlated to earned academic degrees, African Americans are clearly being left behind in a steady downward spiral to poverty.

The elderly and disabled were particularly vulnerable. Those who were confined to home or care facilities due to lack of mobility and other health issues really had little choice about evacuation; there were simply no options available to them. And for some of those who were living in a long-term care facility, the medical staff may have considered mercy killings by the administration of lethal dosages of medications.[51]

So by the time Hurricane Katrina hit and more than 20 percent of the population was left or chose to stay behind in New Orleans, many were in living in conditions that many Americans would find uninhabitable.[52] There were at least one thousand deaths, and hundreds of bodies were left unidentified and unclaimed. Corpses floated down the flooded streets while raw sewage spewed everywhere. This presented significant public

50. Bob Herbert, "No Strangers to the Blues," *New York Times*, September 8, 2005.

51. See "New Orleans Hospital Staff Discussed Mercy Killings," reported on National Public Radio, February 16, 2006. Available online at http://www.npr.org/templates/story/story.php?storyId=5219917.

52. Mayor Ray Nagin of New Orleans had only strongly recommended evacuation. It was not until the morning of Sunday, August 28, that he ordered mandatory evacuation of the city.

health concerns.[53] While there were many heroic individuals and groups working together to rescue people, many believe that the situation never should have reached this point. This point, however, was a long time in the making.

Rebuilding efforts have been slow and uneven. The slowness may be in part a function of the magnitude of the disaster, but other considerations come into play. Shipping interests want the levees rebuilt immediately, while oil companies continue to push for the same drilling practices that contributed to the massive loss of wetlands. Those parts of New Orleans that are huge sources of revenue from tourism have received the highest priority for rebuilding. But these areas are not all that dense in housing. The French Quarter had little to no flooding. It is the oldest part of New Orleans and has one of the smallest populations: 4,200 people with an average income of $58,571. The Mid-City area, on the other hand, has a population of 76,000 people, most of whom are working class or poor. The average income in this area is $25,583.[54]

Blacks' responses in these polls to the government's actions (or inactions) indicate a very different way to frame the issues. These poll results point to very different understandings of the problems. For many African Americans, the government's response is seen as both a cause and consequence of longstanding structural injustices. The oppression is simultaneously material and physical, psychological and ideological. It is structural in the sense of involving the institutions and practices that constitute our world. It is in this way that the realities of blacks and whites are both the same and not the same. Blacks and whites participate in these practices in very different ways, entailing that their experiences and the meanings of these experiences are very different. The oppressive practices very much structure and shape realities. And, while not deterministic, these practices do limit sharply the range of possibilities and options.

As I stated above, one of the ways to understand these radically different views is to see them as involving claims to justice, marking them as species of moral disagreement. These moral disagreements are material and

53. There is also a public health-care crisis with mental health in the post-Katrina era. There are near-epidemic rates of depression and post-traumatic stress disorder. These contribute to a suicide rate that is nearly triple the pre-Katrina rates. The infrastructure of mental health care has collapsed. Adding to these stresses and anxiety is an increasing crime rate, such that the National Guard returned to New Orleans in June 2006 to patrol the streets. See "A Legacy of the Storm," *New York Times,* June 21, 2006.

54. See the diagram "The Neighborhoods That Were Hit Hard and Those That Weren't," *New York Times,* September 12, 2005.

physical; they are more than disagreements among differing sets of moral coordinates of individuals or among systems of attitudes, preferences, and beliefs of broader communities. My concern with Harman's approach to moral disagreement is that the materiality of the disagreements drops out of the picture. The lived realities that give these disagreements and claims to justice their shape recede into the background. The background is not seen as important, if it is seen at all. When this materiality drops out, we are left with few resources for addressing the conflict. We will become mired in nonproductive ways if what we can appeal to is fairly thin. We will have difficulty addressing questions about what justice demands and how we are to meet these demands when the very conditions creating those needs are rendered invisible. When we start from the view about the structural nature of the injustices that blacks' responses point toward, we are simultaneously asking metaethical and first-order questions. This is yet another way to ask about the origin of our moral concepts, of which justice is one of the most basic.

The meaningfulness of justice as a moral concept, which is no different from any other concept, is very much a matter of its use, which is itself a matter of grammar. That is to say, all concepts have a grammar, and we learn the meaning of these concepts by learning how to use them. Justice, no different from the ways our concepts of measurement, for example, develops in interaction with our needs and purposes and the givens of the world. Justice is perhaps the quintessential other-regarding concept. This is a grammatical point and not an expression of some deep metaphysical truth.

I submit that the only way our obligations of justice can be generated are within our social relations and connections, as Iris Young claims.[55] These social connections and relations ultimately rest on acknowledgment and recognition, as I discuss in the previous chapter. In order to avoid the temptation to inscribe the world/language divide anew by calling them "social connections," I prefer to say that our obligations of justice are generated in the context of the stability and certainty of the felted world, with all its constitutive elements. It is only within practices in the felted sense that our obligations of justice can be created, determined, and met. This

---

55. Iris Young, "Responsibility and Global Justice: A Social Connection Model," *Philosophy and Policy* 23 (2006): 103–30. I think that Young would be amenable to this alteration, because it helps keep the material dimensions of our connections and obligations front and center in the analysis.

is also the only way that we can talk about the objectivity of these obligations. These obligations are created and met in conjunction with—or even
in collaboration with—the multiple dimensions of our lived realties. Those
of us who believe that structural injustice was a dominant cause of the
catastrophic effects that are disproportionately borne by blacks, the poor,
the elderly, and the disabled can argue that we have the greatest obligations
to these people. Our obligations of justice are multiple.

In *Oppression and Responsibility*, I argued that the normative focus ought
to be on the oppressive practices and their constitutive grammar that make
up the background in which particular acts have their meanings. By focusing on the practices, institutions, and systemic nature of oppression and
structural injustices, questions of responsibility are at the center. My aim
in that work was to generate an account of moral responsibility that was
able to address the systemic nature of oppression; I also sought to break
out of a mold of assigning responsibility for particular acts primarily to
individuals, and by extension to groups. More specifically, my intent was
to generate an account of moral responsibility that provided the means to
address the responsibility that those who are privileged within an oppressive system have for the maintenance and reproduction of that system.

What are some of the ways that we can see the relationship between
objectivity as responsibility and the generation of our obligations of justice? Defining the "problem" that is the subject of inquiry is itself a form
of inquiry. As we saw above, there are very contested issues about what
caused the devastating effects of Katrina. Many black and poor people
point toward the structural injustices, while geologists point to a steadily
eroding ecosystem, which in part is a consequence of large industrial areas
along the wetlands. These two analyses can be brought together. The area
of North Bywater in New Orleans experienced some of the most significant
flooding and has a population of mostly low-income and working-class
people.[56] Most industrial areas are located in "undesirable" or "wasted"
spaces, even though those areas are often home to thousands of people.

Objectivity as responsibility involves broadening the context of inquiry
by including those whose perspectives have been marginalized or neglected. The context of inquiry with respect to Katrina includes the people,
the places, and the conditions of the people and the places. They are all
participants in the inquiry, though they participate in different ways. It is
important to note that all participants are not equally well situated, with

---

56. "The Neighborhoods That Were Hit Hard and Those That Weren't," *New York Times*.

some participants having a disproportionate amount of power and privilege. Here arises questions about who has the power to speak and to be heard; it is those people who have more of an effect in defining both the "problems" and their solutions.[57] These dynamics rightly focus us back to the conditions or frameworks of these inquiries. Objectivity requires that we attend to these differences, and the obligations of justice are the means to make the inquiry process more democratic.

As an example, one group that has been marginalized in discussions about rebuilding is disabled activists. What is more important in rebuilding—historical accuracy or accessibility? From a tourism perspective, many come to New Orleans for the history. But for disabled people who live in the city, the lack of accessible and affordable housing presents a major barrier to full integration and participation in social life. I would argue that justice requires accessibility and integration, so that one population is not systematically excluded from public life. Safe, affordable housing is an important need for all. There is, of course, a catch-22 character to this situation. Tourists flock to New Orleans for its history, so historical preservation is an important element of the economy. Should tourism decrease, the effects will be disproportionately and immediately felt by those who are already economically and socially marginalized.

Related to social integration and participation is the need for affordable and reliable public transportation. The lack of transportation options has a detrimental effect on employment. Many who work in the service industry, especially in the tourist areas of New Orleans, for example, cannot afford to live where they work. The high cost of public transportation and its unreliability limit employment options. An employer is more likely to fire a worker if she misses work, even though tardiness is far beyond the control of the worker.

Justice also requires that we be concerned with the physical and mental health and well-being of others. So long as medical benefits primarily attach to full-time jobs, and many people lack the jobs that have full benefits, a significant population will continue to live with radical health insecurity. And while there are state and federal programs that provide some health benefits, the bar for these programs in set in such a way that someone must live in extreme poverty before she is eligible. For those who are just above the extreme-poverty line, they most likely will be ineligible. Justice requires some sort of guaranteed health care.

---

57. This also raises the very important question with which feminists have grappled: under what conditions may one person or group speak for another?

Justice also requires that particular attention be given to the educational needs of students. As I described above, the New Orleans public school system was already in serious distress before the hurricane. With high dropout rates and few employment opportunities for undereducated people, the cycle of poverty will grow worse with each generation. A significant portion of the population will not come close to earning a wage that could sustain them and their families. Many of the children who were evacuated and moved into new schools dropped out. The concern of educational and child-health activists is that evacuees fled to areas where education had already fallen by the wayside. The fear is that these children, many of whom have not yet completed elementary schools, will become permanent dropouts.[58]

Justice also requires that people be paid more for their labor. The minimum wage has lagged terribly far behind inflation, and a full-time minimum-wage job might bring one close to the poverty line. Add to it the expense of housing, and there is very little on which to live, never mind thrive. Justice requires a sufficient livable wage, as described above. This might well help to take some pressure off local, state, and federal assistance programs, and it may also help to stimulate the economy.[59]

We have obligations ensuring that victims of the storm receive adequate food in regular, secure ways. When those obligations are not being met as a result of decisions by a government, for example, I would argue that justice requires we protest. And this is just what some did when the Republican-controlled Congress decided that it was necessary to make massive spending cuts to the hurricane relief; one item on the block was $574 million in food stamps.[60]

Justice also requires that these terrible events not be used as an opportunity to roll back hard-won civil rights protections and to subvert mechanisms that are supposed to promote and produce equality and equity. But after the hurricane, this is precisely what happened when the Bush administration awarded multiple no-bid contracts for relief efforts, a move that effectively excluded small or women- or minority-owned businesses. The government also waived the requirement that businesses receiving federal

58. See "For Many, Education Is Another Storm Victim," *New York Times,* June 1, 2006.

59. If the Bush administration and the Republican-controlled Congress can argue that tax cuts for the wealthy will stimulate the economy because those receiving the benefit will have more money to spend and invest, I argue that workers' having and spending more money will contribute to the growth of the economy.

60. See "Storm and Crisis: The Costs, Republicans in Congress Seeks Budget Cuts," *New York Times,* October 7, 2005.

monies have affirmative action programs in place. In addition, federal law that requires that prevailing wages be paid on projects subsidized by the federal government were waived. The recovery will be lucrative business, but those already marginalized have been excluded from participation.[61]

These are just some of the obligations of justice that I see arising in the context of Hurricane Katrina. Of course, this is a context of inquiry, which means that my views can and should be subjected to critical scrutiny. Many readers may disagree, but my hope is that they can see the ways the disagreements are grounded in a context that is very different from the surface conventionalism/relativism of Gilbert Harman. My hope in enumerating some of these was to show some of the ways that our obligations of justice can arise only in the context of the stable felted world. We may well disagree about the content of a particular claim to an obligation of justice, but our obligations of justice have the character of lived mustness that I described in Chapter 4. The normativity here is not metaphysically mysterious. The must or the should has its life in our relations and interactions within the world.

Our obligations of justice cannot be derived from a universal law or rule, but this does not imply that we cannot make demands that we believe are universally binding. But this requires recognizing and seeing the humanity of others, seeing commonality and forging connections with others. But these are not simple tasks. Hiding behind abstract rules makes it much easier not to see the pain and suffering of others and not to see ourselves, in whatever way, as like them. It also makes it easier to feel more allegiance to the rules rather than to people, which may prolong disagreements that could have been resolved or transformed by different means. Living in a society that is oppressive and structured by domination and subordination makes it difficult to see sources of connection or commonality with other groups.[62] But my point is simple: the material we need is always right before our eyes, unglamorous though it may be.

If you assume that the rules have an origin that is somehow separate from us and that their authority is independent of you, then you risk abdicating an important dimension of responsibility. Rules do not make you do anything nor do they determine your actions. Rules have their lives in our actions, practices, and ways of living. What happens when you are

---

61. Robert Garcia, "Race, Poverty, Justice, and Katrina: Reflections on Public Interest Law and Litigation in the United States" (paper presented at the Conference on Public Interest Law in Ireland: The Reality and the Potential, Dublin, Ireland, October 6, 2005).

62. This is one of the main themes in *Oppression and Responsibility*.

disobedient to moral systems in which people exert a normative authority that you want to resist? What does it mean to be disloyal to and a dissident from the formal and informal, overt and subtle rules and norms about oppression and privilege? Rules of all sorts structure our lives and identities, and this should prompt us to ask about the rules to which we have allegiance and those about which we are suspicious or uncomfortable. We are all teachers and learners, transmitters of judgments, and wielders of normative authority in all domains of living. This means that we have responsibilities with respect to the rules that structure our lives and identities.

If you believe that obligations have their origin in the shared stable felted world, and that moral frameworks are not merely rules, preferences, attitudes, or affectional states of individuals or groups (what I have called surface conventions), then no one who shares this form of life is immune from these demands and obligations. What it means to be human is to have these demands and expectations extended to you. It means being treated as a moral being and being subject to moral judgments and evaluations. It also means appealing to justice, fairness, and other concepts when needed, which is precisely what Frederick Douglass did in his "What to the Slave Is the Fourth of July" speech in 1852. Douglass was directly appealing to these concepts, all the while challenging the ways that certain of their applications were restricted, while others were invoked in justification for the inhumane and brutal treatment of blacks by whites. This is also just what I take many of the victims of Katrina to be doing as well.

BIBLIOGRAPHY

Ackermann, Robert. *Wittgenstein's City*. Amherst: University of Massachusetts Press, 1988.

Annas, Julia. "Moral Knowledge as Practical Knowledge." In *Moral Knowledge*, edited by Ellen Frankel Paul, Fred D. Miller Jr., and Jeffrey Paul, 236–56. Cambridge: Cambridge University Press, 2001.

Arrington, Robert. *Rationalism, Realism, and Relativism: Perspectives in Contemporary Moral Epistemology*. Ithaca, N.Y.: Cornell University Press, 1988.

Ayer, A. J. *Language, Truth, and Logic*. New York: Dover, 1952.

Baier, Annette C. "A Naturalist View of Persons." In *Moral Prejudices: Essays on Ethics*. Cambridge, Mass.: Harvard University Press, 1995.

Baker, G. P., and P. M. S. Hacker. *Wittgenstein: Rules, Grammar, and Necessity*. Oxford: Blackwell, 1986.

Balmond, Cecil (with Jannuzzi Smith). *Informal*. Munich: Prestel Verlag, 2002.

Bambrough, Renford. "Fools and Heretics." In *Wittgenstein Centenary Essays*, edited by A. Phillips Griffiths, 239–50. Cambridge: Cambridge University Press, 1991.

Bledsoe, Albert Taylor. *An Essay on Liberty and Freedom*. Philadelphia: J. P. Lippincott, 1856.

Brinkley, Douglas. *The Great Deluge: Hurricane Katrina, New Orleans, and the Mississippi Gulf Coast*. New York: William Morrow, 2006.

Collins, Patricia Hill. *Black Feminist Thought: Knowledge, Consciousness, and the Politics of Empowerment*. New York: Routledge, 1991.

Crary, Alice. "Wittgenstein's Relation to Political Thought." In *The New Wittgenstein*, edited by Alice Crary and Rupert Read, 118–45. London: Routledge, 2000.

Diamond, Cora. *The Realistic Spirit: Wittgenstein, Philosophy, and the Mind*. Cambridge, Mass.: The MIT Press, 1991.

———. "Wittgenstein, Mathematics, and Ethics: Resisting the Attraction of Realism." In *The Cambridge Companion to Wittgenstein*, edited by Hans Sluga and David Stern, 226–60. Cambridge: Cambridge University Press, 1996.

Douglass, Frederick. "What to the Slave Is the Fourth of July." Douglass Archives, http://www.douglassarchives.org/doug_a10.htm.

Dummett, Michael. "Wittgenstein's Philosophy of Mathematics." *Philosophical Review* 68 (1959): 324–48.

Fausto-Sterling, Anne. "Five Sexes: Why Male and Female Are Not Enough." *Science*, April–March 1993.

———. *Sexing the Body: Gender Politics and the Construction of Sexuality*. New York: Basic Books, 2000.

Forster, Michael. *Wittgenstein on the Arbitrariness of Grammar*. Princeton: Princeton University Press, 2004.

Frege, Gottlob. *The Basic Laws of Arithmetic*. Translated and edited by M. Wurth. Berkeley and Los Angeles: University of California Press, 1964.

Garcia, Robert. "Race, Poverty, Justice, and Katrina: Reflections on Public Interest Law and Litigation in the United States." Paper presented at the Conference on Public Interest Law in Ireland: The Reality and the Potential, Dublin, Ireland, October 6, 2005.

Garver, Newton. "Beginning at the Beginning." In *Essays on Wittgenstein and Austrian Philosophy*, edited by Tamás Demeter, 137–54. Amsterdam: Rodopi, 2004.

———. "Philosophy as Grammar." In *The Cambridge Companion to Wittgenstein*, edited by Hans Sluga and David Stern. Cambridge: Cambridge University Press, 1996.

———. *This Complicated Form of Life: Essays on Wittgenstein*. Chicago: Open Court Press, 1994.

Gerrard, Steve. "A Philosophy of Mathematics Between Two Camps." In *The Cambridge Companion to Wittgenstein*, edited by Hans Sluga and David Stern, 139–70. Cambridge: Cambridge University Press, 1996.

Gert, Bernard. *The Moral Rules*. New York: Harper and Row, 1966.

Gewirth, Alan. *Reason and Morality*. Chicago: University of Chicago Press, 1978.

Glock, Hans-Johann. *A Wittgenstein Dictionary*. Oxford: Blackwell, 1996.

Hampshire, Stuart. *Morality and Conflict*. Cambridge, Mass.: Harvard University Press, 1983.

Hampton, Jean E. *The Authority of Reason*. Cambridge: Cambridge University Press, 1998.

Hanfling, Oswald. *Wittgenstein and the Human Form of Life*. London: Routledge, 2002.

Hannaford, Robert V. *Moral Anatomy and Moral Reasoning*. Lawrence: University Press of Kansas, 1993.

Harman, Gilbert. "Is There a Single True Morality?" In *Moral Relativism: A Reader*, edited by Paul K. Moser and Thomas L. Carson, 165–84. New York: Oxford University Press, 2001.

———. "Moral Explanations of Natural Facts." Spindel Conference 1986: Moral Realism. *The Southern Journal of Philosophy* 24, suppl. (1986): 56–68.

———. *The Nature of Morality*. New York: Oxford University Press, 1977.

Harman, Gilbert, and Judith Jarvis Thomson. *Moral Relativism and Moral Objectivity*. New York: Blackwell, 1996.

Held, Virginia. *Feminist Morality: Transforming Culture, Society, and Politics*. Chicago: University of Chicago Press, 1993.

———. "Whose Agenda? Ethics Versus Cognitive Science." In *Mind and Morals: Essays on Ethics and Cognitive Science*, edited by Larry May, Marilyn Friedman, and Andy Clark, 69–87. Cambridge, Mass.: The MIT Press, 1996.

Heldke, Lisa M., and Stephen H. Kellert. "Objectivity as Responsibility." *Metaphilosophy* 24, no. 4 (1995): 360–78.

Jaggar, Alison M. "Feminism in Ethics: Moral Justification." In *The Cambridge Companion to Feminist Philosophy*, edited by Miranda Fricker and Jennifer Hornsby, 225–44. Cambridge: Cambridge University Press, 2000.

———. "Feminist Ethics: Projects, Problems, Prospects." In *Feminist Ethics*, edited by Claudia Card, 78–104. Lawrence: University Press of Kansas, 1991.

Johnston, Paul. *Wittgenstein and Moral Philosophy*. New York: Routledge, 1989.

Kallenberg, Brad J. *Ethics as Grammar: Changing the Postmodern Subject*. Notre Dame, Ind.: University of Notre Dame Press, 2001.

Kober, Michael. "Certainties of a World Picture: The Epistemological Investigations of *On Certainty*." In *The Cambridge Companion to Wittgenstein*, edited by Hans Sluga and David Stern, 411–41. Cambridge: Cambridge University Press, 1996.

Koolhaas, Rem. *OMA/Rem Koolhaas, 1987–1998*. Madrid: El Croquis, 1998.

Lee, Wendy Lynne. "The Sound of Little Hummingbird Wings: A Wittgensteinian Investigation of Forms of Life as Forms of Power." *Feminist Studies* 25, no. 2 (1999): 409–26.

Longino, Helen. *Science as Social Knowledge: Values and Objectivity in Scientific Inquiry*. Princeton: Princeton University Press, 1990.

Lovibond, Sabina. *Ethical Formation*. Cambridge, Mass.: Harvard University Press, 2000.

———. *Realism and Imagination in Ethics*. Minneapolis: University of Minnesota Press, 1983.

Mackie, J. L. *Ethics: Inventing Right and Wrong*. New York: Penguin, 1977.

May, Todd. *Our Practices, Our Selves: Or, What It Means to Be Human*. University Park: Penn State University Press, 2001.

McDowell, John. *Mind and World*. Cambridge, Mass.: Harvard University Press, 1994.

Medina, Jose. *The Unity of Wittgenstein's Philosophy: Necessity, Intelligibility, and Normativity*. Albany: The State University of New York Press, 2002.

Moore, G. E. "A Defense of Common Sense." In *G. E. Moore: Selected Writings*, edited by Thomas Baldwin, 106–33. New York: Routledge, 1993.

———. "Proof of the External World." In *G. E. Moore: Selected Writings*, edited by Thomas Baldwin, 147–70. New York: Routledge, 1993.

O'Connor, Peg. *Oppression and Responsibility: A Wittgensteinian Approach to Social Practices and Moral Theory*. University Park: Penn State University Press, 2002.

Phillips, D. Z. *Religion and Wittgenstein's Legacy*. Aldershot: Ashgate, 2005.

Quine, W. V. O. *Word and Object*. Cambridge, Mass.: The MIT Press, 1960.

Rouse, Joseph. *How Scientific Practices Matter: Reclaiming Philosophical Naturalism*. Chicago: University of Chicago Press, 2002.

Schatzki, Theodore. *Social Practices: A Wittgensteinian Approach to Human Activity and the Social*. Cambridge: Cambridge University Press, 1996.

Sorell, Tom. *Scientism: Philosophy and the Infatuation with Science*. New York: Routledge, 1991.

Stevenson, C. L. *Ethics and Language*. New Haven: Yale University Press, 1944.

———. *Facts and Values: Studies in Ethical Analysis*. New Haven: Yale University Press, 1963.

Stroll, Avrum. *Moore and Wittgenstein on Certainty*. Oxford: Oxford University Press, 1994.

Stroud, Barry. "Wittgenstein and Logical Necessity." In *Meaning, Understanding, and Practice*. Oxford: Oxford University Press, 2000.

Sturgeon, Nicholas. "Harman on Moral Explanations of Natural Facts." Spindel Conference 1986: Moral Realism. *The Southern Journal of Philosophy* 24, suppl. (1986): 69–78.

———. "Moral Explanations." In *Essays on Moral Realism,* edited by Geoffrey Sayre-McCord, 229–55. Ithaca, N.Y.: Cornell University Press, 1988.

Tanesini, Alessandra. *Wittgenstein: A Feminist Interpretation.* Cambridge: Polity Press, 2004.

Toulmin, Stephen. *Return to Reason.* Cambridge, Mass.: Harvard University Press, 2001.

Walker, Margaret Urban. *Moral Contexts.* Lanham, Md.: Rowman and Littlefield, 2003.

———. *Moral Understandings: A Feminist Study in Ethics.* New York: Routledge, 1998.

Weston, Anthony. *A 21st Century Toolbox.* Oxford: Oxford University Press, 2001.

Williams, Meredith. *Wittgenstein, Mind, and Meaning: Toward a Social Conception of Mind.* New York: Routledge, 1999.

Young, Iris. "Responsibility and Global Justice: A Social Connection Model." *Social Philosophy and Policy* 23 (2006): 102–30.

Wittgenstein, Ludwig. *Blue and Brown Books.* New York: Harper, 1965.

———. *Culture and Value.* Edited by G. H. von Wright. Translated by P. Winch. Chicago: University of Chicago Press, 1980.

———. *Last Writings on the Philosophy of Psychology.* Vol. 2. Edited by G. H. von Wright and H. Nyman. Translated by C. G. Luckhardt and M. A. E. Ane. Oxford: Blackwell, 1992.

———. "Lecture on Ethics." In *Philosophical Occasions, 1912–1951,* edited by James Klagge and Alfred Nordmann, 37–44. Indianapolis, Ind.: Hackett, 1993.

———. *On Certainty.* Edited by G. E. M. Anscombe and G. H. von Wright. Translated by Denis Paul and G. E. M. Anscombe. New York: Harper and Row, 1969.

———. *Philosophical Grammar.* Edited by R. Rhees. Translated by A. J. P. Kenny. Oxford: Blackwell, 1974.

———. *Philosophical Investigations.* 3rd ed. Translated by G. E. M. Anscombe. New York: Macmillan, 1968.

———. *Philosophical Remarks.* Edited by R. Rhees. Translated by R. Hargreaves and R. White. Oxford: Blackwell, 1975.

———. *Remarks on Colour.* Edited by G. E. M. Anscombe. Translated by L. L. McAlister and Margaret Schattle. Oxford: Blackwell, 1980.

———. *Remarks on the Foundation of Mathematics.* Rev. ed. Edited by G. H. von Wright, R. Rhees, and G. E. M. Anscombe. Cambridge, Mass.: The MIT Press, 1978.

———. *Remarks on the Philosophy of Psychology.* Vol. 2. Edited by G. H. von Wright and H. Nyman. Translated by C. G. Luckhardt and M. A. E. Ane. Oxford: Blackwell, 1980.

———. *Wittgenstein's Lectures on the Foundation of Mathematics, Cambridge, 1939.* From the notes of R. G. Bosanquet, N. Malcolm, R. Rhees, and Y. Smythies. Edited by C. Diamond. Chicago: University of Chicago Press, 1975.

———. *Zettel.* Edited by G. E. M. Anscombe and G. H. von Wright. Translated by G. E. M. Anscombe. Berkeley and Los Angeles: University of California Press, 1970.

Wong, David. *Moral Relativity.* Berkeley and Los Angeles: University of California Press, 1984.

INDEX

absolutism: conventionalism and, 21–22; foundationalism and, 83–84; Harman's discussion of, 149–53; metaethics and, 3–4; moral relativism and, 139–42; normativity and, 53–55; stability and, 14–15; Wittgenstein's discussion of, 7–11. *See also* moral fact

Ackermann, Robert, 73

acknowledgment of morality: justification and, 127–31; limits of, 131–34; recognition and, 124–27

action, moral epistemology and, 115–17

agency: acknowledgment and recognition and, 125–27; antirealist-realist debate and, 44–45; felted contextualism of, 62–63; moral epistemology and, 115–17

agreement: examples of, 105–12; as morality source, 140–42; normativity and, 100–103; understanding and, 122–24

alienation and isolation, metaethics and, 8–11

Anglo-American philosophy, ethics in, 3

Annas, Julie, 26n.9, 118–19

antirealist/realist debates: moral epistemology and, 115–17; moral properties and, 23–41; naturalism and, 43–60; normativity and, 15–18; world/language dichotomy and, 47–53

arbitrariness of grammar, 92–95

architecture: felted contextualism metaphor and, 62–63; metaethics and, 11–15

Aristotle, final cause theory of, 34–37

attitudes, disagreements in, 143–46

Authority of Reason, The, 33–37

autonomous ethics, Harman's concept of, 148–53

avowals, empirical statements *vs.,* 129n.21

Ayer, A. J., 118–20

Baier, Annette, 2

Balmond, Cecil, 11–15

beliefs, disagreements in, 142–46

Bledsoe, Albert Taylor, 134n.29

Blue Book, 23

bodies: moral acknowledgment and recognition and role of, 125–27; Wittgenstein's discussion of, 66–69

Brink, David, 3, 138

Bush Administration, 166–67

Cartesian ego: moral acknowledgment and recognition and, 124–27; Wittgenstein's language theory and, 65–69

Cartesian epistemology, 78–84

Categorical Imperative, 117

Catholic Church, fundamentalism and, 138–39

causality: in beliefs and attitudes, 144–46; justification and, 128–31; naturalism and, 50–53; normative authority of grammar and, 103–5; objectivity and, 32–33

certainty theory: metaethics and, xi–xiii; stability and, 85–87; Wittgenstein's critique of, 78–84

Christian Coalition, 140n.7

cognitive science: ethics and, 39–41; feminist ethics and, 2

community: certainty and stability and, 85–87; normative authority and, 158n.45; Stroll's discussion of, 83–84

computers, understanding in, 127n.18

context, absolutism *vs.* relativism and, 151–53

contingency: examples of, 105–12; Wittgenstein's discussion of, 19

conventionalism: grammar agreement and stability and, 100–103; world/language dichotomy and, 47–53

correctness: grammar and standard of, 89–91; standard of, 51–53

counting, as normativity example, 106–7

culture, conventionalism and role of, 48–60

"Defense of Common Sense, A," 78–84

depravity, Sturgeon's discussion of, 30–32